W9-BGW-500

THE UNMANAGEABLE
CONSUMER

THE UNMANAGEABLE CONSUMER

Contemporary Consumption and its Fragmentation

Yiannis Gabriel and Tim Lang

SAGE Publications

London • Thousand Oaks • New Delhi

© Yiannis Gabriel and Tim Lang 1995

First published 1995

SAGE Publications Ltd
6 Bonhill Street
London EC2A 4PU

SAGE Publications Inc
2455 Teller Road
Thousand Oaks, California 91320

SAGE Publications India Pvt Ltd
32, M-Block Market
Greater Kailash - I
New Delhi 110 048

British Library Cataloguing in Publication data

A catalogue record for this book is available from the British
Library

ISBN 0 8039 7744-1
ISBN 0 8039 7745-X (pbk)

Library of Congress record available

Typeset by Type Study, Scarborough
Printed in Great Britain at the University Press, Cambridge

Contents

Acknowledgements

In writing this book, we have been helped by many people who have encouraged us to collect our thoughts; or discussed all or parts of our thesis; or fed us ideas, papers and facts; or suggested avenues of reading and research; or all of those! Our thanks to them all, and in particular to: Richard Adams, David Albury, Phil Blackburn, Eric Brunner, Martin Caraher, Liz Castledine, Charlie Clutterbuck, John Cousins, Ross Cranston, Guy Dehn, Martine Drake, James Erlichman, Ignacio Peon Escalante, Steve Fineman, Jane Gabriel, all at the Food Commission and National Food Alliance, David Gee, Edward Goldsmith, David Grant, Andrew Graves, Aubrey Greenwood, Robin Grove-White, Candido Gryzbowski, Rob Harrison, Nick Hildyard, Colin Hines, Uri Huta, Mika Iba, Helen Ingham, Michael Jacobson, Martin Khor, Richard Lamming, Simon Lang, Jerry Mander and all at the International Forum on Globalization, David McNeill, Pradeep Mehta, Melanie Miller, Erik Millstone, Sally Moore, Geoff Mulgan, David Nicholson-Lord, Helena Norberg-Hodge, Michael O'Connor, Hugh Raven, Geof Rayner, John Richard, Jeremy Rifkin, David Robins, Howard Schwartz, Freida Stack, Margaret Ubakuko, Lori Wallach, Andrew Ward, Kevin Watkins, Tony Webb, Diana Whitworth and everyone in the world consumer movement we have talked and debated with over the years, too numerous to mention! Our thanks, too, to our editor, Sue Jones, and all the people at Sage, especially Jane Evans.

Introduction: The Faces of the Consumer

The consumer has become a god-like figure, before whom markets and politicians alike bow. Everywhere it seems, the consumer is triumphant. Consumers are said to dictate production; to fuel innovation; to be creating new service sectors in advanced economies; to be driving modern politics; to have it in their power to save the environment and protect the future of the planet. Consumers embody a simple modern logic, the right to choose. Choice, the consumer's friend, the inefficient producer's foe, can be applied to things as diverse as soap-powder, holidays, healthcare or politicians. And yet the consumer is also seen as a weak and malleable creature, easily manipulated, dependent, passive and foolish. Immersed in illusions, addicted to joyless pursuits of ever-increasing living standards, the consumer, far from being god, is a pawn, in games played in invisible boardrooms.

The concept of the consumer sits at the centre of numerous current debates. Policy-makers, marketers, politicians, environmentalists, lobbyists and journalists rarely lose the consumer from their sights. The supermarket has become a metaphor for our age; choice, its consumerist mantra. A new way of thinking and talking about people has emerged, which engulfs all of us. In the second half of the twentieth century, we have gradually learnt to talk and think of each other and of ourselves less as workers, citizens, parents or teachers, and more as consumers. Our rights and our powers derive from our standing as consumers, our political choices are votes for those promising us the best deal as consumers, our enjoyment of life is almost synonymous with the quantities (and to a lesser extent qualities) of what we consume. Our success is measured in terms of how well we are doing as consumers. Consumption is not just a means of fulfilling needs but permeates our social relations, perceptions and images.

Only relatively recently has the consumer also assumed centre-stage in academic debates. If traditional social theory and political economy approached people primarily as workers and creators of wealth, consumption is now the focus of much theorizing. Psychologists have redirected their sights towards an understanding of what drives modern consumers. Cultural theorists have increasingly recognized the spirit of our age (whether described as postmodernity, late modernity or advanced capitalism) not in modes of production, government, class structure or art but in modes of consumption, life-styles, identities. Since the collapse of communism in the Eastern bloc, consumerism is now commonly described as the unchallenged ideology of our times.

Discussions about consumption and consumerism are rarely value-neutral. Some commentators celebrate the rise of the consumer; having lost faith in religious or political recipes of salvation, the consumer is seen as the mature individual who seeks to enjoy life by making choices. Others lament consumerism as the final stage of commodification, where all relations between people are finally reduced to usage and exploitation. The consumer is not merely an object of theorizing, but almost invariably a central character from a story, now a hero or a heroine, now a victim, now a villain, now a fool, but always central. In some stories, consumers feature as sovereign, deciding the fate of products and corporations at a whim, in others they feature as duped victims, manipulated by producers, advertisers and image-makers. In some they feature as callous villains, indifferent to the plight of the planet or those less fortunate than themselves, in others as addicts, pursuing a chimera that only reinforces their despair.

This book was written because we believe that the word 'consumer' is now so overused that it is in danger of collapsing into slogan. At one level, to state that someone is a consumer is almost as meaningful as acknowledging that she or he is a living being. We all consume, the same way that we all breathe, since life without consumption is as impossible as life without respiration. Plants and other animals consume too. Why then has 'the consumer' in our culture become so loaded with meanings, assumptions and values? From where does this idea draw its power?

In this book, we argue that different traditions or discourses have invented different representations of the consumer each with its own specificity and coherence, but wilfully oblivious to those of others. Some New Right economists, for example, have invented the consumer as a decision-maker and an arbiter of products while some consumer activists look at the consumer as a vulnerable and confused being, in need of help. Many cultural theorists look at the consumer as a communicator of meanings sustaining the social fabric, while most ecologists reproach consumers for their reckless and selfish behaviour. In this way, the concept of the consumer appears to have lost all ability to resist. It can enter different social and cultural agendas, including those of cultural theorists, Marxists, journalists, publishers, advertisers and politicians across the spectrum with equal equanimity, in apparently perfect accord.

The theoretical softness of the concept of the consumer (its readiness to act as an obedient and polite guest in almost any discourse) is accompanied by a moral hardness which it can readily assume. In reviewing what other thinkers have written and after considering the common usage of the term, we became impatient with one-dimensional views, whether they demonize or romanticize the consumer, as if in consuming, people transcend every other level of social existence. Paradoxically, love and fear of consumption cross conventional political and economic boundaries. Religious authorities side with ecologists in denouncing excessive consumption, while co-operative socialists and free market conservatives join hands to celebrate consumer power.

We believe that it is time different traditions of defining the consumer started to take notice of each other. Our first object therefore is to identify, disentangle and juxtapose approaches to contemporary consumption which are rarely found within a single book. Our discussion will address diverse features of consumption ranging from gifts and bargain-hunting to cashless systems of exchange, from fashion and fads in the First World to the effects of Western consumerism for the Third World, from the class dimensions of consumption to children as consumers, from the semiotics of modern advertising to the scope and limitations of the law as an instrument of consumer protection, from the concept of choice to debates about free trade and protectionism.

A crucial feature of this book is that we examine not only different academic and everyday discourses on consumption, but also the views and ideas of organizations and activists who represent or claim to represent consumers. The consumer movement in the United States is sometimes referred to as consumerism, whereas elsewhere the word consumerism is more frequently taken to refer to a life excessively preoccupied with consumption. This book is not a sociological study of the consumer movement, but it does address its contribution to defining and shaping contemporary consumption. We will sketch an ideological map of the consumer movement since its early beginning in the nineteenth century, describing four successive world-views in consumer advocacy, all alive today: co-operation, value-for-money, anti-corporatism and 'new wave' or alternative consumption. Each of these traditions, and the organizations which still carry them forward, has proffered distinct analyses and interpretations of the position of the consumer in society. These vary hugely from reformist to radical, from pragmatic to visionary, from global to local and from class-, gender- and race-bound to highly individualist.

The book's structure is an attempt to organize a truly prodigious, though chaotic, array of arguments according to the underlying image of the consumer which inspires and drives them. Thus, after Chapter 1, which investigates the emergence of contemporary Western consumption, each subsequent chapter until the final one presents a distinct portrait of today's consumer, as it emerges from the writings of academics, journalists, advertisers, consumer advocates, policy-makers and others. We portray in succession the consumer as chooser, as communicator, as identity-seeker, as victim and so forth. It will quickly become evident that each of these portraits highlights a different feature of the consumer's physiognomy, while at the same time obscuring others. We discuss the tensions and contradictions inherent in each portrait and examine the tendencies of each to mutate into different ones. We observe how critical discontinuities and anomalies in a particular tradition of consumer studies are overcome by simply switching from one consumer representation to another. We look, for example, at how the consumer as explorer turns identity-seeker or how the consumer-chooser turns into victim. We argue that each one of these portraits has strengths as well as weaknesses and we try to evaluate each.

Our own purpose, however, is not merely to recreate these images, compelling though they be, nor to criticize each one of them from the vantage point of another. In spite of their considerable complexity, we shall argue that all of these portraits are too civilized and one-sided, failing to come to terms with the fragmentation, volatility and confusion of contemporary Western consumption. By stirring various traditions together, we are seeking to reclaim some theoretical recalcitrance for the concepts of consumption and the consumer. We introduce the concept of the 'unmanageable consumer' to express this recalcitrance, a refusal on our part to allow the idea of the consumer to become domesticated and comfortable within parcelled discourses.

But there is another quality which we seek to capture through the concept of unmanageability, one that pertains not to the concept of the consumer as it features in academic, political and cultural discourses, but rather to the vital unpredictability which characterizes some of our actions and experiences as consumers, both singly and collectively. As consumers we can be irrational, incoherent and inconsistent just as we can be rational, planned and organized. We can be individualistic or may be driven by social norms and expectations. We can seek risk and excitement or may aim for comfort and security. We can be deeply moral about the way we spend our money or quite unfettered by moral considerations. Our feelings towards consumption can range from loathing shopping to loving it, from taking pride in what we wear to being quite unconcerned about it, from enjoying window-shopping to finding it utterly boring, from being highly self-conscious about the car we drive to being quite indifferent to it. Such fragmentations and contradictions should be recognized as core features of contemporary consumption itself, hence the pertinence of the idea of the unmanageable consumer.

To portray consumers as unmanageable does not seek to overlook the difficulties many of us have in making ends meet or the lack of choice that we experience due to the oppressive burden of social expectations. Nor does it skim over the immense resources and effort deployed to observe, monitor, survey, forecast and control our behaviour as consumers, in short, to manage us. Like today's worker, today's consumer is over-managed, prodded, seduced, controlled. Never before has one's every purchase been so closely observed, each credit card transaction so closely dissected. In the pages of this book we will encounter countless modes of consumer management coming from diverse quarters. Consumers, however, do not always act as predictably as would-be managers desire. The very fragmentations and contradictions which characterize our actions as consumers enable us from time to time, in devious, creative and unpredictable ways to dodge management devices and evade apparatuses of control.

Ultimately, our actions and experiences as consumers cannot be detached from our actions and experiences as social, political and moral agents. The fragmentations and contradictions of contemporary consumption are part and parcel of the fragmentations and contradictions of contemporary living.

Being a consumer dissolves neither class membership nor citizenship; it is not the case that one moment we act as consumers and the next as workers or as citizens, as women or men or as members of ethnic groups. We are creative composites of several social categories at the same time.

But the most important reason for writing this book has been our desire to explore the qualities of fragmentation and unmanageability of contemporary Western consumption as part of a long-term historical process. Today's Western consumer is often treated as the terminus of a historical process, which will be duplicated in other parts of the world. Alternatively, Western consumption is viewed as culpable for the escalating plunder of vast sections of the Third World and the continuing deprivation of its inhabitants. We want to emphasize that today's Western consumption is itself but a stage towards something different. The fact that no one can be sure about what lies ahead does not imply that we should treat today's Western consumer as the consummation of a historical development as some political ideologues do. We wish therefore to reassert the importance of the debate about the global and historical implications of Western modes of consumption and the legacy which it is likely to leave for future generations.

This book was written at a troubled time in the world. The demise of the Soviet Union and the end of the Cold War at the end of the 1980s signalled to many the triumph of consumer capitalism. The spectacular rise of the economies of the Pacific Rim was seen as confirmation that the only meaningful choice left to nations (now that the issue of capitalism versus socialism was foreclosed) was that between consumer capitalism and poverty-ridden underdevelopment. Instead, we argue that any triumphalism about Western-style consumption is misplaced. The future of global consumption must remain the object of questioning on economic, cultural, environmental and moral grounds. The rapid globalization of production and markets heralds a decline in many of the conditions which fuelled the rise of Western consumerism: steady jobs, full employment, high wages, rising standards of living, and so on. The efforts of advertisers, publishers and trend-setters to entice Western consumers in the 1990s to resume the riotous pace of spending of earlier years were not conspicuously successful. In the wake of insecurity about jobs and countless cautionary tales of debt and bankruptcy, some perceptive commentators talked about consumers suffering from spending fatigue. Some politicians even started to despair about consumers doing their bit for the economy. Some consumers became notably reluctant to consume. As earlier generations of workers had been accused of being work-shy by their bosses, so consumers were castigated for being spend-shy and failing in their duty to keep the economy going.

The core assumptions of consumerism also came under scrutiny. The foolishness of pretending that the natural environment contains inexhaustible resources and has unlimited tolerance to abuse, was becoming clear. The notion that everyone in the world could 'enjoy' Western standards of living without leading to an environmental and ecological catastrophe seemed increasingly blinkered. Even the axiomatic equation of quality of life with wealth had started to be questioned, as some vanguard consumer groups dared to say the unsayable 'Consume less!'. While we cannot see the end of Western consumerism yet, its future can no longer be taken for granted. For the time being, consumerism, far from resting on its laurels, seems to be going through a period of well-earned malaise.

This book argues that the fragmentation and unmanageability of the consumer are features of this malaise. As long as the consumer could confidently look forward to a future of greater prosperity and affluence, the issue of defining the consumer seemed pedantic. Today, however, defining the consumer has become like a Rorschach Test, the psychologist's tool, where individuals are invited to say what they 'see' in the shape of an inkblot; the idea is that what they each 'see' betrays their state of mind. Similarly, to ask what the consumer is invites us to explore ourselves, our notions of society and our outlook on life. One's tendency is always to search for meaning, cohesion and transparency where there is doubt, ambiguity and uncertainty. By accepting fragmentation and unmanageability, this book invites the reader to unravel some of the paradoxes that make up contemporary consumption and to assess their implications for the future. Is the coming of the twenty-first century going to witness the consumer's resurgence, metamorphosis or demise?

1

The Emergence of Contemporary Consumerism

There is little sign that most of the populace wish for anything other than a continual increase in the availability of such products and the benefits felt to be received by their possession.

Daniel Miller (1987: 185)

Since the fourteenth century, the verb 'to consume' in English has had negative connotations, meaning 'to destroy, to use up, to waste, to exhaust'. By contrast, the word 'customer' was a more positive term, implying 'a regular and continuing relationship to a supplier'. The unfavourable connotations of the word 'consumer' continued to the late nineteenth century. Gradually, the meaning of 'to consume' shifted from the object which is dissipated to the human need which is fulfilled in the process (Williams, 1976: 69). It is mainly since the Roaring Twenties in the United States that the meaning of consumption broadened still further to resonate pleasure, enjoyment and freedom (Lasch, 1991). Consumption moved from a means towards an end – living – to being an end in its own right. Living life to the full became increasingly synonymous with consumption.

By the end of the twentieth century, this has changed. The consumer has become a totem pole around which a multitude of actions and ideologies are dancing. Whether en masse or as an individual, the consumer is no longer a person who merely desires, buys and uses up a commodity. Instead, as we shall see in subsequent chapters, we encounter the consumer in turn as one who chooses, buys or refuses to buy; as one who displays or is unwilling to display; as one who offers or keeps; as one who feels guilt or has moral qualms; as one who explores or interprets, reads or decodes, reflects or daydreams; as one who pays or shoplifts; as one who needs or cherishes; as one who loves or is indifferent; as one who defaces or destroys.

Like the words consumption and consumer, the word consumerism is part of different intellectual traditions which for a long time have knowingly or unknowingly disregarded each other. As a result, the word consumerism has come to mean different things to different people in different contexts. Even within academic research, the word consumerism has acquired a number of distinct uses. It is common when talking about consumerism to slip from one usage to another, hardly being aware of doing so. It is instructive, however, to try to disentangle some of the different meanings which the term has acquired. We discern at least five variants, some of which are contiguous.

1 **Consumerism as a moral doctrine in developed countries.** In developed countries consumption has come to embody a moral doctrine; with the demise of the Puritan ethic of self-denial, consumption has emerged virtually unchallenged as the essence of the good life. According to this view, consumerism is the vehicle for freedom, power and happiness. All of these things lie in the consumer's ability to choose, acquire, use and enjoy material objects and experiences. Within this discourse, style, taste, fantasy and sexuality have come to the forefront; gender makes an intermittent appearance; class has unjustly tended to be obscured.

2 **Consumerism as the ideology of conspicuous consumption.** In addition to defining the meaning of good life (as above), consumption has come to supplant religion, work and politics as the mechanism by which social and status distinctions may be established. Display of material commodities fix the social position and prestige of their owners.

3 **Consumerism as an economic ideology for global development.** With the collapse of the Communist bloc and its productionist rhetoric ('forever more tons of steel per head'), consumerism, the pursuit of ever higher standards of living, is seen as supplying the ideological force underpinning capitalist accumulation in the global system dominated by the transnational corporations. It has become a key feature of international relations from trade and aid to foreign policy. The nurturing of consumers is seen as the key to economic development in countries as diverse as those of the old Soviet bloc, Latin America and South East Asia.

4 **Consumerism as a political ideology.** Formerly the hallmark of the Right, this form of consumerism is increasingly embraced across the political spectrum, from First World to Third World. The modern state has emerged both as a guarantor of consumer rights and minimum standards and also as a major provider of goods and services. Accordingly, consumerism has entered the realm of party politics. Many right-wing political parties in the West, adeptly shifted their rhetoric to present themselves as parties of choice, freedom and the consumer. Old socialist parties belatedly started to shake off their image as champions of the so-called nanny state and its associations with patronizing attitudes towards what people need and sanctimonious admonishments against pleasure. According to this view of consumerism, corporations supply increasingly glamorous, stylish goods, while the state is seen as providing shabby, run-down services, from which proper consumers seek to buy out, if they can afford it.

5 **Consumerism as a social movement seeking to promote and protect the rights of consumers.** Consumer advocacy, dating back to the co-operative movement in the nineteenth century, has developed with changing patterns and scope of consumption. Some consumer advocates today are moving from concerns over quality and 'value for money' to a critique of unbridled consumption in a world of finite resources and a fragile natural environment. Currently consumer advocacy seeking a

better deal for the consumer co-exists uneasily alongside a new wave consumerism with its radical agenda.

Each of the chapters of this book introduces a different face of the consumer and a distinct variant of consumerism. We will therefore not narrow our discussion by offering a strict definition of consumerism. We embrace the ·variety and nuances in the term in order to draw the connections between the five meanings above. In this way, we will develop a more complex account of consumerism, as a phenomenon which both describes social reality but also shapes our perceptions of social reality. In all its meanings, consumerism is neither ethically nor politically neutral, and is therefore a terrain to be contested and argued over. Our object is not merely to clarify current and past debates on consumerism and consumption, but to explore the contradictions harboured by contemporary consumption patterns, the limits to consumerism and the forces which are likely to oppose it in the future.

The rest of this chapter sketches the emergence of Western consumerism. We examine the circumstances which fostered it and argue that, as we approach the end of the twentieth century, consumerism has entered a period of considerable malaise and may be about to undergo another major transformation. It is possible that consumerism has peaked and that affluent societies are now entering uncharted waters of 'post-consumerism' (Lansley, 1994: 234–8). Alternatively it is possible that the centre of gravity of consumerism is about to migrate from the industrial West to the rapidly industrializing East, particularly the Asian Tiger economies. The paths are unclear. Whatever happens, we shall argue by the end of this book that the present phase of consumerism is drawing to a close. A twilight phase cannot last for ever.

The Fordist Deal and contemporary consumerism

How did it all start? Contemporary consumerism in all its current diversity is unthinkable without the unwritten deal pioneered by Henry Ford for his employees: *ever increasing standards of living in exchange for a quiescent labour force*. Ford summed it up thus: 'If you cut wages, you just cut the number of your customers' (Barnet and Cavanagh, 1994: 261). Since that deal was struck, consumerism has come to signify a general preoccupation with consumption standards and choice as well as a willingness to read meanings in material commodities and to equate happiness and success with material possessions (Lebergott, 1993).

The Fordist Deal highlights three dimensions of twentieth century consumer capitalism which are rarely addressed together. They will be at the forefront of our discussion throughout this chapter. The first is its *historical* character. Consumerism did not appear already shaped and formed in advanced industrial societies. It was prefigured in earlier societies

(McCracken, 1988; McKendrick et al., 1982; Mukerji, 1983; Williams, 1982). Contemporary consumerism is the product of long-term historical changes. Fordism (as a phenomenon embracing both production and consumption) signalled the transformation of consumerism from an elite to a mass phenomenon in the twentieth century, in advanced capitalist societies (Williams, 1976). A very different picture emerges if, instead of approaching contemporary consumerism as the terminus of economic and cultural trends, it is looked at as transitional, that is, having to reinvent itself or being overtaken by other social forces.

The second dimension of contemporary consumerism is its *global* nature. While consumerism touches the minutiae of everyday life, it is a global phenomenon in many different ways. It underlines the interconnectedness of national economies, it affects rich and poor alike, it shapes international trade and (as the Gulf War, a war over cheap oil and Western control, crucially demonstrated) politics and peace (George, 1992). The major players in the consumerist game, the transnational corporations, are global players, the stakes are global stakes and the implications of the game itself are global. Just 200 corporations account for a fourth of global economic activity (Barnet and Cavanagh, 1994; Robertson, 1992; Sklair, 1991). Consumers themselves are aware of globalization, increasingly encountering goods which are both similar and familiar all over the world (Lansley, 1994).

This connects with the third dimension, sharply highlighted by the Fordist Deal, the vital links between contemporary consumerism and *production*. To be sure, a central feature of consumerism is the separation of the at times squalid circumstances of the production of commodities from their glamorized circulation and sale (Bauman, 1988; Lasch, 1991). Yet, patterns of consumption are crucially linked with developments in the nature of production (Murray, 1985; Blackwell and Seabrook, 1985; Seabrook, 1979). The consumer is ultimately the same person as the worker or manager now threatened by continuous mechanization of production and distribution or by the flight of capital to lower wage economies. Equally, international capital has a lot at stake in seducing the displaced peasant and exploited worker of the Third World and converting them into consumers aspiring after Western standards (Bello and Rosenfeld, 1992; Durning, 1992; George, 1988; Norberg-Hodge, 1991; Sklair, 1991: 129ff).

The history of consumption

Much consumer research looks at consumers ahistorically; it also approaches consumption as a set of patterns detached from other cultural practices. This is the approach adopted both by market researchers and by the compilers of official government statistics who monitor spending power, spending patterns and changes in buyer behaviour. On such data, many great corporate and state decisions are based – whether to launch a new product; whether to expand into a new market; whether to tax this product or that service; whether the economy is 'overheating'; whether shifts in spending will last; whether this kind of expenditure should be encouraged or discouraged, and if so how.

Expenditure data can be extraordinarily dry and seemingly lifeless, until placed in historical context. Some social historians have devoted considerable effort to identifying changing patterns of spending across the centuries. John Burnett, for example, identifies several distinct phases of the cost of living in England. For about 100 years following 1280, his starting point, prices fluctuated by 50 per cent to 100 per cent around a constant level. From 1380 to 1500, prices stabilized, and were mainly affected by years of harvest failure. From 1500 to 1650, prices went up sixfold, but remained constant from 1650 to the latter half of the eighteenth century, then to shoot up by the 1820s. The next major period of inflation followed the First World War, when prices rose, only to crash dramatically in the 1930s and then rise again following the Second World War. Through these changes, according to Burnett, the cost of living for people in Southern England rose fortyfold between the mid-thirteenth and mid-twentieth centuries (Burnett 1969: 328).

What the cost of living panorama fails to show is the changing nature and meaning of consumption through the ages. As Burnett himself has argued, 'we cannot compare the cost of a mediaeval peasant's cottage with a modern council house, or of the Wife of Bath's habit with a miniskirt, in any meaningful way: all are typical enough of their times, but the times have changed' (1969: 10–11). Recognizing the limitations of focusing mainly on living standards, a number of authors since the 1980s have explored the social meaning of consumption in different historical periods. These authors have studied moments in history when consumption achieved extraordinary opulence and importance, at least for select social strata. In a pioneering study, McKendrick probed into the demand side of the early industrial revolution, notably the commercialization of fashion, which turned the British bourgeoisie into avid spenders (McKendrick et al., 1982: 361) Rosalind Williams (1982) looked at the rampant consumerism of the Parisian bourgeoisie and the arrival of mass consumption through the institution of department stores in the late nineteenth century. Mukerji (1983) went further back and examined conspicuous consumption among Elizabethan nobility, fuelled by the discovery of 'fashion' and the arrival of the nouveaux riches.

What sets modern consumption apart from earlier patterns is not merely the growth of spending power across social classes and strata, but, more importantly, the experience of choice as a generalized social phenomenon. No earlier period afforded social masses the *choice* of what to spend surplus cash on after the means of subsistence had been met. This is well illustrated by the decline in the proportion of household expenditure on food. In Britain, at the start of the twentieth century, working class consumers were spending around a half to two-thirds of their income on food (Burnett, 1966/1979). By the middle of the century, food on average claimed only a

third of household expenditure. By the end of the twentieth century it is
nearer one-tenth (MAFF, 1994). True, for the least well off, the proportion
of expenditure spent on food might be twice or three times that of the rich,
but even for them, the cash available for other forms of consumption are of
an order that most nineteenth century consumers and many twentieth
century consumers in developing countries would find inconceivable.
Similar, if less pronounced, decreases have been noted in most industrial
countries (Lebergott, 1993: 34–40, 77–83).

By the 1960s, Burnett could note an astonishing shift in consumption
patterns compared with the past:

> Far more than ever before goes on services and entertainment, taxation and the
> various forms of saving, less on the traditional luxuries, drink and tobacco, but
> much more on 'conspicuous consumption' – dress, personal possessions and
> adornment of the home. With the exceptions of domestic help and private
> educational expenses . . . it would be a fair generalization to say that contempor-
> ary spending habits have moved towards what was formerly regarded as the
> typically middle-class pattern and away from the traditional working-class pattern.
> (Burnett, 1969: 318–19)

The emergence of contemporary consumption

Most commentators on consumption agree that following the Second World
War, there was an explosion of consumption in the industrialized nations.
Many industries, such as automobiles, chemicals, domestic appliances,
electrical and electronic goods, took off, fuelling as well as feeding off a
culture of consumerism. The basic bargain on which consumerism flourished
was a more docile workforce in exchange for ever-increasing standards of
living, referred to earlier as the Fordist Deal.

> Because Fordism makes the reproduction of labour power and mass consumption
> a decisive basis for the process of accumulation and valorisation, it must aim for a
> tendentially unlimited expansion of consumption, it systematically institutional-
> ises 'wish production' and it constantly extends needs. These can only be satisfied
> in commodity form, which produces ever new needs. The 'endlessness of needs'
> introduced with Fordist society, the limitless nature of consumer demands
> inherent in the Fordist model of consumption, contains an inbuilt tendency to a
> material 'demand inflation'. . . . [This] binds the structure of the Fordist
> individual with consumerism, which may certainly be politically stabilising, but
> also has an economically precarious effect. (Hirsch, 1991: 168)

Governments became vital parties to the Fordist Deal, leading some
commentators like Hirsch (1991) and Jessop (1988, 1991) to speak of the
'Fordist State'. Governments became guarantors of full employment: 'Work
and you will be able to consume; consume and you will be in work'.
Following the post-Second World War reconstruction, politics in the
affluent world came to be dominated by governments' credibility, whatever
the hue, to deliver on promises to improve living standards (Hobsbawm,
1994: 579 ff.). Political economy became a constant 'compare and contrast'

exercise between the different types of contract with consumers (see Hampden-Turner and Trompenaars, 1994). This was signalled in the United Kingdom by the defeat of the Labour government in 1950–1 whose seemingly endless policy of frugality since 1945 was swept aside by the Conservatives' promise of a better deal for the consumer (Hennessey, 1993) and in the USA by the postwar continuation of the 'American Way of Life' that began before it (Mander, 1991: 21–4).

In economic geographical terms, the world's economy is now dominated by three global trading blocs, in North America around the USA, in Europe around a golden 'triangle' of London–Bonn–Milan, and in the Far East around Japan. All three global blocs have been deeply in love with the consumer. Much is made of the differences between the three, particularly in regard to their emphasis on the role of government. It is less often remarked that all three economic blocs offer voters not dissimilar versions of the consumer dream: pleasure through spending.

Throughout the period referred to by Hobsbawm (1994) as the Golden Age of the West (1947–72), this policy was highly successful, with ever-increasing opportunities for consumers to spend on goods such as records, clothes, homes, cars. By the 1960s, standards of living as measured by traditional indicators of consumption had improved spectacularly, with the USA, as so often, leading the way (Lebergott, 1993). In 1920 16 per cent of US households had a phonograph; by 1960 31 per cent had one (1993: 137). In 1900, only 20 per cent of US households had a horse. In 1920, 26 per cent had a car and by 1989, nearly 90 per cent had one (1993: 129). In 1925, 10 per cent of US households had a radio; by 1990, 99 per cent had one and 98 per cent had a television (1993: 137).

Internationally, the USA led a common emerging pattern among rich countries. By 1960, 93 per cent of US households had hot running water, in Great Britain 77 per cent had, in the Netherlands 67 per cent, France 41 per cent, West Germany 34 per cent. 55 per cent of US households had a washing machine, 45 per cent in Great Britain, 69 per cent in the Netherlands, 32 per cent in France and 36 per cent in West Germany. 77 per cent of US households had a car, 35 per cent in Great Britain, 26 per cent in the Netherlands, 40 per cent in France and 26 per cent in West Germany (Lebergott, 1993: 111).

Time studies offer another way of looking at changes in people's behaviour as consumers, signalling the rise of Western consumerism. The major trend here has been for substantial savings of time spent on domestic labour accompanied by considerably increased amounts of time spent on transport and shopping. Gershuny sums up the findings of extensive research in this area:

> . . . The time freed by the reduction in work in the UK throughout the 1960s and 1970s, was taken up by extra time spent in shopping and related domestic travel. In fact, the increase was very considerable – from about 40 minutes per average adult per day in 1961, to about 70 minutes per day in the mid-1980s. (1988: 70)

By contrast, Gershuny estimated that the average time spent on domestic labour including cooking has declined from 161 to 136 minutes per adult, a 'saving' of 25 minutes per day. Gershuny relates these findings to numerous other social and economic trends, like the availability of labour-saving devices in the home, the increasing participation of women in the waged economy, and the increasing size of retail outlets. He draws attention to wide variations by social class; for example, British working class house-wives saw a decline in their domestic work time from the 1950s until the mid-1970s, whereas middle-class housewives saw a twofold increase (Gershuny, 1992: 16). Yet, he insists on a general increase of time spent on consumption activities: Productivity growth [at work] leads to a need for more time to consume the social product. Consumption takes time: the more we produce, the more time we need for consumption. Working time reduction, in short, is a phenomenon of a deeply materialist society (Gershuny, 1992: 21).

Time studies, like those pioneered by Gershuny, provide interesting information. Like expenditure figures, however, they stop short of unravelling the motives and sentiments of the consumer. Both traditions of studying consumer behaviour indicate *how* consumers 'vote' in the marketplace, not *why* they do. The picture which emerges is that in advanced capitalist societies, people spend more money on more goods and spend more time spending money. But what of the meanings of these goods? Are the luxuries of yester-year still regarded as luxuries, or have they become necessities? And is time spent shopping to be regarded as leisure time or as domestic labour time? Is time spent driving an expensive car (or a cheap one) to the supermarket (or to work) to be seen as enjoyable consumption or as routine drudge? Such questions cannot be answered by economic studies alone. The role of consumption within ideology should also be addressed.

Consumption, the Cold War and the New Right

The emergence of modern consumerism can hardly be reduced to spending patterns. Equally, it should not be studied outside the ideological context of the Cold War. Throughout this period, the glamorized consumption of the West as depicted in advertisements and celebrated in television series, was at least as potent an ideological weapon in the superpower confrontation as space exploits or gold medal hauls in the Olympic Games. The patent effectiveness of Western free enterprise in supplying a plethora of constantly mutating and highly desirable consumer products was held as final evidence of the superiority of capitalist market forces, entrepreneurship, free trade and political systems. Chronic shortages of consumer goods, perennial queues and the absurd inefficiencies of the Soviet bogeyman became as important a part of Western propaganda as civil rights abuses and political oppression.

But the eulogies of Western consumerism set against the bleakness of the communist system did not merely originate with the propagandists of the Cold War. Scorning a long sceptical and critical tradition from the nineteenth century to the present, which included Alexis de Tocqueville, Max Weber, Georg Simmel, Thorstein Veblen, R.H. Tawney and culminated in André Gorz and Herbert Marcuse, many Western economists found much to celebrate in consumerism. To them, the planned economies of the Soviet bloc provided a tangible model against which positive comparisons could be made. Milton Friedman and Friedrich Hayek, for instance, argued that consumers under Soviet-style command economies can only walk down the 'road to serfdom'. Command economies offer next to nothing, Friedman argued, compared with Western economies which gain under 'co-operation through voluntary exchange', that is voluntary associations through the free market's price mechanism (Friedman and Friedman, 1980: 3–14). Raymond Aron, no uncritical celebrant of Western consumerism, noted that under the old Soviet system:

> consumer choice has been almost completely eliminated. The distribution of national resources between investment and consumption is dictated by the planners, and even the distribution of resources between various sectors of industry, or between industry and agriculture, is not determined by the consumers. (1967: 109)

In Soviet economies, it was a political choice not to give consumers choice. The state controlled the price of goods, taxing the difference between what it bought and sold products for. Thus planners had the power to decide 'whether or not to satisfy the desires of this or that category of consumers' (Aron, 1967: 110). Socialist economists joined in the critique of Soviet style planned economies. Alec Nove, long before the demise of the USSR, pilloried the idiocy of giving the planner primacy over the end-user (Nove, 1983). Power over economic activity in the USSR, argued Nove, would ultimately have to be given to the consumer: 'To influence the pattern of production by their behaviour as buyers is surely the most genuinely democratic way to give power to consumers. There is no direct 'political' alternative' (1983: 225).

Nove lived long enough to see his prognosis come true. The Soviet system could not last without the market mechanism, continuously failing to meet the aspirations of its consumers. He would have been critical, however, of those like Stanley Lebergott who, since the collapse of Soviet economies at the end of the 1980s, have been singing the praises of the market. Lebergott, a US free market economist, has argued that the consumer-led market economy is simply the best *social* system. Others have been devised, but only when the consumer is in the driving seat is the 'pursuit of happiness' successful and egalitarian. His missionary fervour in favour of consumerist culture leads him into some well-known minefields. For example, he exalts the wide availability of affordable cars to the US consumer which has extended the privilege of travel from the rich to all social strata. If 'tons of steel per head of population' was the sign of economic prowess and social progress for the old-style Soviet planners, for Lebergott 'cars per head of population' is the measure of happiness, freedom and social justice (Lebergott, 1993: 23). Along with ideologues of the New Right, Lebergott idolizes motor cars, choosing to ignore their social and environmental dysfunctions, the injuries and death which they cause, the frustration of traffic jams or lengthy journeys to work, to school or to the shop. For him, like for Margaret Thatcher, the motor car epitomizes the freedom of private consumers to go where they please, without relying on government, business or anyone else to run the buses, coaches or railways on time.

Throughout the Reagan-Thatcher years of the 1980s, a backlash against Keynesian economics in the West ushered in a phase of almost unchallenged supremacy for the free market. Consumerism shifted from an ideological weapon in the Cold War to an ideological weapon for the New Right. It became fashionable for apostles of the free market on both sides of the Atlantic to view consumers as the storm-troopers of freedom. Their foes were no longer Soviet-style planners, but social-democratic politicians who supposedly wished to tax citizens, in order to provide whatever provisions – housing, health, education, railways, parks, roads – they believed were needed. The 1970s and 1980s saw the spectacular resurrection of Adam Smith, whose ideas provided the gospel of the New Right. Markets work, leave everything to the market, became the cry. Adam Smith was right:

> It is not from the benevolence of the butcher, the brewer, or the baker that we expect our dinner, but from their regard to their own interest. We address ourselves, not to their humanity but to their self-love, and never talk to them of our own necessities but of their advantages. (Smith 1776: 119)

Adam Smith's prototypical consumer did not have to contend with advertisers enticing him to have a second and a third dinner, let alone to 'graze' on snacks all day long; nor was he faced with different brands of meat, beer and bread, each proclaiming its own personality. But Smith's present-day enthusiasts believe that neither the increasing concentration of economic activity nor the effects of mass media and advertising alter the underlying workings of markets.

Consumerism and the mass media

The role of the mass media and advertising in fuelling and sustaining contemporary consumerism has been widely debated and contested. What is beyond doubt is that consumerism, in its many guises, found in the mass media the ideal vehicle both for its self-definition and for its dissemination. Modern consumerism really takes off with the growth of effective advertising campaigns, where the systematic moulding of consciousness can take place. Modern media of mass communication enabled advertisers to capture the attention and imagination of millions, to stop chance dictating how a product is seen and to shape thoughts and actions in particular ways. Raymond Williams suggested that the development of modern commercial advertising is highly significant in the creation of consumerism. Under late nineteenth century capitalism, mass manufacture was related to the satisfaction of relatively fixed needs. Early forms of advertising were primarily meant to notify potential customers about available supply (Williams, 1976: 69) Modern advertising, on the other hand, is forged on the assumption that consumers have different means of satisfying needs, indeed, that consumers can derive pleasures and satisfactions which have little to do with needs. Modern advertising makes no secret of its aim to stimulate desire rather than to propose the means for satisfying needs (see, for example, Williamson, 1986).

Much has been written about the genius and creativity of marketing as well as about the effectiveness of the techniques used. Advertisers regularly counter criticisms that they manipulate the public and generate artificial needs for spurious products by pointing at the numerous failed campaigns and at advertisements which backfired (Davidson, M., 1992). They also like to argue that today's 'sophisticated consumers' are not easily taken in by crass salesmanship, that advertisements today are a subtle art form stimulating thinking, and providing humour and entertainment. Some of these arguments will be examined in detail in the chapters which follow. While it is wrong to attribute to advertisers demonic powers of deception and persuasion, it is equally wrong to overlook the cumulative effect of advertising on culture (Baudrillard, 1968/1988, 1970/1988, 1972/1988; Lee, 1993; Marcuse, 1966; Miller, 1987). Irrespective of whether a campaign is successful or not, whether an advertisement is witty or mundane, whether it is addressed to a mass or a niche market, the cumulative effect of advertising is to associate commodities (and especially brands) with meanings, that is to turn commodities into what Baudrillard called sign values (Baudrillard, 1970/1988). Whether one is looking for happiness, identity, beauty, love, masculinity, youth, marital bliss or anything else, there is a commodity somewhere which guarantees to provide it. Through advertising, meanings are spuriously attached to commodities, which are then presented as the bridges to fulfilment and happiness (McCracken, 1988).

The effects of advertisements on the 'unsophisticated' consumer are even more far-reaching. Mandelson and his co-researchers voice a common concern that children are especially vulnerable. Advertisers, they argue, use two approaches to sell products to children, normal advertisements and program-length commercials which promote action figures and products related to the show.

> Young children are unable to distinguish between programs and commercials and do not understand that commercials are designed to sell products. This observation suggests that any advertising directed at young children is inherently unfair. (Mandelson et al., 1992: 343)

Thus the culture of consumption is reproduced within each generation. This culture is exported to the Third World with equal facility. In her study of Ladakh culture in Nepal, Helena Norberg-Hodge charted the impact that television had on a society previously locked into its extraordinary frugal

ecological way of life for centuries. Within a few short years from the introduction of television, children, aged 6 or less, started to see their own food as
primitive and backward, refusing to eat what had been eaten for centuries
and (had been) regarded with pride. In many other areas of consumption,
Western goods came to be regarded as modern, civilized and desirable while
their traditional counterparts were dismissed as backward and uncivilized.
In a couple of decades, that culture was broken up irreversibly (Norberg-
Hodge, 1991). While Norberg-Hodge acknowledged the role of other agents
in such a cultural invasion, her research highlighted the power of the media
and Western advertising and acts as a particularly striking reminder of the
likely effects on local cultures of further globalization of the mass media
through satellite and cable systems (Barnet and Cavanagh, 1994: 137–160).

Consumerism at the fin-de-siècle

The 1980s is retrospectively recognized as the moment of triumph for consumerism. The old moral restraints on consumption (such as remnants of
frugality and thrift associated with the Protestant Ethic, guilt, or vestiges of
snobbery vis-à-vis conspicuous consumption) were swept aside by an extraordinary, credit-led consumerist boom (Lee, 1993). Successful busi-
nessmen, and a few businesswomen, emerged as cultural superheroes,
temporarily joining film and sports stars. Greed lost some of its pejorative,
puritanical connotations. The other side of the coin in the 1980s in the West
was a crumbling social infrastructure, a squeeze on social services and an
ever-growing proportion of the population which was kept out of the consumer party (Keyfitz, 1992; Mack and Lansley, 1985, 1992; Townsend,
1993). The 'new poor', according to Zygmunt Bauman (1992: 111), were
defined not by absolute standards of deprivation but by the lack of choice
and their dependence on state provisions. In a strange way, the new poor not
only did not spoil the party of the rest, but on the contrary tended to make it
sweeter. According to Bauman, the poor were seen as failed consumers who
stumbled in their exercise of choice and were then forced to accept the
state's choices on their behalf: 'The radical unfreedom of welfare recipients
is but an extreme demonstration of a more general regulatory principle
which underlies the vitality of the consumer-led social system' (1988: 69).

In the 1990s the atmosphere changed, nowhere better indicated than in
the tougher tone of many advertisements. Martin Davidson, a former advertising executive, has commented on how the advertising industry responded
to this new brashness with hard threatening images, which underline the
risks and dangers of modern life, inviting consumers to join the select ranks
of 'survivors' who can join the party. In the following passage, he observes
this change in a well-known series of British vodka advertisements:

> There was a new hardness in the air, particularly manifest in the images we con-
> fronted in the ads. Lifestyle had become a commodity in its own right. Take
> Smirnoff, the vodka that for years sent itself up with a campaign style that was the

epitome of camp (all those 'I thought X was Y until I discovered Smïrnoff'). 'Just good friends' [the replacement ad series] has, however, thrown this all over. This was 80s consumerism in its new guise. For a start it looks different; its production values are affected anti glam, and the strapline throwaway cryptic . . . This is life underground, on the edge, on the up, utter self-confidence even when narcissistically threatened. (Davidson, M., 1992: 67–8)

A blip, a crisis or the beginning of the end of consumerism?

The consumerist party ended abruptly with the end of the 1980s boom. It was ironic that just as the collapse of the Soviet empire came as final confirmation of the superiority of the Western economic and social system (at least for Francis Fukuyama (1992) and those like him), the West was entering a period of recession, accompanied by profound self-doubt and unease. The recession had several distinct features compared with earlier ones. For one, it affected strata of society – managerial, professional, home-owning, thoroughly middle class – which had rarely experienced the reality or even the threat of unemployment in recent times (Handy, 1994). Hardship, privation and feelings of profound economic insecurity were more widespread and more pervasive. On both sides of the Atlantic, the spirit of the times appeared to be captured in the poetic justice seen when some of the abrasive 'yuppies' of the 1980s fell on hard times. Jokes were made about the supply of used Porsche motor cars and overpriced studio apartments. More seriously, even those spared the direct effects of the recession seemed to be afflicted by an ethic of parsimony. Surprisingly, even as signs of recovery were heralded, Western consumers found it hard to rediscover their appetite for spending. The term 'spending fatigue' made an appearance (see Lansley, 1994).

The 1990s witnessed the growth in Europe of US-style cheap mass retail outlets, substantially undercutting the prices of both high street shops and out-of-town supermarkets. They also witnessed consumer spending on basics, such as food, being concentrated into fewer supermarkets chains which were competing, or at least giving the impression of competing, for the first time in ages on price (Raven and Lang, 1995). Words like 'savings', 'value', 'free', 'unrepeatable offer', and so on, reappeared in advertisements. There was also evidence that the amount of time spent on shopping as a leisure activity dipped (Gershuny, 1989, 1992).

There is no agreement on whether the current malaise of consumerism is a mere temporary blip which will leave no long-term effects or whether it presages something more radical. The New Right of the American Enterprise Institute or the Adam Smith Institute in the UK are determined to keep their faith in the market to right itself and are unwilling to be dragged by fainthearts back into Keynesian state investment to create demand. Even if Western markets are hovering near saturation, the prospects of new markets in the Asia-Pacific rim seem to provide new opportunities of expansion for Western enterprise. The prospect of more than one billion consumers in China owning washing machines and driving cars is one which fills them with excitement, even as it concerns ecologists, already worried by the damage caused by the world's first one billion members of the excessively consuming class.

Consumers and producers

China and the rapidly industrializing nations of the Far East offer new market opportunities for Western businesses and producers. These nations doubtless represent the new terrains of consumerism, displaying a voracious appetite for prestigious Western goods and rapidly replacing local markets with Western-style shopping complexes and hypermarkets. Whether these nations will come to the rescue of consumerism in the West is rather more doubtful. Their economic success, based on their ability to supplant the West as centres of manufacturing industry, strikes at the heart of the Fordist Deal on which contemporary consumerism has been based. Workers and managers in the core businesses of the Fordist Deal (cars, electrical goods, chemicals, textiles, shipbuilding etc.) have suffered as their industries have contracted ('downsizing'), rationalized production techniques to use fewer production centres or seen their centres shifted to the new manufacturing boom areas of the Far East, the newly industrializing countries (NICs) (Cavanagh and Broad, 1994; Lang and Hines, 1993). As capital is attracted away from the old manufacturing centres to areas where wages are low and where standards of welfare and protection for the workers and the environment are laxer, neither full employment nor ever-increasing wages and improving standards of living seem likely to return. Countries like Great Britain 'could therefore move in the direction of becoming cheap-labour economies themselves, though with socially explosive results and unlikely to compete on this basis with the NICs (Hobsbawm, 1994: 572).

Whether the old capitalist powers move in this direction or whether they continue to suffer from job erosion (casualization, part-time work, insecure employment, zero contract hours etc.), the Fordist Deal, while finding new incarnations in the NICs, appears to be coming apart in the West. Both sides of the Atlantic, governments now argue over how best to invest for the new global age of competitiveness and how to continue to fuel consumer aspirations (Commission of the European Communities, 1993; Thurow, 1993). Some commentators are beginning to question whether, not how, consumerism, as experienced in the Golden Age of the West, can be resurrected, even if a new era is dawning for the East (see, for example, Goldsmith, 1994). Even some Chief Executives are beginning to sense a coming crisis. The Chairman of United Airlines, Stephen Wolf, wrote in July 1993: 'If a growing number of citizens are not functioning as productive members of society and reaping the corresponding rewards, it is easy to see why the progress that defined the early post-World War II era has fallen' (Wolf, 1993).

The precept 'the producer is also the consumer, the consumer is also producer', which was so self-evident to Henry Ford, appears to have escaped some of those social scientists and cultural critics who were busily analysing contemporary consumption in the 1980s, let alone the politicians who were obsessed with enhancing their workers' competitiveness in the global marketplace. Surely, if wages and conditions of employees are held back their enthusiasm for spending is bound to be checked too.

What then are the chief structural factors which are undermining the Fordist Deal? There is a cluster of interrelated forces which promote both the overall reduction of labour required by manufacturing industry as well as the migration of industrial jobs to nations with lower labour costs and lax environmental controls. These leave the mature economies of the West with leaner, meaner or weaker, in any event less labour-hungry manufacturing sectors, and excessive reliance on the service industries. These forces include post-Fordist production techniques, new telecommunication technologies, robotics, the introduction of shorter, fatter organizations, as well as the gradual dismantling of trade barriers under the 1994 General Agreement on Tariffs and Trade (GATT) and regional free trade deals.

The application of computerized technologies to the entire production process, coupled with Japanese management techniques sometimes referred to as 'lean' production, have led to highly co-ordinated systems from design to retailing, which allow massive rationalizations on relatively small runs and differentiated products – hence the term post-Fordist production. Lean production, a system pioneered by Japanese Toyota engineers,

> combines the advantages of craft and mass production, while avoiding the high cost of the former and the rigidity of the latter. Towards this end, lean producers employ teams of multiskilled workers at all levels of the organization and use highly flexible, increasingly automated machines to produce volumes of products in enormous variety.
>
> Lean production . . . is 'lean' because it uses less of everything compared with mass production – half the human effort in the factory, half the manufacturing space, half the investment in tools, half the engineering hours to develop a new product in half the time. (Womack et al. 1990: 13)

These researchers conducted a massive five-year study on the future of the automobile industry at the Massachusetts Institute of Technology, and somewhat prematurely perhaps describe lean production as 'the machine that changed the world' (Womack et al. 1990). Their study demonstrates that lean production marks a qualitative break from mere automation, going well beyond robotics, computer-aided design and so on; it redefines the role of labour in production accentuating skill, flexibility and commitment, at the expense of quantity. Lean production is now being reflected in lean companies, companies which, to put it mildly, do not see it as their business to enrich large numbers of employees.

The effects of lean production and post-Fordism are not limited to the workplace; on a global level, they are often seen as heralding a new phase of capitalism, referred to as 'disorganized capitalism'. During this phase, economic structures are loosened, capital becomes increasingly mobile, and markets, trade and labour become increasingly de-regulated (Featherstone, 1990; Hall, 1991; Harvey, 1991; Lash and Urry, 1987; Lipietz, 1989/1992; Resenthal, 1991). Whether lean production, post-Fordism and the use of global telecommunication technologies contribute to further worker deskilling or whether they promote the generation of new types of skills is the subject of an intense debate. It is possible that post-Fordism replaces traditional competition on price with competition on innovation, and labour-intensive with skill-intensive productions, thereby undermining two of the traditional comparative advantages of Third World countries (Kaplinsky, 1993). The extent to which old manufacturing centres can remain competitive will depend in part on their continuing ability to reduce the proportion of total manufacturing costs accounted for by labour, in short their willingness to break from Fordism. Therefore, even if it is premature to proclaim the end of manufacturing in the old industrial centres, it is beyond doubt that the mass demands for unskilled, quiescent but relatively highly paid labour by manufacturing industries in these centres will continue to decline.

This decline has already been evident for some considerable time. Gershuny estimated that in Great Britain alone the number of jobs displaced by process innovation between 1961 and 1983 was 2.2 million (Gershuny, 1989). A study by Adrian Wood (1991) estimated that, over 30 years, manufacturing employment saw the transfer of 9 million unskilled jobs from the developed to the developing world. New technologies mean that jobs which in the past could not be moved now can, thus exerting pressure to keep wages down in the rich North.

These trends affect numerous industries, where costs in the developing world are but a fraction of those in the developed world.

- In textile spinning and weaving, a 1993 index of labour costs which took the UK wage costs per operator hour as the norm, found that Irish labour costs were 80 per cent, Taiwan 57 per cent, Malaysia 12 per cent and Vietnam 4 per cent. Reporting these figures the *Financial Times* commented that 'clothing manufacturers . . . move production to lower cost countries. . . . The decline is likely to gather pace after the recent deal under the GATT to end the Multi-Fibre Arrangements' (Luesby and de Jonquieres, 1994).
- In the early 1990s, chemical companies like ICI, Bayer and Ciba began to shift bulk capacity to Asia, partly because it was a booming market, but mainly because the latest plant could be run by local labour. According to Bayer, labour costs in Taiwan were 21 per cent of those in West Germany; those in Singapore are 20 per cent and those in Hong Kong are 16 per cent. (Abrahams, 1994).

The effects of these changes in the Third World are far-reaching, culturally, politically and economically. Gender relations are radically redefined as increasing numbers of women are drawn into the manufacturing workforce (see, for example, Fernandez Kelly, 1994). In developed countries, on the other hand, there has been a remarkable decline in manufacturing employment, affecting predominantly male workers (Balls and Gregg, 1993: 13–15). In the UK, for example, it declined by a third in just ten years, 1979–89. This decline of manufacturing employment is likely to be exacerbated by the dismantling of trade barriers, regionally through initiatives such as the Single European Market of 1992 or the North American Free Trade Agreement of 1993, as well as globally through the new GATT. Under these initiatives, 'more standardised, labour-intensive parts of manufacturing in the richer countries will come under pressure from developing countries' (Julius and Brown, 1994: B7).

Post-Fordism at one level enhances consumerism, since it enables manufacturers to produce highly differentiated niche-market products without forfeiting economies of scale; it also brings consumers products from every corner of the globe with a minimum of delay or tariff burdens. At the same time, however, it undermines the expectations of well-paid, regular and reliable jobs for ever-increasing sections of First World workforce, thus checking their eagerness to spend.

Writing in 1984, Lee Iacocca, saviour of Chrysler and heir to the mantle of Henry Ford wrote:

> Back in 1914 the first Henry Ford decided to pay his workers $5.00 a day and created a middle class in the process. He had the right idea, for unless working people . . . are making a good living, we will be wishing away our middle class. The cement in our whole democracy today is the worker who makes $15 an hour. He's the guy who will buy a house and a car and a refrigerator. He's the oil in the engine. (1984: 319)

A bare decade later the cement in the democracy (or the oil in the engine) is wearing thin.

Can the service industries compensate for the loss of manufacturing employment to rescue consumerism?

Throughout the 1980s, a substantial body of opinion held that these job losses would not have a detrimental effect on consumption because they would be compensated for by the continuing growth of the service sector. Politicians such as Britain's Margaret Thatcher took an ambivalent view of the future. On the one hand, they argued that the growth of the service sector offered hope for continuing full employment by soaking up the surplus labour from the decline in primary industrial production. The decline in agricultural employment, after all, was more than amply compensated by the early growth of industry. If a small number of farmers could provide enough food for the multitudes, why could a small number of manufacturing workers not provide enough goods for everybody too? At the same time, the Thatcher vision in Britain was unwilling to abandon hope that British manufacturing could recover its competitiveness, if the power of unions was curbed and if home-based companies were relieved of burdens posed by taxation and expenditure on the welfare state – the so-called social wage.

Numerous voices challenged the wisdom of the first half of this vision. Lee Iacocca declared of the US that 'we cannot afford to become a nation of video arcades, drive-in banks, and McDonald's hamburger stands' and 'without a strong, vital infrastructure, we're a nation bristling with missiles that surround a land of empty factories, unemployed workers, and decaying cities' (Iacocca, 1984: 343). Gershuny provided the academic version of the same argument. No service economy can thrive without a sound manufacturing base, for a variety of reasons, not least that the service industries (including transport, insurance, telecommunications etc.) to a large extent are precisely servicing the manufacturing sector. Gershuny decried the idea of a service economy as a realistic option for the future (Gershuny, 1978, 1989).

By the 1990s the idea that the service economy could provide the basis for long-term sustainable recovery for consumerism was questionable. An increase in consumer demand sucks in imports. Service workers, far from being seen as the new class of wealth creators, could also be seen as 'non-productive', adding to the burden of the true creators of wealth in manufacturing. At the same time, it became clear that, even where new jobs were created, the new employment structure differed substantially from the structure which had nurtured consumerism. Many of the new jobs in the service sector were temporary, part-time, casual, lower quality and less well paid jobs than the jobs which were disappearing. Insecurity due to casualization of employment and the undermining of the idea of 'a job for life', especially prominent in the service industries, further weakens the Fordist knot.

By 1994, according to British employment statistics, 38 per cent of workers were not in full-time employment: 9.7 million people were either part-timers, in temporary jobs, self-employed, on a government training scheme or unpaid family workers. This was a rise of 1.25 million people since 1986, affecting mostly male workers (*Financial Times*, 7 July 1994). According to one study, by the early 1990s only one in three workers had a standard nine-to-five type of working week (Hewitt, 1993). In the USA, Lester Thurow found that between 1978 and 1988, 7.5 million new male jobs were generated, but 18.4 million males in the USA had jobs with wages below 1978 levels. On a net basis, all the new jobs were below-average jobs. While women's median earnings rose from 43 per cent to 54 per cent of median male earnings, Thurow estimated that two-thirds of US workers, male and female, received lower real wages in 1988 than in 1978. Between 1973 and 1990 real hourly wages for non-supervisory workers, about two-thirds of the US workforce, declined by 12 per cent and real weekly wages fell by 18 per cent. At the same time there was a sharp rise in social inequality in the USA (Thurow, 1993: 53, 163). This widening inequality was paralleled globally. According to UN Development Programme data, between the 1960s and 1990s, the income of the richest 20 per cent in the world grew from 70 per cent to 85 per cent of world total, while the share of the poorest one fifth fell from 2.3 per cent to 1.4 per cent (Cavanagh and Broad, 1994: 5).

Environmental limits to consumerism

These technological, economic and social trends indicate that the present malaise of consumerism in the developed world is more than a blip. It is too early to assess whether it will escalate into a fully blown crisis. There are indications, however, that even as the Fordist Deal is undermined, consumerism, as we have hitherto known it, will face pressures from other quarters too. These include demographic factors, such as migration, an ageing population, changes in reproduction rates, and above all a global increase in population (Harrison, 1992). Even more important than these may be environmental factors. Since the 1970s, a nascent environmental movement coupled with a hippie reaction to materialism had decried the ecological impact of unfettered consumption (Fritsch, 1974; Meadows et al., 1972). As one of the earliest and most trenchant critiques put it, 'the combination of human numbers and per capita consumption has a considerable impact on the environment, in terms of both the resources we take from it and the pollutants we impose on it' (Goldsmith et al., 1972: 2).

Twenty years on, if generally less apocalyptic, the questions regarding the capacity of the earth to maintain its population persist. The debate is no longer about absolute levels of population or about the exhaustion of particular types of raw materials, but about the continuing impact on the ecosystem of reckless consumption in the First World and desperate attempts to escape poverty and hunger in the Third. Even if the planet can sustain twice or three times its present population, it is patently unequipped to sustain it at the present wasteful and polluting life-styles of the affluent nations. (Johnson, 1992). Pessimists argue starkly that 'if we attempt to preserve the consumer economy indefinitely, ecological forces will dismantle it savagely' (Durning, 1992: 107). Optimists, on the other hand, place their faith on technical fixes (cleaner cars, recycling, energy-conservation etc.), on the resourcefulness of markets in finding rational solutions (Cairncross, 1991: 153–172) and, less conspicuously, the determination of governments to see that the poor, the disenfranchised and the starving, at home and abroad, are kept at bay.

Environmentalists have reopened a fundamental ideological critique of Western consumption: that it damages even as it gives pleasure to the consumer; that it carries a likely seed of its own undoing; that the nature and scale of production now threatens the maintenance of present styles of consumption. In an appeal to business to change the direction of consumption, Hawken has argued that contemporary capitalism is ecologically unsophisticated, reducing everything to crude annual indicators of profit and loss which are unable to account for the longevity of by-products of consumption such as toxins in the environment

> Our current system [of managing toxins] is based on the fascinating reverse of responsibility and accountability. If my dog gets loose and bites someone, I have to pay, but if a corporation's chemicals get loose and poison groundwater, rivers, fish, and ultimately humans, it is we, the citizens, who pay. (1993: 70)

Ironically, the unparalleled period of postwar consumption has meant that, by the late twentieth century, the word 'consumer' is regaining its older, destructive connotations, as a result of the environmental critique. Concern for the environment draws together people from across the conventional political spectrum. Whether a green movement can redefine politics, consumption and the nature of the good life or whether it will be compromised and incorporated is still unclear. However, in the view of some commentators like Sklair (1991: 71 f)., the Green movement is the greatest ideological adversary to global capitalism, following the collapse of Communism. The Greens are fashioning a vocabulary deeply critical of consumerism and a global consciousness ('we are all fellow travellers on spaceship Earth'). They may be able to tap into the old tradition that sees progress as having limits, and views overweening desire as calling for retribution (Lasch, 1991). Today's reckless consumption may have to be paid for sooner or later.

Looking ahead

As we approach the end of the century, Western consumerism is facing uncertainty. It is threatened by technological, economic, environmental and demographic forces. The future shape of consumption is not forged by the free actions of sovereign consumers in the world's marketplaces. This is not to say that consumers are not daily involved in numerous choices. However, as we shall see in the next chapter, there are serious limits to both range and types of choice available to consumers. Consumerism is the outcome of a complex interplay of forces – political ideology, production, class relations, international trade, economic theory, cultural and moral values. The rest of this book explores these themes by looking at various faces of the contemporary consumer. Each chapter is a variation on a theme, probing deeper into what is meant by the consumer and consumerism. In the last chapter we shall return to address the questions raised in the first two.

2

The Consumer as Chooser

The idea of a satiable human need will be workable in public discourse, however, only if the ruling ideal of the unending proliferation of human wants is relinquished and replaced by a conception of *sufficiency* in which it is the quality of social life, rather than the quantity of goods and services, that is the central objective of public policy.

John Gray (1994b: 45)

Choice lies at the centre of the idea of consumerism, both as its emblem and as its core value. The principal advantages of choice can be summed up in a few brief notions:

- All choice is good; the more choice there is for consumers, the better for consumers.
- Choice is good for the economy; it is the driving force for efficiency, growth and diversity.
- A social system based on choice is better than one without; choice is the supreme value.
- Consumer capitalism means more choice for everyone.

In this chapter, we explore from where the idea of choice draws its power, and ask why it seduces consumers, politicians and intellectuals alike. We question whether all choice is the supreme value that it is meant to be, by examining three distinct intellectual traditions which address it: psychological, cultural and economic. We do not deny the reality of choice for many consumers, but we argue that the limitations of choice are as important.

First, choice without information is not real choice. Almost everyone agrees with that. The contention starts over what sort of information is appropriate, how much and given by whom. Second, choice between similar options is only choice in a marginal sense, like choosing between Tweedledum and Tweedledee. It can be psychologically significant to the chooser, but of minor social or historical significance. Third, choice limited only to those with resources undermines the advantages of choice for all. It helps to be rich, but to be rich is not a pre-condition for happiness through choice. Fourth, the overabundance of choices leads to diminishing returns. It leads to fears of failing, worries about choosing the right option. This applies not just to major decisions (e.g. marriage, career, house, holiday), but to trivial ones (e.g. which dish to order from a menu). Fifth, choice can be used as a smoke-screen for shedding responsibility or for deception. If one is seen as actively choosing a particular option, one is expected not to complain when it goes wrong; for example if a cosmetic operation leads to complications or if a used car turns out wrong.

It is hard to stand back from the notion of choice. Choice is inextricably linked up with morality, notions of right and wrong, good and evil. Even those who set out to take morality out of the study of choice, back into it themselves. Others who deride choice as a mere bourgeois illusion would be up in arms if their choice of newspapers or television channel or books was restricted. Choice is something one gets used to, which is why it is a sensitive issue. As individuals, everyone likes to believe that they have choices, even if they do not exercise them. The last thing they will surrender when everything else is lost is their right to choice. Pandora's Box was Zeus's gift to Pandora, a valuable receptacle containing all the blessings of the gods; when opened, everything escaped, with the exception of hope. Like Pandora, today's consumer may be at risk of losing all the blessings for the sake of retaining choice.

Exploring choice

Every shift in culture invents or reinvents an image of the consumer and applies it to the act of choosing. Trains of academic thought can be traced from theoretical origins through to marketing application. Games theory, a perspective which analyses interactions as a sequence of moves, was taken up and developed in defence studies and ended up being applied in marketing, the consumer being seen as a game player, someone who seeks to win in the consumption game. The consumer has also been modelled now as a probability estimator (Vanhonacker, 1993), now a risk-taker and now an uncertainty reducer, as though these were mutually compatible. Even the choice of something as mundane as breakfast cereals has been submitted to such modelling (Mitchell and Boustani, 1992). The researchers inform us that perceived risks are financial, physical, social, psychological and time. Consumers therefore adopt risk-reducing strategies, drawing upon formal and informal information about products, brand loyalty, the image of the store from which it was bought, price, promotions, and advice from sales assistants.

Another model of choice has consumers as problem-solvers; how they choose depends on how they frame the problem and the consequences of buying this rather than that product (Burton and Babin, 1989). Apparently, they are also information-seekers and processors, too (Coupey and Jung, 1993). Bettman argues that conceiving of the consumer as 'having goals, taking in information, actively processing and interpreting that information, and selecting alternatives' is superior to other psychological models in that it depicts the consumer as chooser as engaged in an active process, which cannot be said of classical behaviourist analyses where the consumer is seen as stimulus-bound (Bettman, 1979: 346–7).

When choosing a holiday from a tourist operator, for instance, the information that would-be customers seek is, from the operator's point of view, infuriatingly complex. One study found that choice depended on gender, age, previous visits to the destination, type of accommodation used, frequency of vacation trips per year and the likelihood of revisiting the location. We learn that consumers are told they *ought* to be information-seekers. By shopping around for a car, for instance, and by pretending to be a sophisticated would-be purchaser, they can get a better deal (Jung, 1988).

We learn, too, that consumer choices can be a vehicle for social contact. One study of 'lonely people' found that they went out shopping looking for social intercourse (Forman and Sriram, 1991). With retailing being increasingly automated and with pressure on staff to be more efficient, the total needs of customers are ignored at the retailers' peril, warned this study.

Others argue that choosing betrays consumers as pragmatic, consciously judging goods as meeting or failing to meet desired purposes. When they choose, they are influenced by how the product meets what they want, its social value, the ability of the product to arouse curiosity and meaning among others, its emotional value and its suitability for the task envisaged (Sheth, 1991). This image from a study of cigarette choice! Market researchers have been keen to explore the changes in consumer motives and context, and they are reported almost before they have become discernible trends. Thus at the height of the 1980s consumer boom, we learnt that consumers choose ethically (Moyle, 1990); environmentally (Rock, 1989); but at the same time, that their choices are swayed by a variety of factors from check-out technology in retailing (Powderley and MacNulty, 1990) to music in stores (Yalch and Spangenberg, 1990).

With all this inquiry into the everyday act of choosing, it is perhaps surprising that consumer choice has been described as schizophrenic (Gelb, 1992; Kardon, 1992) This image is as much a reflection of the marketers' frustration about consumer behaviour towards brands, as of the complexities of people's behaviour as consumers. But underlying many of these different appeals and metaphors for consumer choice is an assumption that choice is undertaken on rational grounds; the entire marketing enterprise depends on and perpetuates this notion (O'Shaughnessy, 1987: 79–97). Modern texts on consumer choice are full of flow charts, diagrams and decision-trees, and little sign of randomness or whim. The intellectual task for marketers is to find order and reason in what might appear emotional or unreasonable.

The rise of product choice: fact and fantasy

Just as the notion of choice goes almost unquestioned within consumer studies, in spite of the frustration it causes, so too it is taken for granted that choice has increased with the growth of product ranges. 'These days, there is so much more choice' is such a common assertion. Older generations say it to the younger. Some postmodernist theorists, as we shall see shortly, unite with market researchers and with the New Right ideologues to celebrate choice. Consumer theorists join in the celebrations, recognizing that most consumer organizations would be redundant without choice in the market-place. Consumer advocates are more measured in their acclaim. Choice, yes. Endless choice, no. John Winward, Director of Research at the UK Consumers' Association argued in the early 1990s that consumer organiz-ations like his own can only be effective in providing information on goods and services for consumers to choose between if there is large-scale production. This ensures a number of broadly comparable options for every type of purchase. Post-Fordism, with its proliferation of niche products, makes product comparison nigh impossible. Thus, it poses a major threat to the existence of consumer organizations which evaluate and compare products for their members (Winward, 1993). For the postmodernists, on the other hand, the demise of mass markets opens up unique opportunities for exercising consumer choice. Each commodity becomes a unique 'sign' capable of carrying virtually any meaning dreamed of by advertisers or arbitrarily imposed by the consumers themselves.

But is it true that product variety is growing? Much depends on the time-frame of the analysis, or the income level of the consumer. Compared with the Middle Ages, there is an increase in the choice of cars and transport, of course. Growth of choice and variety depends on how you look at products. Are the 10 different variants of a car model or the 50 detergents on a shelf different products?

In a rare and fascinating attempt to assess whether consumer choice has increased in one country, Finland, Mika Pantzar of the Finnish Consumer Research Centre concludes – accurately but unsensationally – that the picture is mixed. For some products the range has increased, but for others it has declined. In 1980 there were 10,000 grocers shops in Finland. At the end of the decade only 7,000 (Pantzar, 1992). But the number of daily goods in Finnish shops has increased, from around 2,600 in 1960 to an estimated 10,000 articles by the year 2000: 'Every day one new product appears in the shops, and every 3rd day one product disappears' (1992: 349). In confection-ery, the number of items went up from under 600 in 1971 to over 800 by 1989. For television, the trend is down, from 127 brands of television sets in the early 1960s to 48 in the early 1990s. The number of hours broadcast has risen from 1,400 in 1960 to 5,600 in 1988 but the number of cinemas dropped from 507 in 1950 to 261 in 1988. In publishing, however, the trend is the reverse. In 1950 1,891 books were published in Finland but 10,386 in 1988. For cars, almost everywhere except the Asian Tiger economies such as Korea, the trend is down. In the USA in 1909 there were 69 car manufacturers with their own designs, by 1916 there were half that number and today a handful.

There is an extraordinary fixation within consumerism on ever-increasing ranges of manufactured products, when natural products are disappearing at an alarming rate. Conservationists are deeply concerned about the decline of species and varieties of both animals and plants, wild and cultivated or domestic. In the UK, according to the charity Common Ground, there are

2,000 varieties of apple in the national collection which have been grown commercially or for domestic use, yet just 9 varieties dominate commercial orchards today (Paxton 1994: 10). Likewise, in UK cereals in 1992, the top three varieties accounted for 51 per cent of winter wheat, 86 per cent of spring wheat, 77 per cent of oats and 51 per cent of spring barley (Jenkins 1992: 11) The rhetoric of diversity is belied by a tendency to monoculture, with many processed food products being based on or including a very restricted number of key ingredients. One estimate of the impact of biotechnology on food products suggested that if a genetically modified corn (maize) was widely grown, it would affect four-fifths of the processed food products on sale in an average supermarket, so extensively is corn or its by-products used in food manufacturing; everything from sweeteners used in soft drinks and beers to snacks and breakfast cereals. A distinction therefore can be made between the appearance of choice and its substratum.

Even accepting consumer product choice at face value, John Benson in his review of consumption in Britain, 1880–1980, like Pantzar in his of Finland, points to the contradictory trends in consumer choice. Compared with the 1860s, British shoppers in the 1960s spent less of their income on shopping because they had more fixed costs (housing, etc.); yet new product ranges had also emerged. Women, for instance, saw a broadening of choice in cosmetic and sanitary protection products in the post Second World War period, where there had been little before, but a decline in food shops coupled with a rise in the range of foods on sale in the remaining shops (Benson, 1994: 75). Range of choice frequently diminishes for consumers, when the rhetoric suggests it only increases. In most affluent societies, the number of shops selling basic goods such as food, furniture and textiles, has declined, and consumers have to travel further to get to the shop. There is increasing ecological concern about the necessity of consumers having to use a car to be able to shop, the costs of transport are externalized, with the retailer benefiting from apparent 'bargains' due to the consumer having no choice but to pay for a car and, as taxpayer, pay for the road infrastructure, burdens not internalized in the cost of goods (Raven and Lang, 1995: 7–15).

Choice inequality

If choice is unevenly distributed across product ranges, as we have suggested, it is infinitely more unequally distributed across sections of the population, indeed across the globe. Nowhere is this more starkly evident than in the global distribution of food. While Western consumers may deliberate over 16 brands of breakfast cereal, other consumers face a different predicament. According to UNICEF:

> One in five persons in the developing world suffers from chronic hunger – 800 million people in Africa, Asia and Latin America. Over 2 billion people subsist on diets deficient in the vitamins and minerals essential for normal growth and

development, and for preventing premature death and such disabilities as blindness and mental retardation. (1992: 1)

There is more than enough food to go around, which is why UNICEF in the same document referred to the 'paradox of plenty' (1992: 29). Even in rich countries, as throughout the world, the poorer people are, the worse the diet they eat, yet they pay proportionately more for it, more of their household income goes on food, and the worse time they have shopping for it (Lang and Raven, 1994). So there is a choice, but not equality of choice. The key barrier to consumer choice is money. The message? If you want choice, and who doesn't, you have to get out there and get going. Money gives choice. Choice gives freedom. Whatever the area of consumption, from crime protection to clothes, from health to education, from cultural industries to cars, money is the final arbiter.

The politicians, however, artlessly disregard this reality and elevate choice to the standing of an unqualified value. Since the earliest attempts to bring the state into consumer affairs (see Chapter 7: The Consumer as Victim) choice has been a cornerstone of political rhetoric. President John F. Kennedy's oft-quoted consumer message to Congress in March 1962 is a classic statement in this vein. He proposed four rights:

- the right to accurate and complete information about products at the point of sale;
- the right to products which are reasonably safe in their ordinary and foreseeable uses;
- the right to choose among products of different specifications; and
- the right of consumers to be heard by government regulatory bodies. (Tiemstra 1992: 11).

Similar emphasis on choice was accorded on the other side of the Atlantic in the National Consumer Council's principles which are as follows:

- access: can people actually get the goods or services they need or want?
- choice: is there any? And can consumers affect the way goods or services are provided through their own decisions?
- safety: are the goods or services a danger to health or welfare?
- information: is it available, and in the right way to help consumers make the best choices for themselves?
- equity: are some or all consumers subject to arbitrary or unfair discrimination?
- redress: if something goes wrong, is there an effective system for putting it right?
- representation: if consumers cannot affect the supply of goods or services through their own decisions, are there ways for their views to be represented? (National Consumer Council, 1994: 14)

The psychology of choice: agent or object?

And what has been the intellectuals' position on choice? They have tended to argue that choice is determined, as we will now see by exploring three different traditions. The first is the study of the cognitive and social psychological processes by which consumers make decisions or judgements. The second centres on the cultural context of consumer choice. And the third is the debate on whether choice matters in economic or political economic theory.

From promising roots at the start of the twentieth century, the psychology of choice has diminished into mundane laboratory studies of decision-making: why this product was chosen rather than that. The trajectory of psychology from a discipline interested in Big Ideas to a discipline concerned about 'marginal differences' in behaviour is illuminating. Psychology started the century with such promise – the unlocking of human motivation, no less – and ended a servant to mass consumer enterprises. And yet, the rise and fall of psychology's interest in consumer choice has an important tale to tell: that in the twentieth century, which saw the meteoric rise of the rhetoric of choice, applied psychologists spent much of their time studying what factors determine choice. Motivation, whether applied to the individual as producer or consumer, became the key to constraining, guiding and controlling choice. Psychologists became merchandisers of meaning (Sievers, 1986). For much of late twentieth century psychology, the study of behaviour had become a study of control, along the path laid by F.W. 'Speedy' Taylor, the father of time and motion studies. For Taylor, the purpose of what became known as industrial or occupational psychology was to remove the unpredictability of the human factor in production. The uses of modern psychology emerged as remarkably prosaic. When applied to consumers, this psychology was to help producers understand how consumers discriminate between products. Such was the point of studies like that of R.L. Brown in the 1950s on whether the wrapper on a loaf of bread can influence consumer perception of freshness (Brown, 1958). The answer was that it can; consumers judged wrapped bread, whether one day or two day old, as equally 'fresh' as freshly baked bread! The uses of this type of psychology for advertising and marketing was even then exciting those who saw it as an aid to moulding consumer consciousness.

In contrast to the noble tradition in psychology, pioneered by William James for whom 'the mind selects' (James, 1891: 285); and 'no two men are known to choose alike' (1891: 289), kept alive by existential and humanistic psychology (Armistead, 1974), a large section of modern psychology sought to manage choice and thereby diminish it. For behaviourist psychology, choice was merely learned behaviour, an act of discrimination between stimuli (Hull, 1964). From this perspective, choice was an almost outmoded notion. It was what students did when sitting multiple choice tests, such as to see who in a group they are attracted to or repelled by

(Secord and Backman, 1964: 239). Choice operates within limits set by superior forces, in this case the psychologist.

The other major tradition in psychology, depth psychology, found the promise of marketing applications even more alluring than did the behaviourists. Since the 1950s a section of depth psychology has applied itself to promoting specific products by connecting them to unconscious desires or by presenting them as substitute gratification for repressed or unexpressed wishes. The sexualization of everyday objects (fast cars, big cigars, lipsticks, etc.) was one of the outcomes. Thus, within psychology, there was a strange truce on the subject of choice between the two dominant schools, psychoanalysis and behaviourism, with both stressing the management of and, on occasions, the constraints on choice. Even as these two schools of thought were availing themselves to the management and control of choice, humanistic psychology could naively argue that, other things being equal, humans always choose love rather than hate, affection and meaning rather than fear (Maslow, 1970 (1954): 275–7). Maslow argued that some choices were healthier for the human than others. Give people the choice, and they mostly make the right one, allowing each person to grow psychologically, to become more adjusted, content, at ease, less selfish – a far cry from the brash world of marketing psychology.

The mass psychology of brands

By the 1950s consumer psychology had already taken shape, focusing, as one textbook put it, 'on the *consumer* of the products and services produced by the enterprise. . . . The psychologist applies scientific methods in the effort to understand factors affecting the behavior of individuals in their roles as consumers' (Fleishman, 1967: 735). Drawing on the experimental tradition of behaviourist and animal psychology, this industry-oriented approach was dedicated to finding out who the consumers are (their psychological profile, income, class, etc.); how they decide between goods (studying issues like what sources of information do consumers trust, when is information about products worthy of confidence); but above all on how consumers may be influenced by personality, family, group and peer group dynamics, leaders, as well as by mental processes, such as cognitive dissonance (Britt, 1966, and 1970).

Much of this research was, and is, ad hoc and borrowed from other academic disciplines (Foxall, 1977: 1, 19). Its model of influences on consumer choice was no great advance on common sense. Foxall, for instance, talks of a combination of social structure and individual influences affecting the buying process, which he sees as going through four stages: perception of want, pre-purchase planning, the purchase itself, and post-purchase behaviour such as repeat purchases (Foxall, 1977: 22). Along with many others, his model of choice hardly goes beyond the tautology of 'to choose is to buy and to buy is to choose'.

The purpose of explorations into consumer preferences and the use of techniques like product testing, design and evaluation was to aid marketing and the central mission of the enterprise. This approach was pioneered for social psychologists in the American Soldier study conducted during the Second World War, when they undertook the largest empirical study until then ever conducted, to find out what made soldiers more efficient (Madge, 1963: 287 ff.). Famously, they found that high on the priority list of soldiers on a beach-head during an invasion was the desire for a coke (Stouffer et al., 1949-50). Half a century after that milestone study, in 1993, the Consumer Psychology Division of the American Psychological Association was happy to be described as 'the prime force' behind the then ten year old annual Advertising and Consumer Psychology Conference (Aaker and Biel, 1993).

The marriage of consumer psychology and business was complete and one of its first offspring was the obsession with brands and the power of advertising to place them. Brand research was 'needed' to understand 'consumer pull', how consumers can be drawn to purchase particular brands through advertising. The methods to test for niches in the market and the effectiveness of marketing such as consumer panels and 'blind' tests were falling into place. These could be applied to products as diverse as shaving creams, foods, colas, cigarettes and beers (Fleishman, 1951). Even as consumer choice was being extolled, an entire market research industry was emerging, monitoring every consumer move. By the 1990s, the Landor ImagePower Survey, for instance, was tracking 10,800 brands in 14 developed economies: 2,000 in the USA, 1,600 in the UK, 1,127 in Germany, 800 each in Belgium and Japan (Aaker and Biel, 1993).

Choice henceforth was defined in brand terms. Choice meant switching between brands, an advertising effect and thus theoretically subject to influence (Deighton et al., 1994). Brands took on a human aspect and choice of brands, like choice of friends, was seen as a personality-dictated affair (Sampson, 1993). Brands were even, as we noted earlier, the object of consumer schizophrenia (Kardon, 1992). Brands take on independent lives of their own, being ascribed financial value in themselves. The power of brand anthropomorphism was such that when confectionery giant Nestlé bid for Rowntree in 1988, at twice Rowntree's pre-bid stock value, Nestlé argued that the Rowntree brands such as Kit-Kat were worth it. By the mid-1990s, the issue of brand value continues to be a sensitive issue. In the globalization process, the notion that choice might not be brand-dominated was explosive. IBM, hitherto one of the highest value brands, saw its brand value go negative in 1994, having been estimated as the third most valuable globally only the year before. The cola market previously dominated by a mesmerizing tussle for market share between the two global giants, Pepsi Cola and Coca Cola, began to be undercut by retailer 'own brands' mostly made by the Canadian company, Cott.

The future of brands

It is now being argued by some commentators that one hundred years of brands may be drawing to a close, that 'consumers have become much more promiscuous in their choice' (McRae, 1994: 20). Changes in retailing have encouraged consumers to purchase 'own label' products, thus undermining the value of bigger brands. If the prognosis that the brand era is ending rather than just fragmenting is true, many tears will be shed in the marketing business and as well as in those branches of psychology which feed them. Belief in consumer choice and the power of brands is an article of faith not only for market researchers and their psychological gurus but also for corporations themselves.

Sir Michael Perry, the Chairman of Unilever, one of the world's biggest brand owners, reasserted this article of faith in his presidential address to the 1994 UK Advertising Association, stating that 'brands – in their small way – answer people's needs'. His argument deserves full quotation as a classic statement of the industry's creed vis à vis the consumer:

> In the modern world, brands are a key part of how individuals define themselves and their relationships with one another. The old, rigid barriers are disappearing – class and rank; blue collar and white collar; council tenant and home owner; employee and housewife. More and more we are simply consumers – with tastes, lifestyles and aspirations that are very different.
>
> It's a marketing given by now that the consumer defines the brand. But the brand also defines the consumer. We are what we wear, what we eat, what we drive. Each of us in this room is a walking compendium of brands. You chose each of those brands among many options – because they felt 'more like you'.
>
> The collection of brands we choose to assemble around us have become amongst the most direct expressions of our individuality – or more precisely, our deep psychological need to identify ourselves with others. (Perry, 1994: 4)

He added:

> Our whole skill as branded goods' producers is *in anticipation of consumer trends*. In earlier appreciation of emerging needs or wants. And in developing a quality of advertising which can interpret aspirations, focus them on products and lead consumers forward.' (Perry, 1994: 18; 'our emphasis')

Advertising: the systematic moulding of consciousness?

As we stated at the opening of this chapter, information is a pre-condition for real choice. One can make choices but if one lacks information about alternatives, their pros and cons, their uses, side-effects and dysfunctions, the results of these choices can range from inadequate to catastrophic. Moreover, information can create false choices or guided choices concealing rather than elucidating the full range of options. The relationship between information and choice is captured in the Chinese story recounted by Gregory Bateson (1972: 208). A guru shows a stick to his pupil and says 'if you say this is a stick, I will beat you with it; if you say this is not a stick, I will

beat you with it'. The lesson the guru was trying to teach was not to fall for
false choices. A sensible pupil should say anything he wished other than the
two 'choices' proffered by his master. Is the advertisers' project anything
other than the drawing of false choices?

Is the message from psychology that consumer choice is moulded, limited
and manipulated? The tendency of the academics is to answer yes. Choice
has become a code for something else. The practitioners from advertising
and marketing, however, are more guarded. On the one hand, they argue
that their professional skills can work (or they would be out of a job). On the
other hand when accused of manipulation they assure that their powers are
limited to choice between brands. These battle lines are old and heat up
periodically, notably in both Australia and the UK over advertising
targeting less than wholesome food at children (Barwise, 1994; Dibb, 1993;
Packard, 1981 (1957).

An unalloyed notion of choice is untenable. For consumers to be
sovereign, they would have to have a wide range of options, an unlimited
amount of information and unlimited amount of money. They would also
have to be immune to temptation. In the words of E.J. Mishan, an
economist, nothing could be further away from reality:

> unless the wants of consumers exist *independently* of the products created by
> industrial concerns it is not correct to speak of the market as acting to adapt the
> given resources of the economy to meet the material requirements of society. In
> fact, not only do producers determine the range of market goods from which
> consumer must take their choice, they also seek continuously to persuade
> consumer to choose what is being produced today and to 'unchoose' that which
> was being produced yesterday. Therefore to continue to regard the market . . . as
> primarily a 'want-satisfying' mechanism is to close one's eyes to the more
> important fact, that it has become a want-*creating* mechanism.' (Mishan,
> 1967: 147–8)

Look at the complexity of the information required on something as
'simple' and 'everyday' as choosing with what to wash clothes. Journals and
consumer magazines are full of reports on tests on machines and detergents.
One, for instance, compared 11 non-phosphate detergents with 12 phosphate-containing ones and found that in soft water there was no difference.
In general, phosphate-containing detergents gave somewhat better results
in warm water, but detergents using bleach did not make clothes any whiter
than non-bleach containing powders (Brown et al., 1993). A follow-up study
by the same researchers, compared 11 'unbuilt' liquids and 6 'built' liquids.
In soft water there was no difference between the liquids, whether warm or
cold washed, except for an elaleuca oil based detergent which was
significantly better in hot water. Unbuilt liquid detergents worked a bit
better in warm and hot water, but not to a statistically significant degree
(Cameron et al., 1993). Who, pray, knows the difference between 'built' and
'unbuilt' liquids? And what is elaleuca oil? What difference does this
knowledge make? What are the effects of not knowing this kind of data?
Should the consumer, like the pupil of Bateson's Chinese guru, 'choose' to

ignore manufacturer's advice, for instance on temperature control? (The answer is no! (Cunliffe et al., 1988).)

The consumer society, glorifying choice, bombards its consumers with information rationalized as aid to choice; this simultaneously underlines how under informed they are and creates an information overload which cannot possibly enhance their decision-making. This is partly due to rapidly changing product ranges and specifications and partly due to changing social relations. People in affluent consumer societies rarely live with extended families from whom they might learn what to buy, how to approach the purchasing; that is, they lack the knowledge base for making informed consumer choices (Galbraith, 1974: 59–60). Instead they live surrounded by messages which undermine the potential for autonomous judgements and objects which seduce even as they appear to be chosen.

Choice in cultural studies

Seduction is the point on which numerous cultural theorists of consumption converge. Many of these writers are either postmodernists or in debate with postmodernist ideas. Postmodernism is notoriously difficult to pin down. Here is one attempt at a definition:

> an intense concern for pluralism and a desire to cut across the different taste cultures that now fracture society; an obligation to bring back selected traditional values, but in a new key . . . ; an acknowledgement of difference and otherness, the keynote of the feminist movement . . . ; the re-enchantment of nature . . . ; and the commitment to an ecological and ecumenical world view. (Jencks, 1992: 7)

Bauman as well as Baudrillard, two key figures in this area, argue that much modern consumption unfolds in the realm of seduction, where goods are not chosen for their uses but act as objects of fantasy. Choice is itself a fantasy, an illusion, but like all illusions it serves as a mechanism of control. Seduction is one major mode of control for Bauman, the one which applies to those people with the means to scrutinize, to fall in love and to purchase goods, namely those who can easily persuade themselves that they are choosing. By contrast, the 'new poor', disenfranchised from choice, by being dependent on the state for their livelihood, a livelihood devoid of choice, are controlled through repression (Bauman, 1988, 1992). Giddens takes a less stark view. For him, the contemporary individual pursues an unending project of self-creation through a continuous making of choices; many, if not the majority of these choices are consumer choices:

> On the level of the self, a fundamental component of day-to-day activity is simply that of *choice*. Obviously, no culture eliminates choice altogether in day-to-day affairs, and all traditions are effectively choices among an indefinite range of possible behaviour patterns. Yet, by definition, tradition or established habit orders life within relatively set channels. Modernity confronts the individual with a

complex diversity of choices and . . . at the same time offers little help as to which options should be selected. (Giddens 1991: 80)

For Giddens, like Sartre, 'we all not only follow life-styles, but in an important sense are forced to do so – we have no choice but to choose'. Life-styles are routinized practices around which they define themselves:

Each of the small decisions a person makes every day – what to wear, what to eat, how to conduct himself at work, whom to meet with later in the evening – contributes to such routines. All such choices (as well as larger and more consequential ones) are decisions not only about how to act but who to be. (Giddens, 1991: 81)

This choice, however, is not open to everyone: 'To speak of a multiplicity of choices is not to suppose that all choices are open to everyone' (1991: 82). Choice is an indicator of the demise of traditional society; plurality of choice is both oppressive and exciting. The world is now characterized by an accentuation of difference and the opportunity for people to create their own niches, rather than be controlled by mass markets. Consumption is an opportunity to display one's identity (see Chapter 5: The Consumer as Identity-seeker). Many postmodern theorists stress the creative opportunities of contemporary consumption. Other cultural theorists stress the culturally determined nature of consumption. Bourdieu, for instance, uses the term 'habitus' to indicate a modest but significant elbow room for choice afforded to each individual by his or her social class or stratum. Tastes in food, films, music, art, photographs, and so on, are social demarcators, generally accounted for by a person's 'cultural capital', that is, his or her educational level or occupation (Bourdieu, 1984). Others are still more determinist (Douglas and Isherwood, 1978) (see Chapter 3: The Consumer as Communicator).

These different tendencies within cultural theory – culture as choosing versus culture as ordained – offer a central insight into modern choice. The tension is important. Never has there been so much; never so little. As Giddens notes:

Modern social life impoverishes social action, yet furthers the appropriation of new possibilities; it is alienating, yet at the same time, characteristically, human beings react against social circumstances which they find oppressive. Late modern institutions create a world of mixed opportunity and high-consequence risk. (1991: 175)

According to Rutherford, contemporary culture has changed the rules of consumption: it's no longer about keeping up with the Joneses, it's about being different from them' (1990: 11). Interest in difference as a central feature of consumption long pre-dates postmodernism; it can be traced back to Veblen's and Simmel's pioneering portrayals of consumption styles at the turn of the nineteenth and twentieth centuries. For postmodern theorists like Baudrillard, however, difference is the only object of consumer choice. In other words, people buy goods solely to be different from others. The futility of this project is self-evident, though the project of difference remains (Baudrillard, 1970/1988: 45). The fascination of choice persists, but choice itself is transformed in most postmodern writings into whim and caprice. Postmodernists have been hugely interested in the effects of mass media and the designer industries from art to architecture and fashion (Harvey, 1990). Sophisticated, culture-literate consumers can share the architect's jokes or the designer's references, as they observe (consume) the postmodern building (a shed with a Graeco-Roman portal) or a clothing outfit with different time references (hippie skirt worn with leggings, working men's boots and a body top). Choosing between goods becomes a cerebral in-joke, an impudent gesture whose ultimate rationale lies in 'why not?'. Choosing becomes a witty tour of the cultural super-market; if it degenerates into whim and fancy, 'why not?'. 'Anything goes' becomes the postmodern slogan, par excellence.

The costs of choice and freedom

Bauman, almost alone among postmodernist thinkers, develops a highly sophisticated but also profoundly ambiguous position as regards consumer choice. He argues that choice, and especially consumer choice, is the foundation of a new concept of freedom: 'In our society, individual freedom is constituted as, first and foremost, freedom of the consumer' (Bauman, 1988: 7–8). This freedom, however, is not distributed evenly: 'Those who rule, are free; those who are free, rule' (1988: 23). Modern capitalism, says Bauman, has opened up the possibility of choice to ever-increasing numbers of people, offering 'a wider than ever space . . ., the rapidly expanding, seemingly limitless, world of consumption' (1988: 57). By the same token, however, the very system which offers 'a lot of choice and makes him a truly 'free' individual, also generates on a massive scale the experience of oppression' (1988: 50–1). Bauman argues that precisely because of the importance of choice, those excluded from making choices automatically become disenfranchised and oppressed (Bauman, 1992).

The key to this type of choice is not political struggle for the acquisition of communal rights (like those in Britain which ensured the Magna Carta or the anti-colonial struggles of the twentieth century in India or the anti-apartheid road in South Africa), but the marketplace: 'The consumer market as a whole may be seen as an institutionalized exit from politics' (Bauman, 1988: 82). Yet, this freedom is no less sweet than that which drove the French Revolution:

> What makes the freedom offered by the market more alluring still is that it comes without the blemish which tainted most of its other forms: the same market which offers freedom offers also certainty. It offers the individual the right to a 'thoroughly individual' choice; yet it also supplies social approval for such choice, thereby exorcizing that ghost of insecurity. . . . People are thus pulled to the market by a double bind: they depend on it for their individual freedom; and

they depend on it for enjoying their freedom without paying the price of insecurity. (Bauman, 1988: 61–2)

This double bind of choice lies at the heart of Bauman's ambivalence. Here is the price of consumer freedom:

Thick walls are an indispensable part of consumer society; so is their inobtrusiveness for insiders. . . . Consumers rarely catch a glimpse of the other side. The squalor of inner cities they pass in the comely and plushy interior of their cars. If they ever visit the 'Third World', it is for its safaris and massage parlours, not for its sweatshops.' (Bauman, 1988: 92)

He is right. Consumer activists, especially the new wave and those in developing countries, constantly remind us of this cultural paradox (see Chapter 9: The Consumer as Activist). Bauman's approach to choice resonates with approval and disapproval. Choice, even when exercised, has its downside. More than many theorists, he acknowledges the contradictions of choice. Choice is imagined, yet real; choice liberates some, but exacerbates the oppression of others.

Choosing as economic welfare

In contrast to cultural theorists, neo-classical economists start with the assumption of choice and explore its implications. They take a consistent, if narrow, approach to choice. The fact that resources are scarce and human wants are infinite means that economic agents have to make choices, to allocate the scarce resources between competing uses. 'Every choice involves a range of alternatives' says one economic textbook (Anderton, 1991: 1). To choose one object or course of action means the potential benefit of others is lost. This is the key economic notion of opportunity costs, the benefit forfeited by not choosing the next best alternative. Faced with the choice of buying one out of many newspapers, the opportunity cost of making that choice is the loss of not being able to read the others. To the economists, choice has by definition a downside.

Since the pioneering work of Herbert Simon, economists have also been concerned with establishing the practical psychological and organizational limits to rational decision-making. Simon's concept of 'bounded rationality' sought to highlight the fact that even 'rational' actors will make a choice when they find an alternative deemed good enough instead of endlessly seeking the perfect option (Simon, 1947). Some economists push this notion further, arguing that the economics of consumer behaviour should take greater account of the limits to choice and constraints on choice. Deaton and Muellbauer, for instance, write that 'the part played by preferences in determining behaviour tends to be overestimated' (1980: 3). The economic factors influencing this limited choice are more important: budgets, information, uncertainty. A consumer has no way of knowing which companies have the 'best' prices for a good (1980: 410), an information vacuum which the value-for-money consumer advocates try to end through their testing procedures and magazines. But Deaton and Muellbauer are right; unless everyone has the consumer magazine, unless the information is completely up-to-date, inevitably prices and specifications of the goods will require checking. In theory the consumer can be helped with information. In practice, choice is doomed to be a stab in the twilight. Subsequent information may always undermine the confidence in the choice. Uncertainty 'is pervasive in almost all decision-making', they say (1980: 380). The ice-cream may melt before it is eaten; its taste may not be what is expected. There is risk in all choice. More recently, Deaton has placed even more stress on consumer risk. Choice, he suggests, is 'volatile'; how much should be consumed now, rather than saved or deferred till later? Consumers look into the future even as they gingerly consume in the present (Deaton, 1992: 104).

This model of consumer choice stands in opposition to more traditional views like Samuelson's confident assertion that modern economics is the study of 'how . . . we choose to use scarce productive resources with alternative uses, to meet prescribed ends' (1970: 13). Galbraith, in contrast, has suggested that 'the best economic system is the one that supplies the most of what people most want.' (1974: 1). In spite of this view, Galbraith recognizes that the imagery, if not the reality, of choice is extremely powerful, which is why those with power such as monarchs have so often denied that they have it.

Galbraith presses his attack by pointing out that everything can be explained and explained away by choice. If someone is abused, they asked for it. If there is pollution from consumption, it was the public's choice. The ideology of choice, Galbraith argues, is highly 'convenient' to those with power. Even though at one time when firms were smaller and markets less oligopolistic, consumers might have been sovereign, today that is impossible. Markets are dominated by relatively few producers rather than millions of individuals making choices. In the USA even by 1970, the 333 corporations with assets of more than $500 million owned 70 per cent of all assets employed in manufacturing (Galbraith, 1974: 43). By the 1990s, according to the United Nations, the top 500 corporations of the world controlled over half of world trade (Lang and Hines, 1993: 34) but employed only 0.05 per cent of the world's population (Hawken, 1993: 92). Forty per cent of world trade occurred within each of those corporations, with different subsidiaries trading with others in the same combine. The combined wealth of the top 500 manufacturing and 500 finance houses was $10 trillion, twice the USA's Gross Domestic Product (Lang and Hines, 1993: 34). The ten largest corporations in the world had collective revenues of $801 billion in 1991, more turnover that the world's 100 smallest countries (Hawken, 1993: 92).

Economists, in sum, are divided over the extent, the value and the reality of choice. The critics, from liberals such as Galbraith to the modern ecological economists such as Ekins, deny that free choice is possible since there is no perfect competition (Ekins et al., 1992). The neo-classicists, on the other hand, drawing from the theories of Adam Smith and Ricardo, argue that politicians' duty is to remove barriers to perfect competition in order to allow growth and the market to work its wizardry over scarce resources and infinite wants. They 'assume an ideal of the world and then explain deviations from the ideal' (Abolafia and Biggart, 1992). Unhindered choice is a restatement of the ideal, as Douglas and Isherwood remarked: 'The theory merely assumes the individual to be acting rationally, in that his choices are consistent with each other and stable over the short time that is relevant' (1978: 19).

Choice, the state and the new right

For some economists, choice is no longer just a means, whether towards economic development or individual happiness. It has become an end in its own right. Nowhere is this clearer than in the writings of the political economists of the New Right who were so influential in shifting political culture from the corporatism of postwar Keynesian economics to the anti-statism of the Reagan-Thatcher years. Economists such as Hayek and Friedman attacked the Keynesian state by celebrating the right of the individual to choose. The purpose of the new political economy, they argued, could only be justified if it increased choice:

> An essential part of economic freedom is freedom to choose how to use our income: how much to spend on ourselves and on what items; how much to save and in what form; how much to give away and to whom. (Friedman and Friedman, 1980: 65)

The main barrier to choice according to these thinkers is the state, which however well intentioned almost inevitably both reduces freedom and fails to deliver what is promised. Far better, therefore, to remove the burden of the state and to structure society to maximize choice and consumer power. Daily experience, said the Friedmans, suggests that consumers can make both sensible and elegantly simple choices:

> When you vote daily in the supermarket, you get precisely what you voted for, and so does everyone else. The ballot box produces conformity without unanimity; the marketplace, unanimity without conformity. (1980: 65–6)

The state by intervening in the marketplace stops the consumer from expressing his or her values and from using resources accordingly. Critics of state-dominated economies do not necessarily deny the need for social welfare; but they do argue with others over how it should be produced, controlled and delivered (see Gray 1994a, 1994b). One of the more intriguing and pervasive ideas from the New Right has been the application of consumer choice to welfare. Since the national or local state provide many social welfare services – schools, health, welfare benefits – monopolies tend to build up. This has the advantage of economies of scale, but the disadvantage of diminution of consumer choice. The New Right's solution to this conundrum, besides curtailing state activity altogether and rebuilding family or community reliance, was to propose vouchers, which the welfare 'consumer' can redeem in whichever way she or he 'chooses'. The argument for vouchers was that they give people room to shop around for services, and to top up with their own savings or income, that is that they turn recipients of services into proper consumers.

In theory, choice is maximized, but in practice, equality declines, and social divisions are accentuated, to say nothing of the extra expense of administering this choice, as the contrast between US and UK healthcare systems shows. In the USA, healthcare accounted for 13.5 per cent of GDP in the early 1990s, more than double the UK National Health Service cost. The UK system, prior to market-reform introduced by the Conservative government, served all the population, whereas the US 'choice'-based system left an estimated 30–40 million Americans without health cover (Himmelstein and Woolhandler, 1986; Woolhandler et al., 1993). Despite the rhetoric of deregulation and reduced role for the state ('get the state off our backs'), the overall level of taxation during the New Right years did not decrease. In the UK, income tax levels fell dramatically from 1979 to 1990, but indirect taxes such as Value Added Tax (VAT) more than made up the difference (H.M.Treasury, 1993: Table 2A. 2).

The political and ideological obsession in the 1980s with applying choice to all spheres of government was extraordinary. Provision of choice became a key rationale – a sales pitch, almost – for the privatization of public utilities, for applying market logic to sectors which perhaps were inappropriate (Hambleton, 1988; see also Locke, 1994a; Hutton, 1995). Public sector bodies, it was argued, are unresponsive to consumer tastes, have no incentive to raise quality, to lower costs or to innovate (Carruthers and Holland, 1991). The free market is the optimum mechanism for allocating resources, as could be witnessed by the idiocies of the planned economies which not only failed to get goods to their consumers, but gave their consumers no control over what or how goods were produced. The previously homogeneous UK welfare system was thereafter separated into 'purchasers' and 'providers' of welfare services. Purchasers have the state-funded budgets with which to buy services from the providers. Providers may either be state or independent or private bodies. The key purpose of the purchaser–provider split is to engender a contractual relation within welfare services. The purchasers' task is to find the best value for money on offer from providers and to ensure the delivery of 'packages of care' to the customer as laid down in the Care in the Community Act 1990 (Barker, 1991).

The 1980s and 1990s application of the notion of choice to public administration ranks as one of the great political experiments by the state machine. This could only happen through a strong central state. It is also a wholly political phenomenon. As a result, perhaps, the love affair with choice in welfare began to raise questions about whether choice is transferable from goods to services. Potter (1988), for instance, questioned whether the principles of consumerism – access, choice, information, redress, representation – are at all applicable to public sector management. He further questioned whether they would yield a shift of power from the service provider to the citizen, let alone mould the service to the consumers' needs. Martin (1992) points out that the transfer of a consumer choice ideology to the service sector – exemplified by the explosion of interest among marketers of financial and welfare services – has underestimated the considerable differences between services and goods, from the perspective of the consumer. Services tend to be intangible (cannot be seen or touched), perishable (expire the moment they are created), inseparable (are produced and consumed simultaneously) and heterogeneous (they vary from service to service). Consumers or would-be consumers of services are forced into a number of conflicting roles, between which they have to learn to discriminate, if they are to exercise consumer choice.

So our review of the political economy of choice returns to where it began; that choice, where it is felt to exist, occurs within limits, that the rhetoric about choice is misplaced, that there is a downside to consumer choice, that choice is a political affair. In practice, there is a tendency for producers to coalesce, for markets to be oligopolistic and dominated by large producers, and for information to be dominated by interests of the seller. We agree with Galbraith that in a true market system, the firm should have few resources to expend on persuading the consumer to do other than he or she wanted (Galbraith, 1974: 45). Yet we have seen that in the second half of the twentieth century wholly new opportunities for highly suspect though systematic moulding of consumer choices have been opened up.

Which? or whether?

From our review of the field of consumer choice, we cannot escape a sense that one type of choice has monopolized the attention of writers whether psychologists, economists or cultural critics. This has obscured a different type of choice altogether, a more difficult type of choosing, one that involves dilemmas and morality rather than tastes and whim or a desire for difference. In our view, the notion of choice should be reserved for important matters in life, like choosing whether to take a job, whom to marry, whether to have children, whether to move abroad, whether to live in rented accommodation or to buy a house, whether to take on private healthcare insurance or send your children to private school.

So much that is referred to as consumer choice in mature markets and developed economies boils down to relative trivialities, compared with matters of life and death, political and civil rights, or the future of the planet. To us as individuals, it does, of course, matter if we put Mozart or McCartney on the tape-recorder, or buy this linen suit rather than the cotton one, or buy this soap-powder over that one, or eat this food rather than that. The deep opposition to lack of consumer choice in communist societies meant that the apologists for Western-style consumer choice have received far less critical attention than they were due. The glorification of consumer choice in the post Second World War period is symptomatic of a blind spot in Western cultural values, that choice is not only a matter of which product or service to select, but also to whether and how to consume.

We would prefer to think of choice in connection with significant issues in our lives, involving genuine life changes, as when someone chooses to become a vegetarian, having been brought up a meat eater, or when, as happened to a friend of ours, he decided to buy a pair of shorts to wear in the summer and for the first time to bare his polio-afflicted leg to the eyes of strangers. That is choosing to consume in a more meaningful sense. More everyday concerns regarding preferences among brands or substitute products could be referred to as selection, that is where one expresses a preference for one among fixed options.

Even manufacturers recognize that the range of options they offer to consumers is often restricted. Ton Otker, Marketing Research Executive for Philips International, argues that the 'harsh reality is that differences between the majority of brands within a given type of product (durable or non-durable consumer products) are actually minimal. . . . [C]onsumers are basically lazy and prefer to extend existing experience, rather than continually branching out and trying something new' (Otker, 1990: 32).

This type of everyday consumer decision is not sufficiently momentous to make it the basis for a consumer culture. When it mutates onto the political plane, this type of decision turns politics into a spectator sport and politicians into competing brands, a phenomenon already widely observed among commentators as diverse as Hobsbawm (1994), Postman (1986) and Baudrillard (1983a, 1983b). Economists, of course, will continue to build elaborate models on just this restricted type of choice. In our view, the right of individuals to make infinitesimal selections between close alternatives, important though it may be, should not override other vital human interests, priorities and rights. The fetishization of choice is symptomatic of a large hole at the heart of consumerism.

3

The Consumer as Communicator

Goods assembled together in ownership make physical, visible statements about the hierarchy of values to which their chooser subscribes. Goods can be cherished or judged inappropriate, discarded, and replaced. Unless we appreciate how they are used to constitute an intelligible universe, we will never know how to resolve the contradictions of our economic life.

Mary Douglas and Baron Isherwood (1978: 5)

Few images have dominated discussions of consumption to the same extent as that of the consumer as communicator of meanings. This may be seen as the by-product of the current dominance of language in every cultural debate. It is not merely fashionable to talk of food, clothes, cars, buildings, organizations, politics or even our bodies *as* 'texts', carrying messages. The idea, according to many cultural theorists, is now that all culture *is* text, using different codes, but subject to very similar rules of syntax and grammar. Language no longer serves as a metaphor for understanding culture (let alone as a mere tool); it has become the central paradigm furnishing core concepts and ideas which then migrate into numerous other cultural debates, redefining the terms of these debates. This chapter explores the strengths and shortcomings of looking at consumption and the world of objects as a system through which we communicate to others as well as to ourselves.

Images of consumers as communicators, using material objects to express social differences as well as personal meanings and feelings, considerably pre-date the present privileged position of language within the human sciences. Simmel's theory of fashions as well as Veblen's critique of conspicuous consumption both approach material goods not as useful objects aimed at satisfying different human needs, but as signs defining social status, establishing differences and similarities. More recently anthropologists and sociologists have examined how social differences and status become encoded in systems of dress and clothing, food, transport and other areas of consumption (McCracken, 1988; Sahlins, 1972). An emerging tradition in historiography is currently re-evaluating consumption in the fifteenth and sixteenth centuries, revealing not only ostentatious displays of wealth but also a keen awareness of fashions and a rampant consumerism (Brewer and Porter 1993; McKendrick et al., 1982; Mukerji, 1983). Even the supposedly ascetic Protestants in the seventeenth and eighteenth centuries are gradually being discovered to have cultivated tastes for 'great country houses on their newly acquired estates and filling them with lovely artefacts (portraits, chairs, murals, and chinaware) that testified to their high social position' (Mukerji, 1983: 3). All of these trends have had the effect of dislodging material objects from their automatic linkage with physical and social needs and placing them within a communicative package as carriers of meaning.

The idea of needs goes out of fashion

Material objects are and have always been central to human communication. We communicate through words, but we also communicate through body language and manners, through gifts, through clothes, through food and through the innumerable items which we use, display and discard every day. Large sections of Homer's *Iliad* and *Odyssey* are devoted to detailed descriptions of material objects, armour, swords, shields as well as domestic objects, each object telling a story (Homer, 1974, especially Rh. XVIII; 1983). At a less poetic level, even a sword may serve its aim without actually being used, by communicating deterrence. This appears so self-evident that it is surprising that entire areas of the human sciences have ever been able to study the material world which surrounds us without looking into communication. Yet, large areas of psychology, sociology and economics have in different ways done precisely that. Whether a coat is seen as an item to keep one warm, as the product of a deskilled mechanical process or as an item on an inventory – in all of these instances, its communicative qualities are either ignored or denied. Consider, for example, the opening of Marx's *Capital*:

> The wealth of those societies in which the capitalist mode of production prevails, presents itself as 'an immense accumulation of commodities,' its unit being a single commodity. Our investigation must therefore begin with the analysis of a commodity.
>
> A commodity is, in the first place, an object outside us, a thing that by its properties satisfies human wants of some sort or another. The nature of such wants, whether for instance, they spring from the stomach or from fancy, makes no difference. Neither are we here concerned to know how the object satisfies these wants, whether directly as means of subsistence, or indirectly as means of production. (Marx, 1867/1967: 35)

Marx and many of those who followed him approached material objects, in the first place, in terms of their usefulness, hence the term 'use-value', and subsequently as things that can be exchanged or traded, hence the term 'exchange-value'. Marx held no naive naturalistic views of the ways objects fulfil human needs, being fully aware both of the social nature of these wants and of the polymorphous usefulness of objects. Nevertheless, he did not inquire into the factors that make objects useful or the manner in which they may satisfy human wants. A weapon, a machine, a coat, a clock, a table and a jewel, are all useful objects having use values; they cannot be compared with each other until they are treated as exchange-values. Political economy takes no interest in what makes them useful or what uses they may have: 'To discover the various uses of things is the work of history' (1867/1967: 35).

Subsequent authors have distinguished between luxuries and necessities, but the essential link between the usefulness of the object and need of the consumer remained (see Lebergott, 1993). Conservatives prefer the term 'utility' to the Marxist 'use-value'. As we saw in the previous chapter, the two have argued endlessly whether the state or the individual is a better judge of these needs, and whether a socialist or a capitalist production system is better able to satisfy them. Nevertheless, they agreed on seeing objects as the means of satisfying material, psychological and social needs, that is, as things whose primary raison d'être lies in their uses.

Baudrillard has vigorously contested this view, arguing that use value was always a flawed concept which foreclosed any theoretical study of consumption (1972/1988: 44 ff.). By short-circuiting the uses of objects with putative human needs, use-value reduces consumption to a series of tautologies: 'I buy this because I need it; I need it because it is useful to me', 'I buy this because I like it; I like it because it is nice', and so on. The shortcomings of the idea of use-value are laid bare by consumption patterns in the industrial West. The word 'useful' is surely being stretched to excess when applied to video games, olive pâté, kitchen gadgets, cigarettes as well as numerous other objects we consume daily. To describe an expensive pair of running shoes as 'useful for running' or a perfume as 'useful for enhancing one's self-image' collapses either to tautology or to absurdity–a theoretical impasse. To argue retrospectively that such objects fulfil human needs merely highlights the impasse. (For more equivocal arguments than Baudrillard's on the demise of use value, see Lee (1993) and Kellner (1989).)

An earlier generation of social critics had also expressed reservations about the idea of goods as use-values. One of them, Adorno, argued that under capitalist accumulation the exchange-value of commodities dominates or even obliterates their use-values. Objects are produced if they can be sold at a profit, rather than because of any social or individual uses they may have. Most commodities, argued Adorno, become detached from their use-value; use-values persist as distant memories lost in the noisy symbolic clout of consumer society, whereas commodities acquire new symbolic meanings and associations (Rose, 1978: 25).

The demise of the concept of use-value, precipitated by the Western consumers' apparent willingness or even eagerness to purchase commodities with only the most tenuous use-value or no apparent use-value at all, has opened several possibilities. One is to argue along with Packard (1957/1981), Marcuse (1964) and Lasch (1980, 1984) that consumers are *victims* (see Chapter 7: The Consumer as Victim), duped into buying more or less useless objects by techniques of mass manipulation and marketing. A less pessimistic option is to argue that the attraction of objects in advanced capitalism lies not in their function but in their aesthetic qualities, the consumer being essentially an *artist* whose purchases constitute the brush-strokes of an ongoing creative process; for example, one's home becomes one's creative expression (see Chapter 6: The Consumer: Hedonist or

Artist?). Yet another option is to approach the consumer as an *explorer* of objects, as one who goes out shopping 'just to look' or who purchases without any clear notion of what lies ahead but in the hope of discovering something exciting and unexpected; for example, buying a record or a book because you like the cover or title (see Chapter 4: The Consumer as Explorer).

The meanings of goods

None of these less pessimistic images, however, have quite the currency enjoyed by the image of the consumer as *communicator*. At the core of this image lies the idea that material objects embody a system of meanings, through which we express ourselves and communicate with each other. We want and buy things not because of what things can do for us, but because of what things mean to us and what they say about us. According to this view, goods tell stories and communicate meanings in different ways but every bit as effectively as words. In the first place, material objects stand as evidence that certain events took place, removing ambiguity and fixing meanings. A wedding ring, for example, is the material object which establishes marital status, turning two separate people into husband and wife; its 'use' lies primarily in the story it tells about those wearing it. According to this view, whether a car is a useful device to carry you from A to B is largely irrelevant. There are many ways of going from A to B, and in any event the reasons why one wishes to go from A to B may be related to the availability of a car. A car, therefore, is not a carrier of persons so much as a carrier of meanings about itself, its owner, its manufacturer and the broader culture. It is a part of a symbolic nexus made up of material goods (Firat, 1992; Pandya and Venkatesh, 1992).

The study of consumption as communication proceeds from the cultural values of goods and the meanings which they embody. Economic (exchange) values ultimately derive from cultural values, not from biological or social 'needs':

> One cannot sell objects that do not have meaning to other people. A wad of paper or ball of fluff does not have economic value, unless adopted by an artist for an artwork or otherwise used as a raw material. . . . But objects do not have to have absolute cultural meanings in order to sell. A Mexican blanket may be bought in Mexico to be used on a bed for warmth while it may sell in the United States as a wall hanging. People need only find ways to make objects meaningful to make them economically valuable (without necessarily depending on the meanings of their creators). (Mukerji, 1983: 13)

The recognition that goods are parts of a communication system opens great possibilities of explaining the seemingly insatiable character of modern consumption without recourse to concepts of greed and envy, of exploring how different goods may combine to generate composite stories, and of explaining why people may make do without necessities in order to afford luxuries. Finally, it opens the possibility of assessing the impact of image-makers and 'merchandisers of meaning' (Sievers, 1986: 347) without resorting to the idea of manipulation or deception, discussed in the previous chapter.

Communication and consumption – some early views

Two of the earliest theorists to focus on the communicative qualities of commodities were Thorstein Veblen and Georg Simmel, both of whom were fascinated by the emerging metropolitan life-styles at the turn of the century, especially the ostentatious displays of wealth pursued by the nouveaux riches. In *The Theory of the Leisure Class*, first published in 1899, Veblen explored how, at least for the newly rich, everyday objects lose their functional qualities and become objects of display, establishing the social standing of their owners and users. For the members of the leisure class, the functions of objects are not defined by their uses; their function is to signify that their user does not work with his or her hands, or indeed does not work at all. Goods become status markers, indicating a certain level of income and a life style of leisure. Veblen's conception, as McCracken has argued (1988: 36), did not involve any elaborate theory of communication or any genuine symbolic depth. Goods are 'prima facie evidence' of income, rather than symbols. Fashionable clothes are *insignia* of leisure. Any sensible observer can deduce the wealth of a person by the cost of an item of clothing they wear, without any intricate interpretation or clever decoding.

Veblen shrewdly managed to detach consumption, especially ostentatious and 'excessive' consumption, from notions of greed or acquisitiveness and to account for its driven qualities by linking it to social status. At the heart of his conception lies emulative spending, a heightened propensity to consume in order to keep up with the Joneses. People are tyrannically dominated by fashion, because falling behind the fashion implies one's social decline. McKendrick et al. (1982) have pointed out that what Veblen observed and described is what pioneering entrepreneurs like Josiah Wedgwood had been aware of and exploited for well over a century – that selling pottery, not because of its use-value but because of its snob value, pays (see also Wernick, 1991). Conspicuous consumption may be aggravated by capitalism, but can be seen as a feature of all cultures; it is based on Veblen's central assumption, that social competition for status induces imitation.

Imitation is a central feature in the other early theory of consumerism, developed by Georg Simmel. Like Veblen, Simmel approached consumption essentially as a process whereby social status and rank are established and communicated. Display is no side-effect of consuming, according to these two views, but its very essence. In an article entitled 'Fashion' (1904/1971), Simmel argued that social groups for ever seek to emulate the clothing patterns of their social superiors. However, Simmel argued that status competition inspires not only imitation but also differentiation. The higher social strata seek to distance themselves from their close subordinates by endlessly adopting new fashions and new trends. These act as the new status markers, while yesterday's status markers fall into disrepute to them, even as they are adopted by social groups below them. In this way, imitation and differentiation drive fashion. He wrote:

> The peculiarly piquant and suggestive attraction of fashion lies in the contrast between its extensive, all-embracing distribution and its rapid and complete disintegration; and with the latter of these characteristics the apparent claim to permanent acceptance again stands in contrast. (1904/1971: 322)

Leading social groups set new trends in an attempt to distinguish themselves from the masses; the new trends are then adopted by those next in the pecking order until eventually they 'trickle down' to lower social groups. By this time, the trend-setters have moved onto new pastures. Even more than Veblen, Simmel was able to show that acquisitiveness, the seemingly irrational change of fashions, the psychological obsolescence of outmoded, though perfectly functional commodities and the obsessive interest in style, fashion and trends are all fuelled by an underlying competition for social status and prestige.

Veblen's and Simmel's ideas have had considerable influence on subsequent theories of consumer behaviour. Their plausibility, when applied to many of the goods we consume in everyday life, is remarkable. Consider, for example, the plight of parents whose children nonchalantly discard yesterday's expensive toys only to embrace a new fad, smartly displayed by their friends in the school yard. In the early 1990s, parents of all incomes and classes fought pitched battles in toy shops to obtain the precious sets of 'turtle ninja warriors'; a mass marketing exercise had induced turtle mania to children throughout the Western world. The coveted turtle logos featured on every conceivable item of children's clothes, furniture, kitchenware, and so on. It may seem ridiculous, but any child who failed to sport at least some turtle merchandise could be described as culturally deprived. What was even more remarkable was the speed with which turtles became passé. Within a few months what had been treasured objects turned into objects of derision. Children who turned up at school still wearing clothes with turtle logos or carrying turtle-emblazoned bags or pencil-cases found themselves teased and ridiculed. It was now the turn of the turtles to become symbols of cultural deprivation. There is nothing new about this phenomenon; whole commercial empires have been built on it, most conspicuously that of Disney (Goulart, 1970).

Holiday destinations can also be seen reflecting status competition among different social groups. New tourist resorts are 'discovered' by the trend-setters, who scorn to visit the mass destinations. Yet, these new resorts gradually trickle down to become mass destinations themselves. Snobbery, hardly concealed contempt and disparagement are reserved for those who cannot afford the new fashionable resorts, even worse for those who have not realized that the resorts they visit are no longer fashionable. Like children's toys, holiday destinations are not innocent or risk-free; they are part of a process whereby meanings of social worth are established and elaborate hierarchies of social standing are sustained.

Simmel, like Veblen, did not develop a theory of how particular meanings come to be attached to particular objects, how meanings migrate across different categories of objects or the changes which they undergo as they are interpreted and decoded. Nor did he explore the circumstances under which subordinate groups may choose to reject the fashions set up by their social superiors and set up fashions of their own (something central to the work of Bourdieu and Douglas). He did, however, argue very cleverly that rejection of fashion and affected indifference to it very quickly becomes 'imitation, but under an inverse sign' (1904/1971: 307), that is, a fashion in its own right. His views on the fickle, arbitrary quality of fashion anticipated current postmodern thinking on 'the arbitrariness of signs' and 'free-floating signifiers', as we shall see. But the paramount value of his work on fashion lies in its convincing portrayal as at once irrational, capricious, tyrannical but also a central force in our lives as consumers:

> Judging from the ugly and repugnant things that are sometimes in vogue, it would seem as though fashion were desirous of exhibiting its power by getting us to adopt the most atrocious things for its sake alone. The absolute indifference of fashion to the material standards of life is well illustrated by the way in which it recommends something appropriate in one instance, something abstruse in another, and something materially and aesthetically quite indifferent in a third. (1904/ 1971: 297–8)

More recent views

The pioneering qualities and originality of Simmel's and Veblen's work is gradually being recognized. Their theories suffer from a number of theoretical shortcomings (McCracken, 1988; Tilman, 1992), yet the fact remains that by looking at the goods which we consume, not as material necessities or useful objects, but as markers of social standing, Veblen and Simmel placed consumption at the heart of social theorizing, long before this became a theoretical fashion in its own right. Their views prefigure many current ideas regarding consumption as a system of communication. An oft-quoted statement of this position is provided by the anthropologist Mary Douglas and the economist Baron Isherwood in *The World of Goods: Towards an Anthropology of Consumption* (1978). Unlike Veblen and Simmel, however, Douglas and Isherwood argued that there had been too much sniping at excessive consumption. For too long, the study of consumption had suffered from 'a tendency to suppose that people buy goods for two or three restricted purposes: material welfare, psychic welfare, and display' (1978: 3). Much of the sniping would be silenced if consumption was seen as a *live information system*, through which cultural meanings are conveyed and contested. The essence of objects lies in the social symbolism which they carry:

> Instead of supposing that goods are primarily needed for subsistence plus competitive display, let us assume that they are needed for making visible and stable the categories of culture. It is standard ethnographic practice to assume that all material possessions carry social meanings and to concentrate a main part of cultural analysis upon their use as communicators. (1978: 59)

Douglas and Isherwood are more concerned than the earlier theorists about the fine nuances of meanings which may be communicated through material objects, as well as about the creative choices which consumption require:

> The housewife with her shopping basket arrives home: some things in it she reserves for her household, some for the father, some for the children; others are destined for the special delectation of guests. Whom she invites into her house, what parts of the house she makes available to outsiders, how often, what she offers them for music, food, drink, and conversation, these choices express and generate culture in its general sense. (1978: 57)

Instead of passive imitation or compulsive differentiation, they argue that 'the most general objective of the consumer can only be to construct an intelligible universe with the goods he chooses' (1978: 65). Goods do not only communicate social categories and hierarchies (e.g. superior/ subordinate, avant-garde/conservative, new rich/old rich) but a highly varied, specific and symbolically charged range of meanings. In this sense, they are far richer than signs or insignia, and more like stories through which we communicate with each other and express our emotions. As Miller has noted (1987: 99), children are able to articulate a wide variety of feelings and desires through objects at a much earlier age than through purely linguistic symbolism and although language may supplement the usefulness of material objects in communication, it never quite nullifies it.

Consider, for example, the range of meanings communicated through food, an area of consumption on which Douglas has devoted considerable attention over many years. In her classic article 'Deciphering a meal' (1972/1975), she examined in detail what exactly constitutes a meal. She argued that the definition of a meal varies across cultures and has little relation to the nutritional qualities of what is being consumed. Instead, it depends on the types of utensils used, the kinds of ingredients used, the type of cooking and so on. These not only differentiate meals from other occasions when food and drink is taken (e.g. 'drinks', 'snacks', 'quick bites', etc.) but also define what kind of meal is being consumed as well as what the relations are among those who participate. To most middle-class Britons, a sequence of soup and fruit simply does not constitute a meal, just as eating without utensils cannot be described as a meal (at least until the arrival of US-style 'fast food'). A dish with two staple items on a plate, such as potatoes *and* rice, sounds a discordant note, just as a misspelt word on a printed page or a mispronounced word in a sentence.

Food on a plate, then, constitutes a system of communication, with its own rules and its own ambiguities. It is a coded message: 'If food is treated as a code, the message it encodes will be found in the pattern of social relations being expressed. . . . Food categories encode social events' (Douglas, 1972/1975: 249). Particular types of meal are signalled through the use of special dishes or trimmings. The use of special items, such as turkey with all the trimmings at Christmas, a roast on Sunday, or a first course followed by an entrée for a dinner party, communicates specific messages. For Douglas, unlike Veblen, ostentation does not necessarily imply social competition, but rather a fixing of meanings. Social and moral judgement is withheld. The use of special cutlery or luxury china during a meal may be less a means of impressing an important guest than a way of stating that a meal is a special one in comparison with others.

While Douglas has been persistently critical of Veblen (for example, Douglas and Isherwood, 1978: 4 and passim), Veblen's argument about competitive imitation can be seen as a special case of Douglas's more general view that goods establish social categories. For it can hardly be denied that one of the range of social categories which *may* be communicated through a meal is social superiority, especially if a highly ostentatious meal is served to a visitor who can hardly reciprocate at the same level. Nevertheless, Douglas's argument considerably enlarges the communicative potential of material goods, well beyond the establishment of social hierarchies to the general maintenance of meanings. Without material goods, argues Douglas, meanings become unstable, ambiguous, they tend to drift or even disappear. Meanings require rituals to sustain them, and rituals depend on material objects:

> More effective rituals use material things, and the more costly the ritual trappings, the stronger we can assume the intention to fix the meanings to be. Goods, in this perspective, are ritual adjuncts; consumption is a ritual process whose primary function is to make sense of the inchoate flux of events. (Douglas and Isherwood, 1978: 65)

Douglas and Isherwood carry the argument well beyond those of Veblen and Simmel, by highlighting the interconnections of material objects as a feature of their communicative potential, instead of treating each object as a separate icon. Objects do not make individual statements, but rather they communicate together with other objects, just like individual items on a menu or on a plate acquire their significance in the light of the other items. Silver cutlery next to crystal wine glasses and expensive porcelain tells a very different story from silver cutlery in the midst of rustic tableware.

The Diderot effect and product constellations

The combined effect of material objects is graphically captured in what McCracken terms the 'Diderot unity', prompted by an intriguing observation made by the great French thinker Denis Diderot (1713–84). In a little essay entitled 'Regrets on parting with my old dressing gown', Diderot describes how upon receiving a gift of a magnificent scarlet robe, he discarded his 'ragged, humble, comfortable old wrapper'. He then started getting dissatisfied in turn with every other item in his study for failing to live up to the splendour of the new item. He therefore set about replacing chairs, engravings, bookshelves and everything else. With every new acquisition, however, he found new things to be dissatisfied with, so that eventually he looked back nostalgically at his study the way it used to be, crowded, humble, chaotic but happy. 'Now the harmony is destroyed. Now there is no more consistency, no more unity, and no more beauty', he reflected (quoted in McCracken, 1988: 119).

McCracken, prompted by Diderot's reflections, observes that objects do not communicate in isolation but in concert with other objects (the 'Diderot unity'). Once a particular component is replaced, the harmony is undermined, precipitating further changes. According to this view, individual purchases are not motivated by envy or social competition or display, but by an urge for consistency and completeness. The quest for completeness, consistency and unity, is, of course, a driving force in every collector; but it is also a more general cultural phenomenon. Buying a new set of speakers for one's stereo system is likely to lead to dissatisfaction with one's amplifier; the replacement of the amplifier is likely, in turn, to cause dissatisfaction with the other musical components. The owner of a new Rolex watch soon begins to be discontent with his or her modest motor car and starts dreaming of 'upgrading' it. This phenomenon is well-known to advertisers who perennially try to entice us with offers of products which complement or 'bring out the best in' what we already have. Product constellations can be seen as objects which somehow reinforce each other's message and reduce the scope for ambiguity or conflict. Even more commonly, we are enticed with 'complete sets', packages or collections which have already been designed to communicate in unison.

Moving from the public statements of goods in Mary Douglas's arguments to the solitary concerns of Diderot, it may be thought that we have lost sight of the consumer as communicator. After all, Diderot's study, like his dressing gown, were private, not meant for public display. Are there some forms of solitary, personal consumption which simply repudiate the idea of consumption as communication? Douglas and McCracken do not think so. Douglas argues that even the solitary consumers submit to the rules and categories of their culture, when, invisible to others, they eat their meals with knives and forks and shirk away from beginning with pudding and ending with soup, or eating mustard with lamb and mint with beef (Douglas and Isherwood, 1978: 67). Somewhat similarly, McCracken describes goods both as 'bulletin boards for internal messages and billboards for external ones' (1988: 136). Through the goods which we consume, we may be communicating with ourselves, reinforcing social categories and classifications. Like old family photographs which are not for public display, we may use those private goods to remind ourselves of who we are, what we have achieved, what we have lost and what we may wish for the future.

It is questionable, however, whether many consumer goods fall into this category of purely personal story-telling, entirely devoid of a social dimension. Consider for example some increasingly popular types of consumption in the West, such as body piercing jewellery or tattoos in intimate places. The very fact that such practices are now seen as fashionable indicates that, for all their privacy and intimacy, they comply with the trends described by Simmel and elaborated by Douglas and McCracken. Like whispered secrets, private and hidden jewellery and tattoos can be seen as a unique type of communication, confirming the special standing of both those who don them as well as of those allowed to see them.

Gifts

Even Diderot, in his solitary study, was hardly removed from a process of communication. In the first place, he was interpreting his friend's opulent gift as a message confirming the eminence which he had attained, rather than purely as a token of esteem or as a mere luxury in which he might indulge without further ado. Moreover, through the hapless sequence of subsequent replacements, he might have been seeking to communicate to himself an image of himself as someone who, adorned by his magnificent scarlet robe, deserves something more sumptuous for his den than his simple study of old. His friend's gift turned inadvertently into a Trojan Horse.

If virtually all goods carry meanings, gifts are self-conscious of their meaning-carrying capacities. By their essence, gifts are laden with symbolism, punctuating important ritual occasions, like weddings, anniversaries, birthdays, name-days, bar mitzvahs, christenings, house moves, Christmas, Mother's and Father's Days, Valentine's Days, and so on. Gifts must not be regarded as a small class of objects and exchanges at the margins of consumption. From the 'treats' indulged by parents on deserving children, to flower bouquets dispatched by Interflora, to the purchasing of rounds of drinks or the holding of parties, to corporate hospitality, to the generalized consumer delirium as Christmas approaches, gifts are an important feature of Western culture and a cardinal feature of many others. A new and unique merchandising operation called 'The Gift Shop' has confidently taken its place in shopping malls, high streets and airport lounges. Whole areas of the economy from jewellery and perfumes to book and record tokens, are now fuelled by gift-giving. It is not accidental that the study of gifts has attracted considerable research interest and offers important insights into the consumer as communicator.

Since the pioneering work of Marcel Mauss (1925/1974), it is widely accepted that gifts, unlike donations, are not just free goods, but parts of reciprocal exchange relations. Gifts reflect the nature and importance of the occasion, they communicate meanings and emotions (such as respect, gratitude, love, and even pity, disdain and scorn) as well as defining the social and emotional distance between giver and receiver. The meanings of gifts are often ambiguous and far from easy to interpret (Sahlins, 1972) and the choice of gifts can become a cause of major headaches. Yet, the very ambiguity in the meanings of gifts makes them highly effective. Like myths, gifts can carry meanings which are at once ambiguous and powerful. And like myths, gifts can reconcile the irreconcilable (Barthes, 1973), bridging vast differences of culture and interest, though of course they can equally lead to gigantic misunderstandings and conflict. For this reason, most of us treat gifts with special respect, as if we recognize that they are a risk. A gift is something which both the giver and the receiver will be judged by. It is also something through which both giver and receiver will judge the other's opinion of them, as well as the importance which the other accords to the occasion. It is not surprising then that the amount of time we spend in choosing a present is considerably greater than that which we spend in buying similar items for personal consumption (Belk, 1979; Belk, 1982; Pandya and Venkatesh, 1992).

Gifts communicate in many ways and are judged by many of their qualities. Consider one of the simpler ones, price. The price of a gift is an important part of its meaning, yet it can be highly ambiguous. An inexpensive gift from a rich relative may be interpreted as a rebuff, as a discourtesy, as a sign of a loss of money or status on the part of the giver or as a sign of increasing social and emotional distance which the giver tries to establish. Yet an inexpensive gift may equally be accepted with relief for not imposing too severe demands for its reciprocation. A costly gift from a rich relative may be gratefully received with an acknowledgement of the relative's superior economic and perhaps social standing. It may, however, be interpreted as an attempt to humiliate, since it may not be reciprocated in kind. Gifts are a highly delicate area of consumption.

Price is not the only feature by which gifts are judged. Appropriateness, originality, presentation and personal time are highly valued qualities in gifts, as is the personal touch. Children may delight their parents with presents which they make themselves, until somehow they get the idea that things which they make themselves and are not paid for are not 'real presents'. A less well-off relative may be able amply to reciprocate an opulent present with a less expensive but very well-chosen one, a beautifully wrapped one, an exotic one or one which required a lot of his or her time. Skill, judgement and above all time can all enrich the meanings of a gift, compensating for its low cost. As Bourdieu (1979) has argued, time can be the most precious of gifts, and the time it takes to locate, to choose, to wrap and to present become parts of the story which the gift tells. The wrapping, the ribbons and cards which accompany a gift are no mere ornaments, but of the very essence.

Nor do gifts cease to communicate once the ritual of presentation has taken place. Some remain as reminders of the occasion or of the giver, keeping or even increasing their symbolic power as the years go by. These are treasured objects, whose damage, theft or loss is experienced as a personal injury by their owner. The anthropologist Levy-Bruhl (1966) noted that in some cultures, everyday objects like ornaments, clothes and tools, become literally incorporated in the self. In a similar way, Belk (1988) has argued that certain objects (especially things like cars, or houses) become vital elements of our identity as if they were physical extensions of our bodies. Lacan (1953) even went as far as to suggest that our car's mechanical failures are exactly equivalent to neurotic symptoms, its fits and starts are neurotic twitches. Such objects clearly provide a bridge between the consumer as communicator and the consumer as identity-seeker (see Chapter 5: The Consumer as Identity-seeker). Most gifts, however, have more mundane careers, being used and forgotten, or being sold as second hand goods at knock down prices, being given as 'half-gifts' to new receivers or simply being thrown away.

In an intriguing article on consumerism in Japan, Clammer describes how shopping habits are conditioned by the gift economy, 'a perpetual and enormous circulation of commodities – a gigantic kula-ring-like cycle of obligations and reciprocities' (1992: 207). Gifts, exchanged by the Japanese on a considerably larger scale than most West Europeans or Americans, come mostly to an inglorious end:

> A certain day each month is 'heavy rubbish day' when unwanted large objects can be put on the sidewalk for collection by the municipal rubbish collectors or by private contractors. The most astonishing variety and volume of things are discarded – furniture, TVs, bicycles, golf-clubs, all kinds of electrical appliances and just about everything that a modern household needs, . . . often in almost mint condition. (1992: 208–9)

From an economic point of view, endless rounds of gift giving may represent waste and may be dented by recession. All the same, in Japan, they strengthen networks of social relations and define social hierarchies in an effective way. In these respects, gifts highlight Douglas's and McCracken's arguments concerning the consumer in the capacity of gift buyer and gift receiver as someone who essentially creates, communicates and interprets meanings.

Gifts to one's self?

Is it possible to give gifts to oneself? Levy (1982) and Mick (1986) have argued that self-gifts differ in character from other personal consumption; they are quite common in Western cultures. Self-gifts can mark special occasions, like private anniversaries or special visits. Souvenirs are often purchased in this way, as markers of specific events. Even more commonly, they appear as rewards for achievement or consolations for failure, reasserting pride and self-respect. Pandya and Venkatesh give this graphic example:

> In the film 'Crimes of the Heart', Diane Keaton, a lonely middle aged single woman, thinks her family has forgotten her birthday. She gets a cookie for herself,

lights a candle on it and sings 'Happy Birthday' to herself. She gives herself a
birthday party the others forgot to give her. Her gift to herself accentuates her
loneliness but also affirms her selfhood. There are many such examples of self-gift
in real life like vacations as a reward after a year of hard work. But when families
discuss their vacations with their friends these often become signs of their status,
competition and success. (1992: 152–3)

Such self-gifts can be seen as part of a continuing dialogue one has with
oneself. One can almost imagine old Diderot, as he ruminates in his study,
on what should replace the threadbare tapestry hanging from the wall and
finally deciding to treat himself to a fine new one. The need which we have to
present special purchases as treats or rewards highlights the symbolic
importance of the objects we purchase. In this way, we use objects to
construct meaningful stories about our efforts, our successes and failures
and this is one of the factors which doubtless drives modern consumerism. A
new compact disc or video may be thought of as an unnecessary luxury which
we resist. If, however, we can present it as the just dessert for a successful
effort or as the rightful consolation for an unsuccessful one, it becomes
irresistible.

One could very well ask why success or failure need be marked in this way,
through the use of a newly acquired object? Is it impossible to construct
meaningful stories about ourselves and others without the assistance of the
objects? For example, is it necessary to mark an important anniversary with
a costly gift rather than a kiss and a hug? Why are singing, dancing, poetry
and speech-making not adequate enough rituals for a wedding, without
having in addition an arsenal of gifts? Is it impossible to construct a story of a
meaningful holiday without the material reminders of photographs,
souvenirs and other costly tourist paraphernalia?

Objects and sign values

Mary Douglas has argued that material objects are indispensable for fixing
the meanings and the categories of events. Long after the singing and the
dancing at the wedding has finished, the wedding ring will still be the
material evidence of the event. Primitive cultures as well as modern cultures
rely on material objects to fix meaning. Baudrillard, on the other hand,
whose early studies into consumer culture have much in common with
Douglas's, takes a different view. Like Douglas, Baudrillard viewed
material objects as forming a system of classification, though his assessment
of their value is more ambivalent: 'Objects are *categories of objects* which
quite tyrannically induce *categories of persons*. They undertake the policing
of social meanings, and the significations they engender are controlled'
(1968/1988: 16–7).

Having convincingly challenged the concept of objects as use-values,
Baudrillard approached each object as the carrier of a sign-value. This is
where his argument departs from Douglas's view of physical objects as

material repositories of social meaning. For Baudrillard the sign-values of objects are mobile and precarious, more so since the beginning of the industrial era, and infinitely more so at the present time. Like neurotic symptoms, where each symptom can easily be replaced by another (e.g. a neurotic cough may be replaced by colitis), the sign-value of objects can quickly migrate from one commodity to another:

> A washing machine *serves* as equipment and *plays* as an element of comfort, or of prestige etc. It is the field of play that is specifically the field of consumption. Here all sorts of objects can be substituted for the washing machine as a signifying element. In the logic of signs, as in the logic of symbols, objects are no longer tied to a function or to a defined need. This is precisely because objects respond to something different, either to a social logic, or to a logic of desire, where they serve as a fluid and unconscious field of signification. (1970/1988: 44)

Baudrillard is arguing here that for the individual consumer, the desire for a washing machine may inexplicably be transferred onto a desire for a dress, a record or a car, just as the signifying effect of the washing machine may be achieved through a dishwasher, a carpet or a ring. Unlike Douglas who stresses the stabilizing influence of objects, Baudrillard views sign-values as fleeting and migratory. For Douglas, a wedding ring is solid, timeless, reassuring; for Baudrillard, a wedding ring is a transmitter of spasmodic, indistinct and ambiguous messages. This is what makes sign-values both fiercely contested as well as ideally plastic material in the hands of advertisers and marketers. This is also why, in the last resort, they are unable to provide the basis for real identity or selfhood. Ultimately, goods lose all signification, standing for nothing whatsoever beyond themselves. From being repositories of social meaning they become black holes into which meaning disappears (Baudrillard, 1983a, 1983b).

Brands, advertising and the destruction of meaning

> If I can describe a cake, a cigarette, a fishing rod, or a bottle of whisky in such a way that its basic soul, its basic meaning to modern man, becomes clear I shall, at the same time, have achieved direct communication. I shall have established a bridge between my advertisement and the reader and come as close as possible to motivating the reader or listener to acquire this experience via the product which I have promised him. (Dichter, 1960: 92, quoted in Lee, 1993, 150)

Selling things by making them tell stories was well-known to Dr Ernest Dichter, Director of the Institute of Motivational Research. He saw advertising as the art of making commodities communicate to us, by making goods speak with human voices (see Chapter 2: The Consumer as Chooser). Brands were humanized and brand names became condensations of stories. Like the 'crown' which stands metonymically for all things royal, majestic and imposing, brand names become embodiments of special qualities, values and images. Meaning travels from the whole to the part and from the part to the whole. A small bar of soap carrying the logo of Harrods, the famous London department store, becomes the embodiment of the Harrods values, tradition, soundness and quality, the best of Old British values. By purchasing the small bar of soap, one purchases all that Harrods stands for, and makes these attributes of Harrods one's own. Exploiting these metonymic qualities of goods has long been the task of advertisers and market analysts; it has been explored by academics, like Williamson (1986), Lee (1993) and McCracken (1988).

> Advertising works as a potential method of meaning transfer by bringing the consumer good and a representation of the culturally constituted world within the frame of a particular advertisement. The creative director of an agency seeks to conjoin these two elements in such a way that the viewer/reader glimpses an essential similarity between them. When this symbolic equivalence is successfully established, the viewer/reader attributes certain properties he or she knows to exist in the culturally constituted world to the consumer good. The known properties of the world thus come to be resident in the unknown properties of the consumer good. The transfer of meaning from the world to good is accomplished. (McCracken, 1988: 77)

McCracken argues strongly that material objects act as a means of encoding and communicating meanings, but do *not* constitute a language. One of the main differences between language and objects is that objects are constrained in the range of meanings which they can assume. In language, onomatopoeic words apart, a particular sound may signify virtually anything, there being no necessary connection between signifier and signified, between word and meaning. Objects, on the other hand, 'bear a "motivated" and "non-arbitrary" relationship to the things they signify' (1988: 132). In this view, a Rolex watch cannot signify a poor man, since a poor man could not afford to buy one. Equally, an inexpensive 'unglamorous' pair of shoes may signify parsimony or poverty or inverted snobbery or various other qualities, but it *may not* by its very nature signify certain things like, for instance, wealth, power or discriminating taste in shoes.

Not so, argues Baudrillard, who, since his early book *The System of Objects* (1968) has seen brands as capable of telling virtually *any* story, however unconnected to any putative need or use. Even a Rolex may be but a cheap fake, bought at a hundredth of the price, though looking similar. And even a 'real' Rolex may appear as nothing but the kind of model that is much imitated and faked. Once Rolex watches, real and fake, are seen worn on the wrist of any taxi driver, the meaning carried by them becomes plastic. This argument develops Simmel's idea on the whimsical nature of fashion, whereby anything can become fashionable, provided that it stands out from the rest. Baudrillard takes this argument to its logical conclusion, that signification means simply difference and nothing else. The only meaning that signs retain is their difference from other signs; and this is the end of meaning:

> Diverse brands follow one another, are juxtaposed and substituted for one another without an articulation or transition. It is an erratic lexicon where one brand devours the other, each living for its own endless repetition. This is undoubtedly the most impoverished of languages: full of signification and empty of meaning. It

is a language of signals. And 'loyalty' to a brand name is nothing more than the conditioned reflex of a controlled affect. (1968/1988: 17)

The more brands like McDonald's, Marlboro, Harrods and Nike become temporary repositories of 'meaning' the more emaciated and burnt out the meaning becomes. The more obsessively we interpret, analyse and classify others in terms of the messages emitted by their shoes, their clothes and their preferred drinks, the less we know about them. Ultimately, medium becomes message, signifiers float freely and meaning implodes. Nike, the ancient Greek goddess of victory, no longer stands for victory, for the meaning of victory is swallowed up by the shoe. Clio is no longer an ancient Greek muse; nor do her classical qualities survive in the product; she has become momentarily a French motor car, a pretty girl, a youthful longing, a clever advertisement, before she is drowned by the noise of other brands, lost and forgotten.

In Baudrillard's view, within the media-dominated world of Western societies, boundaries between reality and representation, substance and image, have imploded, just like the difference between the real and the fake Rolex. A photograph no longer captures the essence of a real event, nor does it claim to do so. A photograph becomes pure image, the product of a photo-opportunity, a staged event which may link, for example, a perfume brand to a tropical island or a politician to a cause. But the viewer of the picture is aware that the picture is the product of a temporary marriage of convenience between two free floating signifiers, which will soon go their separate ways. Ultimately, the perfume, the tropical island, the politician and the cause lose any meaning, outside the photograph. Like photographs, other consumer goods cease to express meanings and they too become self-referential. The gift is no longer the material proof of Christmas, nor is the wedding ring the material proof of the wedding. Both become opportunistic carriers of ever-decreasing fragments of meaning. Christmas becomes *the* gift; its meaning apart from gifts, photo-opportunities, television images, drink and food opportunities shrivels to almost nothing. What makes you a mother is not having had a baby but the fact that you shop at a specialist shop called Mothercare. The wedding ring and paraphernalia procured from a shop called Pronuptia become *the* marriage. Disneyland is the photographs and merchandise one brings back. Ultimately Christmas, marriages, Disneyland and the other institutions of postmodern society become photo-opportunities, object-opportunities, spending opportunities and little else.

New wave advertising

The names adopted by rock bands, seemingly laden with meaning, yet ultimately completely meaningless, highlight Baudrillard's notion of the arbitrariness of the sign. They are entirely self-referential, making no attempt at signification or classification, their only point being to make a temporary impact on our consciousness, without getting lost in the general clamour of which they are but an infinitesimal part. The same can be said of the postmodern advertisements which have become common since the 1980s. These advertisements, pioneered by a number of new advertising agencies which challenged the functional and pragmatic approaches of the older more traditional agencies, eschewed both hard-sell and soft-sell approaches in favour of images and compositions from which 'selling' is effectively banned (see Davidson, M., 1992; Lee, 1993; Wernick, 1991). Instead of appealing to our reason or to our emotions, such advertising, along with other postmodern artefacts, celebrates visual images, 'decontextualizing "great" works of art and established aesthetic conventions, raiding the iconographies of religious beliefs and political struggles, or incorporating the forms of other cultures into its own discursive frame and for its own ends' (Lee, 1993: 149).

Many of these advertisements are intertextual, openly borrowing text or ideas from other advertisements and adding a twist. Alternatively, they are reflexive, being essentially advertisements about advertising. 'Aren't conventional ads a bore', they seem to say. 'Do they not treat consumers like dullards, presuming to manipulate their choices through silly images and naive stories. Now *we* know that *you* would not fall for such crude tricks, would you? In fact, we know that you cannot be manipulated at all. You are cool, sophisticated. So, let's forget about us selling you a product. Forget about the product altogether. Let's have some fun together.' Such is the message of this new generation of advertisements. Fun assumes the form of a joke, a pun, a parody of a competitor's advertisement or product, a puzzle, a guilty pleasure or the breaking of a taboo. Such fun, undoubtedly creates a degree of solidarity between the advertiser and the reader/viewer based on a shared sense of non-conformism, cleverness, originality, rebelliousness. A conspiracy is sometimes orchestrated between clever advertiser and smart consumer at the expense of supposedly dull advertisers, dumb consumers, or even the very manufacturer who is paying for the commercial. Whether consumers are flattered by such treatment and whether they appropriate the positive qualities residing in the hypertext are as questionable as whether such advertisements help sell products at all.

According to Davidson (1992), these advertisements tell no story about a product; their stories are at best about themselves and those who conceived them, at worst they would seem to have no story at all. They are pure signs without meaning, signs which almost coincidentally collide with 'products' (which are themselves but signs) only to destroy them, part of the 'hyper-real' world of the mass media, which in Baudrillard's later arguments completely defines the 'real' world. In the hyper-real world everything mutates into everything else, all is image, appearance and simulation. The television soap opera is more real than the viewers' own personal reality, the brand is more real that the product. In this hyper-real world, the consumer is no longer a communicator, nor are commodities sign-values. The consumer becomes a Pavlovian dog salivating mechanically at the sight of simple images, his or her emotions are conditioned responses to the sight of brands. Communication dissolves into seduction.

Baudrillard's insights unlock some of the mysteries and mystifications of modern advertising, mass media and communications, pointing at a very real crisis of meanings and signification. They highlight the fragility of systems of signification which are built around seemingly solid objects. They also act as a constant reminder that when we believe that we are most aware that we know what is going on, that we have objective, up to the minute, information from CNN, the BBC and other media organizations, we are in fact being transported in a world of special effects, simulations and virtual reality. (See, for example, Baudrillard's discussions of the Gulf War as a consumer spectacle in Gane (1993).) At the same time, one cannot escape the impression that Baudrillard's views on the omnipotence of modern media, their ability to shift signs and signifiers, to define reality and to destroy meaning, these are the products of one fixated on the mass media, living through the media and ultimately becoming himself part of the hyper-real world which alone interests him. "I live in the virtual. Send me into the real, and I don't know what to do', (Gane, 1993: 188) was Baudrillard's response to an offer to go to the Gulf and see for himself what was going on during that War.

Even if a good deal of modern consumption unfolds in the realm of virtual reality, simulations and make-believe, Baudrillard underestimates consumers' ability to *alter* rather than just receive and carry messages. It may be quite true that everyday reality is cluttered by the noise of commodities, signs and images, yet most of us have learnt to ignore much of this noise, screen it out and live with it, just as we can enjoy listening to music over the noise that surrounds it. We also learn to experiment with objects, to try them in different ways, and discover meanings in the *uses* we find for them. As de Certeau (1984) has argued, through makeshift arrangements and creative combinations of objects, we learn both to discard the spurious significations of the media and to redefine objects, replenishing them with meanings and significations (see Chapter 8: The Consumer as Rebel). Advertising agencies today are only too aware how deft consumers have become at subverting some sign-values, ridiculing others or appropriating others for the 'wrong' purposes (Carter, 1994; Cook, 1994).

In addition, Baudrillard simply disregards those areas of consumption which are rooted in the functional qualities of goods. A washing machine *is* after all a device for washing clothes, and one can hardly imagine doing without if one can afford it, sign-value or no sign-value. Many of the ordinary, unbranded, quiet, unobtrusive objects which surround us never seem to quit the mundane realms of the real for the fantasy world of simulations. And even when they become fantasy objects, they are just as likely to take on the robust cultural symbolic qualities highlighted by Douglas (a Valentine card stands for romantic love and roast turkey for Christmas) as the volatile, nervous and transient qualities of the hyper-real.

Conclusion

Consumption as communication opens numerous windows into our re-lations to the physical objects which surround us and the ways we use these objects to express meanings, feelings and social distinctions. This approach can account for the seemingly endless and absurd variety of products which we seek and use, without resorting to tautologies regarding the use-values of such objects or reducing everything to greed. Once we recognize that goods tell stories, that these stories resonate with symbolism and express meanings that cannot be expressed effectively through language, consumption becomes strangely re-humanized. Even irrational, absurd consumption, can be seen as a muddled, ambiguous, contested but ultimately sensical activity, rather than a zombie-like delirium. This is part of being human. Consider the following example from everyday experience:

> I am looking at a kitchen gadget, described on its package as an olive/cherry pip remover. It is a shining stainless steel contraption, a cousin to that other object which can be found in many kitchens, the garlic crusher. To describe this object as useful would be simply absurd. As a cooking implement, the object is an insult to my intelligence. As an object for which money was paid, it is an insult to my sense of thrift and economy. As an object for which natural resources were used up, to manufacture it, package it, transport it and display it, it is an affront to my 'green' conscience. As an object which clutters my already over-full kitchen drawers, it is a nuisance. Dear old Marcuse might have seen this object as evidence of the spiritual bankruptcy of modern culture and the alienation of the consumer. From most points of view, this is exactly the kind of object I abhor.
>
> Yet, my feelings towards it are tempered, once communication is brought into the picture. This olive/cherry pip remover was a present from a friend, who may have meant it as a joke (and a rather good one to someone who thinks he knows all there is to know about olives) or as a compliment of my cooking skills. Come to think about it, several friends have offered me kitchen gadgets over the years. It is possible that my friend might have been lured into buying this object by its claim to make a fine gift 'for the cook who has everything'; or more simply, my friend might have wanted to share a laugh with me at the expense of a plainly ridiculous object, whose uselessness is evident to all. In any event, the object resolved my friend's aporia, the difficulty of expressing something in words. It was not the perfect gift, I shall not be using it very much, nor will it become a permanent feature of my identity, but I do not reproach my friend for giving it me. I too have succumbed to the temptation of buying silly presents for friends, expecting a degree of clemency in their reading of them. A bit like a joke, which though not very funny, serves its purpose.

The point of this example is to show how objects can be useful as communicative devices. In this way, the idea of usefulness is brought very close to that of communicating meaning. For many objects, use has always involved communication. This applies not only to purely decorative objects with no proclaimed functional purposes or to objects which will serve as media in communication (such as telephones, television sets etc.), but also to a class of largely functional objects whose mere display may forestall their physical use. Weapons, guard dogs and burglar alarms (including fake ones), for instance, can be useful without actually being used, for their deterrent effect, which is achieved through communication. In a similar way, the olive/cherry pip remover was useful as a gift, even if I can never envisage using it.

In spite of its remarkable ability to explain numerous aspects of consumption, the image of consumer as communicator presents only a partial picture of consumption. Gifts, status symbols, fashion and branded goods, designer products, and goods which are self-consciously displayed, these are objects for which it seems tailor-made. For goods which are consumed without fuss, in privacy, it is less illuminating. The idea of self-gifts, which turns personal consumption into part of self-dialogue, seems more like an excuse or rationalization for behaviour rather than an explanation of it. The fact that an object can equally be a self-reward for success or a consolation for failure would support this scepticism. Unless we accept unconditionally Baudrillard's challenge and provocation, a hyper-real world of simulations and mirages, of fleeting signifiers and black holes of meaning, it is not clear from the idea of consumer as communicator why objects which require payment have such unique significance in our lives, what drives our desire for them and why we need excuses for purchasing them. Unlike myths, with which we argued commodities have much in common as carriers of symbolism, the resonance of most objects which were once desired and subsequently purchased fades away quickly. The image of consumer as communicator simply fails to account either for the kick we get when we acquire a new and much longed for commodity or for the frequent disappointment we feel for yesterday's purchases. The portrait of the consumer we next turn to, that which approaches the consumer as explorer, holds the promise of insights into these excitements and disappointments.

4

The Consumer as Explorer

When you start on your way to Ithaca,
then pray that the road is long,
full of adventure, full of knowledge.
. . .

Stop at Phoenician markets,
and purchase fine merchandise,
mother-of-pearl and corals, amber and ebony,
and delicious perfumes of all kinds.
. . .

And if you find her poor, Ithaca has not deceived you,
With the wisdom you have gained, with so much
     experience,
you have surely understood what Ithacas mean.

Kavafis, *Ithaca*

Who could fail to experience the eternal fascination of exotic markets, their
strange displays, their unfamiliar smells and sights, their mystifying rituals of
coaxing, bargaining and bluffing? There are no signs anywhere around you,
no empty Marlboro packets, no Coca Cola logos on refrigerated displays.
American Express is not known here. These markets are ageless, chance
alone has taken you there. You are surrounded by unfamiliar things; or
familiar things in unfamiliar guises, at unfamiliar prices. These are not
generally friendly places. Excitement is mixed with danger. Are things what
they appear to be? Is the amber real or might it be a clever plastic imitation?
Would you be taken for a ride if you paid the asking prize for a local
wood-carving? And what would it look like back in your house, miles away
from its siblings and forced to mix with your other valuable possessions? A
good topic of conversation or an eyesore?

Now picture yourself in a shopping mall, not perhaps the one you visit
regularly whose features you know well, but one slightly less familiar. It may
have been purpose-built or it may be housed in an old canning factory or a
converted and 'preserved' warehouse. This too is a place to explore, a place
to discover, but it is certainly more user-friendly. This is a space that has
been *designed* for exploration. An invisible hand has planned everything for
your delectation. The reassuring quality of its anchor supermarket at one
end, the familiar array of boutiques next to the intriguing shop selling
Peruvian parrots and Colombian hammocks, the bars, the restaurants, the
soft background music, the discreet lighting, the comfortable climatization,
the instantly meaningful signs – this is a synthetic oasis, and none the less
stimulating for being designed with people like you in mind. It is a clean,

genial, graffiti-free space, where a cultural oxymoron can be acted out, relaxed exploration. There are no worries here, no pushy salesmen, no invisible pickpockets, goods have fixed price-tags and are covered by the Trades Description Act; if you run short of cash, plastic money is welcome. To be sure, this is a fantasy world; it brings exotica to the consumer instead of taking the consumer to the exotic. Yet it is a space of exploration.

Exploring and shopping have become one. Bargain hunting, discovering new lines, new fashions, new 'product ideas' and new forms of fun; these are all part of the excitement of shopping. But exploration can begin before you leave your home; it can take place in a relaxed, poised manner, merely flicking the pages of glossy magazines, brimming with new ideas for entertaining guests, decorating your home or stimulating your partner (Barthes, 1973: 86) You can explore the lives of the rich and famous, study the interior of their houses and scrutinize every particle of their face. You can savour dream-like cuisine and be transported to magical places, hardly needing to leave your armchair or strain your purse. Alternatively, you may join the armies of energetic explorers, travel to distant places and fill your bags with souvenirs and your camera with images. Or you may explore the latest changes in your own high street's array of shops, window displays, signs and street life. Tele-shopping hopes to bring the excitement of high-street exploration into your own home. Whether we envisage the consumer browsing a magazine or touring, it is hard to imagine consumption without exploration or exploration without consumption.

This chapter looks at contemporary consumers as explorers of goods, marketplaces and signs. We examine the curiosity which is manifest in the act of shopping in all its diversity and the quest for novelty that drives some of our consuming behaviour. Some of the approaches which we will introduce may seem far-fetched and removed from the world of mundane day-to-day consumption. They lend themselves to easy ridicule as hopelessly indulgent and middle class, oblivious to the world of poverty and privation, as portrayed by theorists like Townsend (1979, 1993), Mack and Lansley (1985, 1992) and Seabrook (1985). Nevertheless, the image of the consumer as explorer was implicit in much of the work on consumption done by cultural theorists in the 1980s. It also inspired an entire generation of retailers and their designers who sought to transform shopping areas from hypermarkets to boutiques into terrains of exploration. By making explicit what has hitherto been implicit, namely the view of the consumer driven by insatiable curiosity, we seek to highlight both the strengths and, later, the serious deficiencies of these approaches.

Bargain hunting

Exploration takes many forms. Bargain hunting is perhaps the most evident. Even unfamiliar foreign markets may contain goods which can easily be obtained 'back home', though perhaps at different prices. Prices exercise undoubtedly a strange fascination on consumers. How is it possible that exactly the same item of clothing, the same bar of chocolate, the same shampoo, can cost different amounts in different shops? How is it possible that exactly the same train journey can incur dozens of different fares? How can the price of an electronic toy be halved in less than a year? Or for a pack of four video-tapes to retail for less than a pack of three identical video-tapes on display in the same shop? Not for nothing did Marx argue that commodities are enigmatic things, shrouded in mystery, long before marketers adopted pricing as one of the four Ps (the others being product, place and people) of their métier and decided to make these things still more confusing.

In spite of the growth of non-utilitarian, esoteric advertising, words like 'free', 'extra', 'more', 'value', 'savings' and, above all, 'bargain' dominate numerous commercials. What is a bargain? Clearly a bargain is in the first place quality at low price, good value for money. But this cannot make bargains the subject of a hunt, or fuel the kind of fever that is generated by the sales of large department stores, let alone explain the joy and delight generated by the discovery of a bargain, which parallels that of discovering a secret or sharing a good joke. Dry beans may represent excellent value for money, especially if value is defined in nutritional terms, though they could hardly be described as a bargain. Conversely, discovering a designer scarf at half its normal price may seem like a great bargain, even if the last thing you want is another scarf. A free bottle of champagne with every dozen you buy can look irresistible. Bargain hunting has little to do with sound management of household budgets, and more to do with discovering a secret, which few may share, a secret of getting something for nothing, in a world where everything has to be paid for. For years immemorial, the secret of commerce has been spotting bargains, buying cheap and selling dear. Whole areas of trade, from antiques to houses, and from second-hand cars to coin or stamp collections are driven by the craving for bargains. The discovery of a bargain performs great services to our self-esteem. It is not uncommon for individuals to fashion their identities around their uncanny ability to spot bargains and take advantage of them. Their exploits are often recounted to others (who may feel bored to tears or, alternatively, envious at having missed an opportunity) and embroidered for greater effect, while the spoils of their adventures are displayed with considerable pride.

While much energy and money is spent by advertisers to inform consumers of the bargains on offer, it seems to us that, like secrets, bargains cannot be known to everybody. Nor can a shop or a retailer be perceived to make a living by always offering bargains. In these cases, goods on offer cease to be bargains. They may be cheap or economical but not bargains. Looking for a bargain then, is not the same as looking for value for money. It is more like looking for opportunities to discover anomalies in the market and take advantage of them. The bargain spotter is akin to a trickster figure who exposes fissures in the system and triumphs against its dictates through cunning and opportunism. Bargain hunters are not always solitary creatures. Informal networks of information exist through which individuals can share their discoveries with friends and neighbours. Finding a bargain marks the triumph of opportunism, like scoring an undeserved goal, which is all the sweeter for being undeserved.

A duty to explore?

It is paradoxical that bargain hunting, which is central to value-for-money consumerism and to consumer advocacy (see Chapter 9: The Consumer as Activist), has not attracted much attention in studies of consumption, whether undertaken by economists, sociologists or psychologists. Economists, in particular, have been reproached for ignoring curiosity as one of the consumer's motives. Scitovsky, one of the few economists who has introduced the concept of exploration in to the discussion of modern consumption, has criticized other economists for failing to recognize 'that most important motive force of behavior, including consumer behavior – man's yearning for novelty, his desire to know the unknown. The yearning for new things and ideas is the source of all progress, all civilization; to ignore it as a source of satisfaction is surely wrong' (1976: 11).

By contrast, however, curiosity was a notion of considerable interest in cultural theory circles, coupled with the idea of difference. When applied to the study of consumption, these generated immense excitement: the consumers' quests for new pleasures, new meanings and even new identities, through tiny differences in what they purchased, through their sorties to the market were endlessly probed. Today's Western consumer is constantly exhorted to savour new tastes, to discover new pleasures and to explore new worlds. As Baudrillard, a major figure in this trend, noted:

> the modern consumer, the modern citizen, cannot evade the constraint of happiness and pleasure, which in the new ethics is equivalent to the traditional constraint of labor and production. . . . He must constantly be ready to actualize all of his potential, all of his capacity for consumption. If he forgets, he will be gently reminded that he has no right not to be happy. He is therefore not passive: he is engaged, and must be engaged, in continuous activity. Otherwise he runs the risk of being satisfied with what he has and of becoming asocial. A *universal curiosity* (a concept to be exploited) has as a consequence been reawakened in the areas of cuisine, culture, science, religion, sexuality etc. (1970/1988: 48)

Being true to oneself as a consumer means being eager to browse and to explore. A vast number of consumer products, ranging from books, magazines, videos and films, to holiday packages, have materialized arousing consumer curiosities, exciting them, nurturing them and satisfying them. Newspapers are filled with curiosity features, exotic places, exotic cuisines, exotic people, and so on. 'I don't like travelling' is an instant conversation stopper at parties, just as 'I don't have a TV' can be an instant conversation starter! The local grocery store has been metamorphosed into the hypermarket which may stock up to 40,000 different items. This jungle of consumption offers a bewildering array of goods, whose prices, packages, sizes, formats and names, to say nothing of contents, are constantly changing. Thus, shopping for groceries turns from a habit or a rational choice into an exploration (see Chapter 2: The Consumer as Chooser).

Consumer explorations are not searches into deep unknowns, inner or outer. Instead they are explorations of minute variations, of infinitesimal idiosyncrasies of style, products, brands, signs and meanings. This type of exploration is the discourse of *difference*, the discovery of difference, the establishing of difference and the appropriation of difference. Even modest bargain hunting is a quest of a certain type of difference (that is, to be the person who spots the bargain) and the reading of meaning into this difference.

The quest for difference

Images of consumers as explorers, restless and impatient, driven by insatiable curiosity, constantly looking for difference, underscore the ideas of numerous prominent cultural theorists, including Bourdieu, Bauman, Featherstone, McCracken and the early Baudrillard. Reekie argues that 'shopping appears to have undergone re-skilling, from a management task defined by the shopper's ability to select "bargains" (or quality at low cost), to a creative task defined by the shopper's ability to locate unusual, unstandardized or personalized goods' (1992: 190). Difference drives the modern consumer, argues Baudrillard, effectively obliterating the concept of *needs* which can be satisfied through material objects, since 'a need is not a need for a particular object as much as it is a "need" for difference (the *desire for social meaning*)' (1970/1988: 45).

Consumer explorations routinely assume this form of a quest for difference. It is not surprising then that even our local mall, our local supermarket and our local high street can be places of exploration, where the consumer pursues difference, just like the primitive huntsman pursues his prey (Ginzburg, 1980). And just like the primitive huntsman, the consumer/explorer is avidly and restlessly looking for tiny clues and disturbances for signs that a new fashion may be about to explode on the scene, that a new pleasure has been discovered or that a new signifier has been born.

The quest for difference has all the compulsive qualities of the 'Spot the Difference' game, something that manufacturers and advertisers have long appreciated. The consumer is presented with countless puzzles to unlock, countless catches to decode, countless knots to untie. Examples of semiotic puzzles include:

- misspelt words or brand names;
- puns, word games, double entendres or innuendoes especially in advertisements and corporate logos;

- unpronounceable words, especially in brand names;
- ambiguous newspaper headlines;
- advertisements which do not display the name of a brand or conceal the product in a collage of images.

The current trend among some car manufacturers, following BMW, of *not* marking their products with prestigious model signs is another play on difference. To the 'untrained' eye, two cars may seem identical, yet, to the connoisseur, tiny details of trim reveal enormous differences in price, specification and prestige. Such devices highlight the importance of the minuscule, heighten the consumer's state of alertness, provoke curiosity and reward perseverance.

Freud's concept of the 'narcissism of minor differences' captures well the symbolic and emotional importance of tiny details, especially when they distinguish social groups and individuals which are geographically and socially close to each other (Freud, 1921, 1930). In such situations, group members are held together not by the force of shared ideals and powerful leadership, but rather through the signs which differentiate them from their immediate neighbours. It is to those little badges, emblems and colours that the group's and the individual's self-esteem become, as Freud would put it, condensed. Postmodern theorists would say that they act as metonymies for the group (Culler, 1981). Under the regime of the narcissism of minor differences, signs become essential differences and, therefore, essences. This is how small differences become big differences. Being able to read such differences is vital, since these differences become sources of in-group solidarity and out-group hostility. In this way, supporters of a football team reserve the highest hostility for supporters of the team based in a neighbouring part of the same town (Gabriel, 1982, 1983). Local accents, slang, anecdotes, badges, stories, myths and folklore can also provide similarly charged symbolic differences, as can consumer products. In this way, clothes, watches, compact discs, shoes, cars, bikes and other visible products offer the symbolic means of self-identification, through which individuals align themselves emotionally with those sharing their life-styles, forming what Maffesoli (1988) aptly described as 'neo-tribes'. These neo-tribes are transient and volatile, mutating and cross-fertilizing, but they are a reliable source of narcissistic satisfaction for their 'members'.

Being able to identify and decode what to others may be imperceptible differences between products, solving those semiotic puzzles which either defeat or escape others, give people a sense of uniqueness. In this way, they can become sources of narcissistic pleasure, similar to the pleasures of people who solve the *New York Times* crossword puzzle before breakfast or hack their way into any secure computer for the thrill of unlocking what is seemingly impregnable. This may explain the compulsive puzzle-solving responses generated by unmarked products, cryptic advertisements, unorthodox hairstyles and other mildly unusual signs of difference. The ability to decipher such signs, as well as a selection of the signs themselves, are incorporated in the consumers' idealized images of themselves (what Freud (1914) calls 'ego-ideals') which fuel their further explorations. Being street-wise means being able to recognize instantly signs like those above.

If Freudian theory may indicate that narcissism is the fuel of the individual's quest for difference and compulsive puzzle-solving, Simmel's trickle-down hypothesis (see Chapter 3: The Consumer as Communicator) offers an interesting sociological parallel, linking these phenomena with the impersonal qualities of modern urban life and the decline of traditional fixed status markers. For Simmel (as indeed for Veblen), consumption turns into an arena for status explorations, where subordinate groups constantly seek to imitate the consumption patterns of superordinate groups, which, in turn, strive to differentiate themselves by adopting new fashions and generating new status markers. Imitation and differentiation act as a motor for social change. Discovering *difference*, becoming different and discovering ways of becoming different are all, in Simmel's view, responses to the pervasive *indifference* of urban cultures:

> This leads ultimately to the strangest eccentricities, to specifically metropolitan extravagances of self-distantiation, of caprice, of fastidiousness, the meaning of which is no longer to be found in the content of such activity itself but rather in its being a form of 'being different' – of making oneself noticeable. (1903/1971: 336)

In this remarkable passage which anticipates the concept of 'cool' as well as theories of free-floating signifiers, Simmel captures two important themes; first, that consumers set interpretive puzzles for each other so that manufacturers and advertisers may be seen merely as riding rather than causing this tendency; and, second, that difference is not a fact, but a way of looking. When consumers are looking for difference, they are in effect looking for different ways of looking. Whether or not two pairs of trousers are alike or different has less to do with the qualities of the trousers themselves, than with the meanings attached to them by different groups. A pair of jeans may stand out from an ocean of grey suits; a pair of bleached jeans may stand out from a sea of jeans; a pair of torn and bleached jeans may stand out from the rest – only to the practised eye. In this way, 'decoding the minutiae of distinctions in dress, house, furnishing, leisure lifestyles and equipment' (Featherstone, quoted in Tomlinson, 1990: 21) turns into a compulsion for all of us. It is because we strive for difference, that we become compulsive 'readers of signs', experimenting with different interpretations.

The shopping space becomes a jungle of signs and symbols where products and people alike seek to present themselves as, what the marketers would call, 'unique selling propositions'. Shoppers are at once explorers and explored. New shopping design incorporates the shoppers as part of the adventure, as they try different clothes, stare at themselves in mirrors, or simply display their enigmatic hairstyles, clothes or 'looks' (Nixon, 1992).

> Shopping is . . . adventure, safari, carnival, and contains unexpected 'risks' in what you may find and who you may meet. It is a kind of self-discovery. And by its

very nature it possesses theatricality: one dresses up to go out and one shops to acquire the new persona, to modify the old one or to perfect the setting in which one is seen and known. (Clammer, 1992: 203–4)

Not that the malls and redesigned department stores are the only spaces of consumer exploration and discovery. Browsing at 'exciting new titles' from academic book catalogues one notices that many of these 'titles' present little semiotic puzzles to be deciphered, such as puns, metaphors, para-doxes, oxymora, caricatures, or, most commonly, spoofs on famous titles. The books' covers are equally exciting and inviting. Collages, distorted photographs, parodies of famous images, decontextualized cuttings all help to create the feeling that not only is the catalogue a space to be explored, but each book is itself a little mystery, having an utterly unique and personal story to tell. It is easy to regard these qualities as uniquely 1980s consumption phenomena. They have in fact been the hallmark of con-sumerism since its early phase, whether in Parisian department stores (Williams, 1982), the Army and Navy stores throughout the British Empire or the famous Sears catalogue to US homesteaders since the turn of the century. Whether looking at goods directly or through their images in catalogues, contemporary consumers are constantly invited to become explorers of differences.

Goods and their stories

Just like goods in the catalogue, so too other consumer objects cry out loudly that they have their own personal stories to tell (see Chapter 3: The Consumer as Communicator). The consumer as expert semiotician can disentangle the voices of the different objects, and quickly reads the clues about their stories in their appearance, their name, their packaging, their relationships and, unnoticed to postmodern thinkers, their prices. If, as Baudrillard argues, commodities are 'sign values' rather than use values, price is an important aspect of the story which they tell. For example:

'I am pricey, I know it and I invite you to find out for yourself if I am worth it.'

'I offer no-nonsense value for money; I may look plain, but if you choose me you will receive loyal and reliable service.'

'I am really inexpensive, but what do you lose by trying me?'

'I look pricey, but I am not really.'

Of course, price is by no means the only feature of goods which tells a story. The story told by a shampoo or a motorcycle is fashioned by numerous other features as well: brand name, packaging, advertisers' images for the product, the images of people displaying or using the product, the images of those who eschew it, the images of other products with which it is associated or against which it competes. All these things and many others shape the stories told by a particular commodity. Consumers listen to these stories and make their own decisions about the products. Some goods are quickly discarded as boring, uncool, poor imitations of the 'real thing', sheep in wolves' clothes, phoney, unfashionable. Others, are appreciated as clever challenges, such as a witty advertisement, an amusing package, a clever spoof on an existing product or an imaginative new *product idea*. Being phoney does not necessarily diminish a product in the eyes of today's consumer, if it can be interpreted as an imaginative, cheeky or defiant simulation rather than as an inferior copy, seeking to conceal its inferiority or the fact that it *is* a copy. Such products may generate a desire to acquire them, not because their stories are untold to the prospective purchaser, but because they can provide semiotic tests to others. Will they be able to 'read' them, or will *they* be fooled by them? We go exploring for such objects which will serve as puzzles which we enjoy setting for others.

There is another category of objects which appear more reluctant to reveal their story to potential buyers. Such objects are either difficult to decode so long as they are not owned, or stimulate curiosity about, for example the truthfulness of their claims. The resistance offered by these objects increases their aura and stimulates desire. They seem to cry out for further exploration, an exploration which cannot proceed unless the consumer can get them, either by paying for them, borrowing them or by 'liberating' them from their ownerless state (see discussion of shoplifting in Chapter 8: The Consumer as Rebel). A new arrival on a supermarket shelf or a sealed cartridge with a computer game act in this manner.

Such objects cannot be fully consumed, that is tell their full story, unless the consumer can make them his or her own and appropriate them. Objects that require no payment seem hardly worth exploring; their value in the eyes of the consumer is reduced, the quality of the exploration is diminished in his or her own eyes. How unalluring are the various free-sheet newspapers that are dispensed through our letter-boxes; how unexciting the various experiences on offer 'for free'; how insipid the water that comes out of our taps when compared with the sparkling glamour that pours out of a delicately tinted bottle that we have paid for! Notice that 'something for free' is not at all the same as 'something for nothing' which, as we saw, is the trademark of the true bargain. If the bargain represents a little symbolic triumph at the expense of the system, free handouts carry many of the dreary marks of philanthropy, the dispensation of second-hand or second-rate goods with a symbolic or moral catch. Payment then is far from incidental to consumer explorations. Paying for a product signals the start of a new phase of exploration, the exploration of the owned object. Think of the excitement of bringing a new acquisition back from the shop or of receiving an order in the morning's mail. What will the new armchair look like in your sitting room? How will the new compact disc player perform with your amplifier? What will the new blouse look like with your green skirt?

The careers of objects

Once an object has been paid for, rented or stolen, safely tucked away inside a bag, it begins a new life as an object of consumer exploration; this life can assume several different twists. Many authors have commented on the tendency of objects to disappoint once they have been paid for and numerous explanations of this phenomenon have been offered (Baudrillard, 1968/1988; Bocock, 1993; Campbell, 1989; Galbraith 1967; McCracken 1988). In these instances, the consumer finds that the object has no story to tell, no secret to reveal. Like Kavafis's poem *Ithaca*, it has no special magic of its own. Its promise is the journey, not the final destination. Such objects lose their charm instantly and sink into an anonymous existence, forgotten at the bottom of a drawer or quickly discarded in a dustbin. Occasionally, they may be rediscovered, as gifts to someone who unaccountably values them, as items of kitsch value, as antiques or even as souvenirs of one's consumer follies. Many end up in charity shops and jumble sales, where they can be discovered as bargains and start new careers.

Consumers may or may not feel cheated at such inglorious turns of events (see Chapter 7: The Consumer as Victim). What is interesting is the extent to which they are prepared to weather disappointments; after all, exploration is full of dead-ends, and if they paid good money for what turned out to be quite ordinary or a dud, so be it; perhaps the price was worth paying for the satisfaction of knowing that the product was quite ordinary. Sometimes disappointment is swift. There are instances, however, where the consumer stubbornly refuses to relinquish faith in a product, against considerable evidence to the contrary as illustrated by the following experience.

> I remember purchasing what had seemed like a marvellous Italian motor car, much to the amusement of my friends and relatives who teased me endlessly about the car's poor reputation for reliability and its general 'tackiness'. No matter. Since my childhood this make of car, famous for its sweetly purring engine, had held an overwhelming fascination for me. It did not take long for me to realize that every allegation against the car was true, as hardly a week went by without the car needing garage attention. The story told by the car was very different from the one I was longing to hear. Yet, the car's aura refused to wane. Each time I took it to be repaired, I thought it would be the last visit, the one that would finally get the car back into full health. This was no love-hate relationship; it was straightforward love. I was prepared to forgive the car its every misbehaviour, as one forgives a pampered child. It took me fully 18 months before I was willing to recognize that the car was simply a fiasco. I employed every conceivable rationalization to defend the car, until I finally gave up and sold it. Yet, I felt no anger or disappointment for having bought it; I paid good money for what turned out to be a bad car. But I felt that I had owed it to myself to buy this car, and the money was spent to very good effect. It was like staking some money on a bet and losing. As a consumer-explorer, I was philosophical about losing money on bad bets.

In addition to objects that sooner or later disappoint, there are objects which stubbornly refuse to yield their full stories. How often is it that we discover that having purchased something, we may not obtain full advantage of it unless certain accessories are purchased, which in turn emerge as nothing but preambles for further purchases. We may suspect that such objects are mere entrapments, that they try to lure us into explorational impasses, yet, as in the case of the Italian car, the temptation to throw good money after bad is powerful. Explorers find it very difficult to turn full circle and return to base.

There is yet another class of products, those with which we develop a relationship of sorts. Some of them are quickly absorbed in our self-perceptions; they pose no further puzzles but offer the prospect of quiet contentment. A new track suit in which we feel comfortable, a trusted brand of virtually anything, a no-nonsense watch, such items do not challenge us, though in their quiet way they may be important parts of our identity. Then, there are objects which cannot be incorporated so easily: a 'loud' jacket, a flash car, an eye-catching hat, a suggestive T-shirt. They may need to be used at first in private before we feel confident to present them as part of our public persona. These things may make us self-conscious, they cannot be readily accommodated in our identity, which needs to stretch or adjust itself in order to absorb them. It is then that exploration of the world of objects initiates an exploration of identity, the quest for outer difference becomes a quest for inner meaning. This will be the main focus of the next chapter, which examines the consumer as identity-seeker.

Strengths and weaknesses of the image of the consumer as explorer

Few images capture the driven qualities of modern consumption, its excitements and disappointments, as vividly as that of the explorer. And yet, few figures can so easily be ridiculed and disparaged as the explorer who never left his or her backyard, the explorer who dreamed it all up. The worlds explored by modern consumers are certainly not natural worlds; the discoveries they make along the way are carefully orchestrated by producers, designers and retailers to greet them at the appropriate time in the appropriate place. Many surprises are premeditated, many wonders staged (Gardner and Sheppard, 1989). Here lies one of the paradoxes of modern consumption – the experience of exploration can be genuine, even if the object is simulated and the subject knows that it is simulated. Why go looking for real alligators, unpredictable as they are, when you can catch a grand view of them in the theme park, where they are guaranteed to make an appearance? And why indeed go to the theme park, when you can put your face right inside the mouth of one through the lens of a camera or virtual reality?

Consumer 'explorations' easily end up in quotation marks, as simulated pseudo-explorations in the virtual pseudo-realities generated by the magicians of postmodern spectacle societies. Yet, even if theme parks, shopping malls, museums, galleries, tourist attractions and other sites are pre-arranged and man-made, does this disqualify them from being sites of exploration? Does the fact that others, sometimes thousands or even millions, have been there before, invalidate their experience of exploration, excitement and discovery? Hardly. It is perfectly possible to explore human artefacts, whether they be the pyramids of Egypt, a Gothic cathedral or a Doris Lessing novel. If it is possible to explore a novel, a symphony or a building, why not a compact disc, a suit or a shopping mall? Nor does the circumstance that many have been there before, diminish the experience of one who, for the first time, 'discovers' Mahler. With innocent eyes and ears, he or she may even discover a line of interpretation, a symbolic twist, a coded melodic reference which has not been noticed before. A young student recently discovered an extended quotation from Pergolesi in Mozart's Requiem, which had escaped the notice of experts, who had spent life-times studying the piece. Besides, leftovers by previous explorers can be fascinating in their own right; one, for example, may remember one's first forays into an area of literature through second-hand paperbacks, which have been read and underlined in different colours by several previous owners, each leaving their own comments in the margins. This can enhance one's experience of exploring.

In sum then, neither the artificial quality of the terrains of exploration, nor the presence of numerous fellow-explorers detract from the aptness of a metaphor of exploration, which captures admirably the restless, exciting, insatiable qualities of modern consumption, its endless fascination with tiny differences, and its obsession with puzzle-solving, interpretations, clues and signs. The metaphor highlights curiosity as a driving force of Western consumers, the desire to know the unknown and the yearning for innovation and change. In this sense, it accounts for consumers' unique vulnerability to lucky draws, mystery presents, promises of exotic trips and other marketing gimmicks, which rely on our state of excited curiosity and our longing for the unknown as a leverage for sales. Curiosity, once aroused, makes us highly vulnerable to the merchandisers' tease 'Discover X', where X can range from Turkey to a new brand of lavatory cleaner, a new food product or a new sanitary towel.

What the perspective of the consumer-explorer fails to do is to illuminate what makes things or spaces worth exploring in the first place and at what point they lose their charm and are discarded in favour of new ones. Equally, it obscures the wide range of instances when consumers appear to strive after the familiar and the safe. Brand loyalty would seem incongruous from a perspective which stresses change, innovation and adventure. Surely one of the defining paradoxes of modern consumption is the consumer's need to mix the familiar with the unfamiliar, the simultaneous travel to exotic places with patronage of McDonald's and Holiday Inns (logo: 'No surprises'), the simultaneous capitulation to the comfort of habit and the pursuit of adventure. This is an instance of fragmentation in contemporary consumption which frequently goes unnoticed.

In general, the explorer metaphor presents a somewhat individualistic concept of consumption, underplaying its social character except for the interpretative puzzles that consumers set for each other, known as fashion.

Even then, the metaphor is more successful at illuminating why individuals seek to decode and solve these puzzles than why they are inclined to set them for others. In these different ways, this metaphor draws attention to consumption in the first place as a range of relationships between people and things and only to a much lesser extent as relationships among people, consumers and producers or among consumers themselves (as highlighted in Chapter 3: The Consumer as Communicator).

All in all it is a metaphor which creates rather too heroic an image of consumers. It is also too cheerful and, perhaps, frivolous an image. What if the driven qualities of modern consumption, instead of being a quest for novelty and adventure amount to little more than an attempt to escape reality, to find solace in fantasy and self-delusion (Marcuse, 1964)? In any event, the sorrows, deprivations and frustrations of modern consumption are far from the sight of the consumer as explorer. The drudgery of routine shopping, the furtive sorties to shops between family and work commitments, the sacrifices necessitated by demanding children and social expectations, above all, the anxiety about making ends meet or stretching the family budget, these things have no place in the realms of consumers as explorers.

No other image of the consumer studied in this book is quite as firmly middle-class as that of the consumer-explorer. It is remarkable that in a period which spawned several important studies of poverty and deprivation (see, for example, Brandt, 1980; Mack and Lansley, 1985, 1992; Seabrook, 1985; Townsend, 1979, 1993; Walker and Walker, 1987), so many commentaries on consumption simply chose to turn a blind eye on the hardships experienced by increasing numbers of consumers, both in developed countries and the Third World. Disregarding the difficulties involved in precise definitions and measurements of poverty in different parts of the world (Chaudhuri and Ravallion, 1994; Cornia, 1994; Delhausse et al., 1993; McGregor and Borooah, 1992; Slesnick, 1994; Ravallion et al., 1991), one suspects that large numbers of people on the breadline would regard the idea of consumers as explorers as a cruel joke. One suspects that consumer-explorers, in their youthful enthusiasm and exuberance, their constant desire to experiment and try, their naive fascination with puzzles, signs and symbols and their obsession with difference, were a wish-fulfilling fantasy of glossy marketers and excitable semioticians in the 1980s. It is a fantasy on which, from time to time, some consumers became fellow-travellers.

5

The Consumer as Identity-seeker

That which is for me through the medium of *money* – that for which I can pay (i.e. which money can buy) – that am *I*, the possessor of money. The extent of the power of money is the extent of my power. Money's properties are my properties and essential powers – the properties and powers of its possessor. Thus, what I *am* and *am capable* of is by no means determined by my individuality. I am ugly, but I can buy for myself the most *beautiful* of women. Therefore I am not *ugly*, for the effect of *ugliness* – its deterrent power – is nullified by money. I, in my character as an individual, am lame, but money furnishes me with twenty-four feet. Therefore I am not lame. I am bad, dishonest, unscrupulous, stupid; but money is honoured, and therefore so is its possessor.

Marx 1972: 81

Debates on Western consumption rarely stay clear of the theme of identity for long. Identity is Rome to which all discussions of modern Western consumption lead, whether undertaken by Marxist critics or advertising executives, deconstructionists or liberal reformers, advocates of multi-culturalism or radical feminists. The consensus of otherwise irreconcilable perspectives appears to be that in late capitalism, consumption is the area where personal and group identities are fought over, contested, precariously put together and licked into shape. As previous chapters have indicated, the Western consumer readily transfigures into an identity-seeker. Whether choosing goods, exploring them, buying them, displaying them, disfiguring them or giving them away, consumers are, above all, frequently presented as thirsting for identity and using commodities to quench this thirst. This chapter examines this popular image of the consumer as identity-seeker, highlighting some crucial ambiguities in the concept of identity.

Identity, like stress, is a concept whose currency and expedience belies its relatively recent pedigree in psychology. It is a concept which we all feel we grasp intuitively and is given great explanatory weight in discussions of consumption. For these reasons, it is important to investigate how this idea achieved its privileged place in contemporary cultural discussions and then to ask what it adds. We start by examining some of the ambiguities acquired by the concept of identity, as it migrated from objects onto people and as the quest of identity came to be regarded as the cause of most major social and individual problems. How did identity turn from a fact into a problem and what is its relevance to consumption? We will also indicate some of the ways in which the obsession with identity, brands and consumption among cultural theorists has hogged the limelight and obscured some other promising lines of study into the relationship between the individual, their sense of self and what they consume.

Fixed identities: from people to goods

Initially, the word 'identity', drawing on its Latin derivation, stood for the sameness, continuity and distinctiveness of things. It applied equally to humans, animals and material objects. Establishing the identity of a person, a flower or a mineral amounted to giving it a name and specifying its uniqueness and distinctiveness in terms of similarities with and differences from its relatives. Even in this early conception, identity is not merely a property of the object being identified; it is equally an expression of the interest of those who identify it. The identity of minerals or plants generally coincide with the name of their species – the particular specimen at hand generally requires no further identification to establish it as something singular and unique. This, however, is not the case with a famous diamond which has been given a name, like the Koh-i-noor; its identification, notably if stolen and recovered, is not complete unless confirmed to be the very specimen which is missing. Simply establishing the identity of a recovered gem as a diamond is not enough. It is immediately apparent that forensic investigations crucially depend on the identity of objects as absolutely unique items.

The identity of animals in many cases is adequately fixed by the species name alone, or species plus gender. Gardeners are quite happy to know the species of caterpillar which is ruining their crops without concerning themselves about the particular individuals which are most to blame. Knowing the species is enough to dictate the measures which may be taken against it. Likewise, bird spotters are generally content to establish the species and gender of a rare specimen which they catch sight of. Ornithologists, on the other hand, may be interested in knowing the habits and history of a particular specimen or pair; to do so, they may then seek to identify them through the use of coloured rings or other unique marks. Such marks would establish not just species identity but individual identity and where they have been. In a similar way, family pets, race horses or animal celebrities carry identities beyond their species and gender, names which establish them as unique individuals. As we shall see presently, the question of whether identity refers to species or specimen is not unconnected with the strivings of Western consumers.

People too are generally identified by names; but different people may have the same name, hence it is often necessary to specify the identities of the father and mother, the date of birth or some other feature to establish the identity of an individual. Identity, in this sense, is fixed. No matter what transformations are undergone by the individual, his or her identity cannot change. Nor is identity a matter of choice, will or desire; identity is the outcome of family lineage. Confusion over identity amounts to confusion over parenthood, confusion about facts not about meanings. This theme lies at the heart of drama, both in its tragic and comic senses. Establishing the identity of an individual, whether a person is accused of a crime, or is claiming to be somebody or to own something, is not always easy, but essentially it is a technical, forensic question. Odysseus, returning home after 20 years, had to prove his identity and establish that he was who he claimed he was. This he proceeded to do with the aid of signs – a scar on the knee as well as knowledge of several intimate secrets which no-one else could know (Homer, 1988).

Why is this important? As Ginzburg (1980) reminds us, the problem of identity was in the first place a *political* one, not an existential one, to which consumer theorists have narrowed it down. Claims to power and property depended crucially on establishing the identities of individuals making the claims. Equally importantly, the maintenance of criminal records and the administration of legal justice and discipline hinges on establishing the identity of people as unique individuals. This can be an immensely difficult problem if individuals are unwilling to co-operate. In a memorable scene from Kubrik's film *Spartacus*, the Romans ask the captured rebels which one of them is Spartacus; to protect their leader, each and every one of the rebels claims to be Spartacus, to great dramatic effect.

The branding of offenders was meant to establish their identity permanently, marking their criminal record, so to speak, on their bodies. Branding was not an option available to colonial administrators, though of course it was rediscovered by the Nazis in the twentieth century. A different type of branding has now assumed great importance as a way of marking a product on consumer consciousness. The problem of identity was especially pressing for the administrators of the British Empire, having to administer what they saw as justice, to 'natives' who seemed deceitful, disputatious and, who to their Western eyes, all looked the same. Fingerprinting, introduced by Sir William Herschel in Bengal in the 1870s, seemed to provide a technical solution to the political problem of identity, a far more discreet but also more efficient solution than branding had been to the slave-owners. Each person carried permanently on their fingertips indelible evidence of their identity; no subjective claim or denial could thenceforth discredit the objective evidence of ink on paper. The fingerprint was proof of the person's identity. Thus a person's identity is, in the first place, part of a system of political practices which seek to classify, distinguish and differentiate each individual from others.

The political dimension of practices like identity cards, fingerprinting, random identity checks or unobtrusive surveillance in shopping malls and elsewhere has led to endless controversy surrounding their introduction. We shall refer to this conceptualization of identity as 'forensic identity' to underline its political nature, and to distinguish it in this chapter from the 'psychological' and 'group' identities. This discussion leads to two conclusions. First, we note that branding has shifted from being a mark to discriminate between people to being a device for according identity and individuality to products. Second, we note that forensic identity, unlike psychological identity, was a problem not for the individuals concerned but for those who sought to control them. The importance of these ideas for the study of consumption will become apparent presently.

Identity as a psychological and sociological concept

The migration of identity into psychology and sociology has maintained some of the qualities of forensic identity, reversed others, and introduced several new features of crucial relevance to consumption. It is interesting that psychoanalysis which virtually invented the idea of psychological identification, did not seriously turn to identity until Erikson coined the expression 'identity crisis'. He used this term to describe the condition of soldiers severely traumatized by the battlefield during the Second World War. These soldiers appeared to have lost their sense of sameness and continuity with their former selves. This suggested to Erikson the idea that psychological identity is not something given or fixed but something which one achieves with the aid of others. Subsequently, Erikson developed his theory that identity crisis is a normal stage of ego development in late adolescence and early adulthood which may lead to different outcomes. Some individuals uncritically adopt identities derived from their parents, others endlessly experiment with different identities (a process Erikson refers to as 'moratorium'), at times failing to emerge with any coherent identity (a process he refers to as 'diffused identity'). The happiest conclusion of this process is the achievement of an identity in which the individual is both conscious of his or her uniqueness and which provides him or her with an anchoring into the here and now (Erikson, 1968: 42). In these ways, self-esteem and self-image, as Erikson has acknowledged, are conceptually very close to ego identity.

Erikson's ideas of identity crisis and of identity confusion and diffusion gained substantial popularity in the 1950s, when the search for identity came to preoccupy psychologists, especially American ones, very considerably. This led to a very different concept of identity from the fixed, stable and immutable forensic identity. The new concept was to serve very well psychologists intent on delivering the consumer as a manageable package to merchandisers. This identity is subjective; it is an individual's answer to questions like 'Who am I?' and 'In what ways am I different from others?' This is a changing, precarious and problematic entity, the product of an individual's perpetual adaptation to his or her environment. Uniqueness is not given, but is achieved; continuity can be undermined or ruptured. Psychological identity is the product of psychological work; it must be nurtured and defended, worked for and fought over. The importance of material objects to these processes was to prove seminal.

The sociological itineraries of identity took off from where psychological discussions left. Psychologists themselves had prepared the ground in their 'mass psychology', where it was argued that in crowds people lose their individual identities and become one with the mass, part of a collective mind, entirely derivative from it (Freud, 1921; Fromm, 1942; Le Bon, 1895/1960; Reich, 1970). The implicit assumption that identity is a free-flowing entity which pours from the collective to the individual characterizes much of the sociological literature on the subject; by contrast, the pursuit of forensic identity has been to distinguish the individual from the masses. Thus, members of ethnic groups, sexual preference groups, political movements, occupational and professional groups are often seen as drawing their sense of identity from their group, sharing its ideals and aspirations. A group's identity, like personal identity, is problematic; it must be fought over and forged out of shared experiences and traditions; it must discard attributions imposed upon the group by others; it must discover and celebrate its own continuity with its past; it must choose who its friends and enemies are, where its boundaries lie, what its symbols are and so on (see Anthias, 1992; Hall, 1988, 1989; Omi and Winant, 1987). However, as groups shape their identities, their members' individual identity problems recede; individual identity derives from identification with the group. So long as the group is unique, uniqueness need no longer be part of the individual identity.

Modernity and identity

Most cultural commentators agree that psychological and social identity is a uniquely modern problem. In a pre-modern society, psychological and group identities coincide with forensic identities, since they

> are easily recognizable, objectively and subjectively. Everybody knows who everybody else is and who he is himself. A knight *is* a knight and a peasant *is* a peasant. There is, therefore, no *problem* of identity. The question, 'Who am I?' is unlikely to arise in consciousness, since the socially predefined answer is massively real subjectively and consistently confirmed in all significant social interaction. (Berger and Luckmann, 1967: 184)

Urban living, anonymous organizations, impersonal work, mass production, social and physical movement, the proliferation of choice, in short modernity itself conspires against fixed identities. In late modernity, the media of mass communication assume extraordinary significance in shaping our perceptions of the world we inhabit, saturating our physical and mental spaces with images, yet producing a massive vacuum to the individual's question 'Who am I?' With the possible exception of brief glimpses we may catch of ourselves on television monitors in shopping malls or very rarely on a real television programme, our personal identities are emphatically denied by the world of simulations, where, as Baudrillard insists, only what appears on television is regarded as real. One of the authors had maintained a totally impersonal relationship with his newsagent, until one morning the newsagent greeted him excitedly like a long lost friend by saying: 'Mr Lang,

Mr Lang, I saw you on TV last night!' Appearing on television had certainly made the author a real person in the eyes of the newsagent, whereas countless personal encounters had failed to elevate him above the status of 'another customer'.

Faced with a modern world which falls far short of providing the massive confirmation noted by Berger and Luckmann, identity becomes a major and continuous preoccupation of each individual. Unlike Erikson, who saw identity crisis as a temporary phase, eventually resolved and left behind, current cultural theory approaches identity as an interminable project, involving not only crucial life-choices and decisions but, equally, their translation into a narrative, a life-story. One of the clearest statements on identity has been offered by Giddens:

> In the post-traditional order of modernity, against the backdrop of new forms of mediated experience, self-identity becomes a reflexively organised endeavour. The reflexive project of the self, which consists in the sustaining of coherent, yet continuously revised, biographical narratives, takes place in the context of multiple choice as filtered through abstract systems. In modern social life, the notion of lifestyle takes on a particular significance. The more tradition loses its hold, and the more daily life is reconstituted in terms of the dialectical play of the local and the global, the more individuals are forced to negotiate lifestyle choices among a diversity of options. (1991: 5)

Identity, in this formulation, does not lie in any fixed attributes of personality or self, still less in certain fixed forms of behaviour. Nor can past achievements and glories form the basis of identity. As Schwartz reminds us, a '"has been" [is] somebody who once was somebody, but is no longer anybody' (1990: 32). Instead, as Giddens states, identity lies now 'in the capacity *to keep a particular narrative going*' (1991: 54). Identity, then, can be seen as a story which a person writes and rewrites about him- or herself, never reaching the end until he/she dies, and always rewriting the earlier parts, so that the activity of writing becomes itself part of the story. In this sense, it is both reflexive and incomplete. Identity and identity-seeking are, at least in Western culture, essentially the same thing.

Consumption and identity

What then do individuals write in the precious life-stories which constitute their identities? How do they construct their selfhoods? What are the identity structures which distinguish late modernity from earlier periods? Various answers have been provided to these questions, though increasing emphasis is placed on consumption at the expense of personal and family histories, membership of occupational and professional groups, work and personal achievement, character and temperament, as the terrain in which identities are sought. Bauman (1988, 1992), has been one of the strongest champions of the view that the 'work ethic' has, at least in Western societies, been dislodged by a 'consumer ethic'. He argues:

If in a life normatively motivated by the work ethic, material gains were deemed secondary and instrumental in relation to work itself (their importance consisting primarily of confirming the adequacy of the work effort), it is the other way round in a life guided by the 'consumer ethic'. Here, work is (at best) instrumental; it is in the material emoluments that one seeks, and finds, fulfilment, autonomy and freedom. (1988: 75)

Consumption, not only expands to fill the identity vacuum left by the decline of the work ethic, but it assumes the same structural significance that work enjoyed at the high noon of modernity:

The same central role which was played by work, by job, occupation, profession, in modern society, is now performed in contemporary society, by consumer choice. . . . The former was the lynch-pin which connected life-experience – the self-identity problem, life-work, life-business – on the one level; social integration on the second level; and systemic reproduction on the third level. . . . Consumerism stands for production, distribution, desiring, obtaining and using, of symbolic goods. (Bauman, 1992: 223)

How do consumer choices fashion identity? At its simplest, the argument would suggest that individuals can buy identities off the peg, just as corporations can buy themselves new images, new brands and new identities by adopting new symbols, signs and other similar paraphernalia. Numerous commentators on consumption appear to regard this as self-evident, requiring little explanation or elaboration.

Shopping is not merely the acquisition of things: it is the buying of identity. (Clammer, 1992: 195)

The identity of the consumer is tied with the identity not only of the brand, but of the company that produces it. (M. Davidson, 1992: 178)

At their most mechanistic, such arguments suggest that images and qualities of products are simply transferred onto the consumer, either singly or in combinations. Identity is essentially a self-image resulting from the endless displacements and condensations of product images. 'Ours is a world in which it is our products that tell our stories for us', argues Davidson (1992: 15). The consumers' main preoccupation then is being able to afford those goods which they require to sustain their identities. This approach, however, disregards the reflexive qualities underlined earlier and only transposes the question 'Who am I?' On what basis do individual consumers make their choices? Why are some objects liked and others disliked? Why do some objects easily blend with individual identity and others not? Why are some images convincing while others rejected as phoney? And if the qualities of objects are mechanically transferred onto their owners, like branding for slaves, why does the project of identity remain uncompleted? What drives the consumers' desires for new products and new identities?

These questions can be foreclosed if we were to accept Baudrillard's argument that the *only* product image which today's consumers want is one which is perfectly unique, different from all others. Only this will make each consumer unique, for ever standing out from the crowd. This is impossible, of course, though not merely because today's products are mass-produced and lack the required uniqueness. In a hyper-real world of self-devouring signifiers (see discussion of Clio and Nike in Chapter 3: The Consumer as Communicator), where each new arrival on the scene consigns its predecessors to the undifferentiated state of also-rans, standing out from the crowd is an entirely futile project. Free-floating signifiers wreak havoc with our individual identities, which are ransacked by wave after wave of semiotic invaders. In this case, as Miller puts it, 'our identity has become synonymous with patterns of consumption which are determined elsewhere. Taken to its logical conclusion (and the advantage of Baudrillard is that he does just this), this view entails a denial of all signification' (1987: 165). The project of identity, once it has been hijacked by hyper-real consumerism, is doomed. Uniqueness, continuity and value will for ever elude it.

Many of the writers exploring the connection between consumption and identity in the 1980s and 1990s do not share Baudrillard's rather bleak view. Nor, however, do they take the view that identities can be constructed unproblematically by purchasing a particular set of images. Between the life-story that constitutes identity and the images of the consumer world, most of these authors seek to interpose human agency, a kind of creative *bricolage*, whereby identities are fashioned through an active engagement with product images. This relationship between identity and the world of material objects will be the main focus of the rest of this chapter.

Objects and extended selves

The view that material objects are a vital feature of our identities, forensic, psychological and cultural, is neither novel nor particularly original. Owning a unique object, a sword or a crown, might have been as solid a proof of forensic identity as any branding or distinguishing mark. The qualities of material objects and their past history confers prestige and status onto their holders. Furthermore, there are categories of objects, such as family heirlooms or valued gifts, which may be so dear to us that we end up seeing them as parts of an extended self (Belk, 1988; Csikszentmihalyi and Roschberg-Halton, 1981; Dittmar, 1992; Lee, 1993: 26). Winnicott (1958, 1964) noted that in early childhood certain objects, like Teddy bears or pieces of soft rag, acquire a great significance for children. These objects, which he calls 'transitional objects', are half-way between the infant's inner and outer realities, providing bridges between the internal and external worlds. Transitional objects are instrumental in the child's development and may be replaced later by other objects which have the same bridging function. From a very young age, we learn to look at such objects as extensions of ourselves. In the words of George, a 7-year-old boy, to his dad:

> My owl collection is very valuable to me; it is part of me. It's like my hair. If you lose your hair you are sad, if I lost my owls I'd be sad.

In this way, some material objects can become central characters of our personal histories, without which our histories would be unthinkable. The quest for a particular object, whether it be the Holy Grail or another owl in George's collection, may be an important part of a person's life-story, and the finding of the object may confer fame and generate pride. In this way, the search for particular objects, the adventures encountered along the way, the glory and fame achieved by its discovery, these can all become part of an individual's identity.

As we saw in Chapter 3 (The Consumer as Communicator), Levy-Bruhl (1966) noted that in preliterate cultures, ornaments, clothes and tools, are seen as parts of the self. Over a century ago, William James (1892/1961: 44) argued that a man's 'me' is made up of everything that he can call his, including his body and his mind, his clothes, his house, his wife, his children, his parents, his land, his yacht and his bank account. In all these instances, material objects become ensconced in our identity because of the closeness of our relationships with them, our physical and emotional attachment to them.

In contrast, however, to all these instances, Western consumption is unique in that identity becomes vitally and self-consciously enmeshed in stories which are read by consumers into innumerable, relatively mundane, mass produced objects which they buy, use or own. These unexceptional objects are not so much carriers of meaning, as carriers of vivid and powerful images, enabling us to choose them consciously from among many similar ones, promising to act as the raw material out of which our individual identities may be fashioned. Unlike children who form attachments to their cuddly toys, Western consumers do not establish profound relationships with the majority of the goods they consume. Instead, they use them in opportunistic but highly visible ways, being very conscious of the inferences which others will draw from them, and by the ways their image will be affected by them.

Children spontaneously like certain things and dislike others; they do not construct identities around them (Baumeister, 1986: 192). Yet, by the time they reach school age, likes and dislikes lose their innocence. Liking unfashionable toys, making friends with unpopular children, wearing old-fashioned shoes, these things become tied to image and identity. By early adolescence, virtually every choice becomes tainted by image-consciousness. Smoking, drinking, eating, clothes, accents, hairstyles, friendships, music, sport and virtually every like and dislike become highly self-conscious matters. Whether this phenomenon exists in most cultures or not, it is beyond doubt exacerbated by the targeting of children as consumers (Barnet and Cavanagh, 1994: 137 ff.).

For young people today, consumption appears as the key to entering adulthood. Abercrombie argues that 'young people will experiment with different identities, by ignoring the way in which class, gender and race construct the boundaries of identity' (1994: 51). Commodities, under consumer capitalism, rich in image, become young people's main accomplices in these attempts to reach adulthood (Lansley, 1994: 96–7). As Willis argues, adulthood 'is now achieved, it seems, by spending money in a certain way rather than "settling down" to a life of wedded bliss' (1990: 137). Consumption becomes the core element in the rite of passage to adulthood. It is not enough for young people to be seen spending their own money on cigarettes, clothes, stereo and computer gear and so on, though this in itself is not unimportant. What is more important is constructing out of these ingredients an individual style, a convincing image. Identity then does not mean the creation and projection of any image, but of one that commands respect and self-respect.

Shopping malls become the arenas for such explorations where young people try out different images and experiment with precarious selfhoods. Today's teenage identity-seekers are not a marginal social group; nor do they go through a temporary phase which will be overcome with triumphant entry into adulthood, as Erikson might have envisaged or anthropologists debating rites of passages. Instead teenagers become pioneers of a new-lifestyle revolving around television and the mall which, in a somewhat hackneyed metaphor, emerges as the Gothic cathedral of today:

> Malling confirms consumption-based activities, lifestyles and identities; teenaged mall-rats and bunnies may be the prototypical group of amusement society. This is all the more the case as television, having hurried if not destroyed childhood, has created the grown-up child and immature adult as the whole of a life course is sandwiched between infancy and senility. (Langman, 1992: 58)

As Featherstone has argued, 'youth styles and lifestyles are migrating up the age scale and that as the 1960s generation ages, they are taking some of the youth-orientated dispositions with them, and that adults are being granted greater licence for childlike behaviour and vice versa' (1991: 100–1). This is especially noticeable when adults go on holiday or even on business trips, when, relieved of the hardened personas they assume at work and at home, they experiment with different styles, images and identities. They wear strange clothes, develop unusual mannerisms, let the hair down and feel free to explore pleasures which they would otherwise deny themselves. The transformation of airport and hotel lobbies into Meccas of consumption can be seen as testimony of the travelling consumers' thirst for experimentation with identity as well as of the loosening of their inhibitions towards spending (see Chapter 4: The Consumer as Explorer).

Experimenting with identities and images of self can at times be seen to stretch into explorations of inner worlds, spiritual Ithacas and Idahos of the mind. Vast areas of the economy, including some of the so-called leisure industries, the hobby industry, the body industry, the personal growth industry, appear to be fuelled by individuals' thirst for self-exploration (Lasch, 1980, 1984, 1991). Many of these explorations become quests for reaching one's own limits, whether in sport, art or learning. Occasionally buying or being given a new object, such as a trumpet, a tennis racket or a set of water-colours, may signal the opening of a new phase of selfhood. Yet, in truth such inner explorations seldom go beyond ephemeral daydreams or the volatile fantasies. Compared with the explorations of the colourful world of objects and their images out there which many consumers pursue with skill and virtuosity, inner explorations seem murky, dull and not terribly productive.

Postmodern identities, images and self-esteem

Images of the consumer as identity-seeker are compelling and feature centrally in postmodern theory. They account for the obsession with brands, the willingness to read stories into impersonal products, the fascination with difference, the preoccupation with signs, and above all the fetishism of images. They also account for the fragmented and precarious nature of selfhood, which has been a favourite theme of those writers who postulate a radical discontinuity between modernity and postmodernity, the phase of human history we are currently meant to be entering. One leading feature of this discontinuity concerns the final demise of the idea of a sovereign self, the managerial self which reflects, compares, decides, creates and takes responsibility. Following Freud, Mauss and Foucault, many postmodernists argue that this image of the sovereign self is an illusion reflecting the grand narratives of modernity – such as work, gender, happiness, healthy life, moral choice, and achievement – but fatally undermined by postmodernity. According to Firat (1992), consumers of modernity fashioned their identities by purchasing products, whose stories and images echoed those grand narratives. By contrast,

> the consumers of postmodernity seem to be transcending these narratives, no longer seeking centered, unified characters, but increasingly seeking to 'feel good' in separate, different moments by acquiring self images that make them marketable, likeable and/or desirable in each moment. . . . Thus occurs the fragmentation of the self. In postmodern culture, the self is not consistent, authentic, or centered. (1992: 204)

Firat argues that fragmentation and discontinuity become themselves the dominant narratives of postmodernity, sweeping all in front of them and shattering the self into numerous self-images coming in and out of focus. If modern consumers could be seen as victims of self-delusions, their needs manipulated by image-makers, postmodern consumers suffer from no such self-delusions. They do not search for authentic, integrated, wholesome selves (Suerdem and Sinan, 1992; Venkatesh, 1992). They do not demand that product images should be authentic, integrated or wholesome. They are sophisticated enough to recognize that these images are only fleeting mirages, spawned in the imaginations of clever image-makers who want to sell them things. But they do not mind. They are content with diverse personas, all products of artifice, all inauthentic, often at odds with each other. Schizophrenia becomes a perennial condition for the postmodern consumer (Jameson, 1983).

Group identities too become fragmented. Groups themselves lose their boundaries, becoming transient, ephemeral and largely fictitious. Individuals will identify with each other through shared life-styles or shared fantasies, their self-images temporarily shaped by memberships to imaginary clubs and societies, 'imagined communities' (Anderson, 1983), 'invented traditions' (Hobsbawm, 1983) or 'neo-tribes' (Bauman 1992; Maffesoli, 1988). Some of these groups are the ephemeral result of converging identity projects, sharing imagined heritages, qualities or interests. Others exist purely in individual imaginations.

Some thinkers draw rather optimistic conclusions from images of consumers as identity-seekers. Bauman, one of the most insightful theorists of the intersection of consumption, identity and postmodernity, sees in consumer freedom the possibility of a healthy competition, which does not disintegrate into warfare and destruction:

> In the game of consumer freedom all customers may be winners at the same time. Identities are not scarce goods. If anything their supply tends to be excessive, as the overabundance of any image is bound to detract from its value as a symbol of individual uniqueness. Devaluation of an image is never a disaster, however, as discarded images are immediately followed by new ones, as yet not too common, so that self-construction may start again, hopeful as ever to attain its purpose: the creation of unique selfhood. (Bauman, 1988: 63)

Can the idea of identity survive the many fragmentations and discontinuities celebrated by postmodern writers? Is the idea of the consumer as identity-seeker meaningful, when identity has turned into nothing more than a succession of mirages? And can Bauman talk plausibly of this succession of mirages as 'selfhood' (Warde, 1994)? The above extract illustrates well some of the paradoxical implications of postmodern thinking which at once obliterates unity, sameness, continuity, fixity, and independence, the features which defined identity as a concept, while at the same time giving it pride of place in cultural discussions. If, as Bauman, correctly points out, the overabundance of signifiers undermines their value, is it possible to view identities as non-scarce goods? While there may well be an overabundance of images, we think that there is a scarcity of value-laden images, images which command respect. While identity, in the fragmented, anarchic postmodern sense may not be in short supply, the same could hardly be said of esteem and self-esteem. To individuals craving recognition and self-esteem, Bauman's pronouncement that 'identities are not scarce goods' (1988: 63), sounds a bit like the sanctimonious preaching of conservative politicians to those living on state benefits. If uniqueness is so highly prized as a prerequisite for esteem and self-esteem, the notion that any image can be the basis of identity begins to sound like a cruel joke.

Postmodern thinking scorns to distinguish between identity and self-image, self-image and self-love; it also cheekily conflates image and self-image. If identity is treated as narrative pure and simple, not only is the issue of authenticity obviated (any story can be valid as a story), but also the traditional concerns of sociologists and psychologists regarding the differences between self-identity and presentation of self to others melts away (see, for example, Goffman, 1959; Hewitt, 1984). If self-image and image are only mirages, to ask whether they coincide becomes irrelevant. Yet, experience suggests that today's consumers are highly preoccupied both with the authenticity of their own identity and with the recognition of this authenticity by others. They spend much time scrutinizing each other for inauthentic personas, contrived styles, yesterday's fashion and false identities. To argue that in the postmodern carnival, every mask adds to the generalized delirium fails to recognize the high levels of policing and self-policing that governs styles, fashions, images and identities. The follies of those who assume images above their station, those who seek to deceive others with cheap imitations or those who deceive themselves with studied and affected life-styles attract the same ridicule and censure today as they did in the age of Molière's Bourgeois Gentilhomme, the classic statement of a man who makes a fool of himself by seeking to give the appearance of one above his station. The struggle for identity is much less benign than Bauman envisages, and may indeed be ridden with malice, envy and contempt, clearly delineated by Veblen and Bourdieu (see Chapter 6: The Consumer: Hedonist or Artist?)

To summarize: if Western consumers are to be seen as identity-seekers, as numerous postmodern theorists invite us to do, the craving for authenticity, unity and consistency must be seen as intrinsic features of their searches. Any image will simply not do. While today's consumers may be willing to adopt multiple personas in different circumstances, as Giddens has argued, life-styles, are 'more or less *integrated*' sets of practices, through which self-identities are constituted (1991: 81). Cohesion cannot simply be wished away from identity, simply because it has become problematic. (Bourdieu's concept of 'habitus' is pointing in a similar direction.) Identity which does not command the respect of others and does not lead to self-love is quite pointless; even if image is in ample supply, the same can be said of neither respect nor self-love. Without these qualifications, the theme of fragmented identities and the figure of the consumer as identity-seeker threaten to collapse into meaningless, though fashionable, clichés. Identity, self, image, self-image and subjectivity threaten to become free-floating signifiers, easily substituting each other, merging and dividing up, losing their moorings and distinctiveness.

Identity, the ego-ideal and narcissism

Can money buy us identity? If identity were seen as pure image or as the respect of anonymous others, then, as Marx surmises in this chapter's opening extract, money would rule supreme. In spite of reservations expressed by theorists like Bourdieu, since the decline of the aristocratic ideal, matters such as taste, style, refinement, adventure, and image are things which may be bought, if one is not born with them. In today's world, it is not unknown for rock stars to become country gentlemen. Identity should then not be a serious problem for the rich. Yet, one searches in vain for confirmation of this view (see McCracken, 1988: 112). Instead, we propose that to the extent that identity constitutes a 'problem' or a 'project', it must encompass not only image (which may be purchased) and narrative (which may be constructed) but, contrary to some postmodernist thinking, meaning and value as well. This is far more problematic, for rich and poor alike. It involves the fashioning of an image in which one may admire oneself and through which one may gain the respect of significant others. Identity is no mere life-story but a life-story which commands attention, respect and emotion. Extending Giddens's idea of identity as narrative, we would see identity not merely as the story of who we are, but also a fantasy of what we wish to be like. Identity is not only an embellished account of our adventures, accomplishments and tribulations, but also that vital web of truths, half-truths and wish-fulfilling fictions which sustain us. This accounts for identity being at once fragmented and discontinuous, as well as united and continuous; it also brings the project of identity surprisingly close to the psychoanalytic concept of the ego-ideal, an amalgam of idealized images, phantasies and wishes against which we measure our experiences.

The ego-ideal can be built around different themes, frequently drawing on cultural or organizational achievements, nostalgic recreations of a golden past or utopian visions of glorious futures (Gabriel, 1993; Schwartz, 1990). The ego-ideal represents an attempt to recreate, in later life, the condition of primary narcissism, the period of our infancy when we imagined ourselves the centre of a loving and admiring world. Our primary narcissism is doomed to receive numerous blows, starting with the realization that the world is generally not a loving place and that, contrary possibly to the impression created by mother, we are not its centre (Freud, 1914; Schwartz, 1990: 17 ff.). We may still cling to the fantasy that we are unique and special, but this too will receive a cruel blow during our first encounters with schools and other impersonal organizations, which consign us to the status of a number on a register or a face among unknowns (Gabriel, 1993; Mannoni, 1971). Thereafter, we discover that admiration is hard to come by and love even harder. For this reason, the fact that young children have little problem of identity is hardly surprising. With every injury to their narcissism, however, the need to erect an ego-ideal becomes more pressing. The ego-ideal, then, emerges as a wishful fantasy of ourselves as we wish to be in order to become once more the centre of an admiring and loving world.

> What man projects before him as his ideal is the substitute for the lost narcissism of his childhood in which he was his own ideal. . . . To this ideal ego is now directed the self-love which the real ego enjoyed in childhood. The narcissism seems to be now displaced on to this new ideal ego, which, like the infantile ego, deems itself the possessor of all perfections. (Freud 1914: 94)

At times our ego-ideal merges with our ego; these are moments of triumph and joy when admiration and love is lavished on us, either for our individual achievements or for the achievements of groups, organizations or cultures with which we identify. Traditional societies supported individual ego-ideals with cultural ideals, powerful role models and overbearing symbols. Members of religious or political sects, today, may derive total narcissistic fulfilment through their membership of these organizations, which promise them not only omnipotence and salvation but also immortality in one form or another.

Western culture not only exacerbates the need for an ego-ideal by inflicting numerous injuries to our narcissism, but it also places formidable obstacles to its formation. Gone are the days of sweeping cultural ideals and moral certainties. Gone are the powerful role models, untouched by scandal and corruption. Gone are the stirring symbols. Gone too are the great cultural accomplishments, artistic, scientific or military, in which we may take unalloyed pride. In a world where heroes are for ever cut to size and perfection remains elusive, the gleaming surfaces of material goods, their pristine packaging and virginal existence inevitably attract our attention, even before the image makers get down to work. As Lasch (1980, 1984) has powerfully argued, the world of objects appears to hold the promise of delivery to our ailing narcissism. Consumerism promises to fill the void in our lives.

Lasch has provided vivid pictures of the narcissistic personality which he sees as dominating American culture. Today's Narcissus spends endless amounts of time looking at himself in mirrors, but is not lost in self-admiration. He is not happy with what he sees. He worries about growing old and ugly. He sets down busily constructing an ego-ideal around idealized qualities of commodities, aided and abetted by the propaganda of the makers of dreams. He pours money into anti-ageing cosmetics, plastic surgery, and every conceivable beauty aid. He yearns for admiration and recognition from others, striving for intimacy, yet he is unable to establish long-term relationships; after all his only interest lies in himself and his ego-ideal, for ever elusive, yet for ever appearing within reach. Although blemished, the narcissist always finds something to admire in himself; his life-story may not have been crowned with glory yet, but the happy end is within sight – if only he tries a little harder, gets a lucky break, or, above all, finds a bit more money.

The usefulness of material objects now becomes quite apparent – these objects hold the promise of bridging the distance between the actual and the ideal. The view of commodities as bridges has been developed by McCracken (1988), who regards them as instances of displaced meaning. 'If only I could buy that car I would be what I would ideally like to be'; the car becomes a fantasy bridging the actual and the ideal. The less accessible the car, the greater the promise it holds. As focal point of a fantasy, the longed-for car becomes a magnet for displaced meaning; the flawlessness of the paintwork, the power inside the bonnet, the overwhelming sense of perfection which it radiates, are thinly disguised narcissistic delusions transferred onto the idealized object. Once acquired, the object may at least temporarily act as a powerful narcissistic booster. Grown-up men have been known to cry in the arms of their mothers, on seeing a tiny scratch on that gleaming bodywork (Becker, 1962: 44). In such cases, the car is incorporated in the ego-ideal, its every affliction experienced as a personal calamity.

In as much as it provides a reason for self-love and the respect of others, such an object can be said to support the consumer's identity quite effectively. Yet, as McCracken argues, once acquired, often at considerable sacrifice, the spell of the commodity is exposed to falsification:

> The possession of objects that serve as bridges to displaced meaning is perilous. Once possessed these objects can begin to collapse the distance between an individual and his or her ideals. When a 'bridge' is purchased, the owner has begun to run the risk of putting the displaced meaning to empirical test. (1988: 112)

Once the fantasy built around the product has accepted the test of reality, its value to the ego-ideal decreases; almost invariably, it is bound to be found lacking, not because the product is not good, but because such extraordinary expectations had been built on it. A new fantasy will already start to develop around some new product. It is this process which consumer capitalism thrives on.

Consumerism: addiction or choice?

In this chapter, we have argued that behind the consumer's ostensible quest for identity lurk more fundamental cravings for respect and self-love, born out of the injuries that modern life inflicts on us. These generate anxieties which cannot be allayed by image alone or narratives spun around commodities; they demand far more radical measures. These anxieties are the result of injuries sustained by our narcissism, whose healing requires nothing less than the formation of an idealized fantasy of the self, an ego-ideal, commanding admiration, respect and self-love. In a culture shorn of role models and ideals, consumerism throws up ephemeral images to identify with (pop-stars, sportspeople, television celebrities) and a promise for boosting our ego-ideals, by proffering commodities around which fantasies of perfection, beauty and power may be built. These fantasies are wish-fulfilments which transform mundane everyday objects into highly charged symbols.

How successful is consumerism as the means of restoring our ailing narcissism? Cultural critics like Christopher Lasch are in no doubt that consumerism merely reinforces the discontents for which it promises consolations. Individuals become constantly more insecure and image-conscious, looking at themselves in mirrors.

> A culture organized around mass consumption encourages narcissism – which [we] can define, for the moment, as a disposition to see the world as a mirror, more particularly as a projection of one's own fears and desires – not because it makes people grasping and self-assertive but because it makes them weak and dependent. (1980: 33)

In the last resort, the self-illusions of uniqueness, power and beauty cannot be sustained in such a culture. As Horkheimer and Adorno put it in their memorable lament of lost individuality:

What is individual is no more than the generalities' power to stamp so firmly that it is accepted as such. The defiant reserve or elegant appearance of the individual on show is mass produced like Yale locks, whose only difference can be measured in fractions of millimeters. The peculiarity of the self is a monopoly commodity determined by society. (1972: 154)

In a more recent work, Lasch argues that Western consumerism, sustained by mass production and celebrated in the mass media, amounts to a mechanism of addiction.

Shop till you drop. 'Like exercise, it often seems to present itself as a form of therapy, designed to restore a sense of wholeness and well-being after long hours of unrewarding work. 'I feel like hell and I go out for a run, and before I know it, everything's OK.' Shopping serves the same purpose: 'It hardly matters what I buy, I just get a kick out of buying. It's like that first whiff of cocaine. It's euphoric and I just get higher and higher as I buy.' (1991: 521)

At this point the consumer as identity-seeker turns into a victim, a willing victim, an unknowing victim perhaps, but a victim all the same. While the addictive qualities of consumption epitomized in the 'shopoholic' are widely recognized (for example, Baudrillard, 1968/1988; 1970/1988; Bocock, 1993; Campbell, 1989; Lansley, 1994; Lebergott, 1993), Lasch's pessimism is not shared by everyone. A more equivocal picture emerges from the work of Bauman who argues that consumption is the new 'pioneer frontier' in which individuals may successfully assert themselves, with no insecurity and not harming others (1988: 57) An earlier herald of the liberating potential of consumer freedom, Philip Rieff, argued:

Confronted with the irrelevance of ascetic standards of conduct, the social reformer has retreated from nebulous doctrines attempting to state the desired quality of life to more substantial doctrines of quantity. The reformer asks only for more of everything – more goods, more housing, more leisure; in short, more life. This translation of quantity into quality states the algebra of our cultural revolution. Who will be stupid enough to lead a counter-revolution? (1966: 243)

Rieff's views are echoed by numerous less eloquent conservative theorists, who view consumerism, not only as offering delivery from the drudgery of self-reliance, but also as the begetter of genuine variety, choice, freedom and true individuality. Such enthusiasts dismiss the arguments of critics like Lasch as sanctimonious nonsense, flying in the face of all evidence. Lebergott (1993: 26–7) pours scorn on intellectuals who dismiss the choice presented by supermarkets while revering libraries full of unread tomes. Consumers' freedom to choose from 200 different beers, 600 different motor cars or 160 different magazines is no less meaningful than the intellectuals' freedom to read or write what they please. Freedom of choice, in the view of conservative commentators, far from being empty or meaningless is the very foundation of our cultural identity, which has rejected apocalyptic messages and faith as the roads to the good life (Rieff, 1959, 1966). The consumer Garden of Eden, according to this view, with its limitless choice, endows us with narcissistic pride, even if its most alluring packages remain beyond our reach. A brief look at the images of poverty, warfare, hunger and suffering on our televisions or at the plight of those surviving on state benefits, deprived of the freedom of choice, suffices to convince us of the spiritual superiority of the culture of the mall, the supermarket and the gleaming surfaces (Bauman, 1988, 1992; Miller, 1987). (See Chapter 2: The Consumer as Chooser).

Conclusion

Our pursuit of the consumer as identity-seeker has brought us to a junction. In one direction, we can pursue the consumer exercising freedom, making choices, accepting satisfactions and set-backs, reaching compromises and, to a greater or lesser extent succeeding in building an ego-ideal which commands the respect of others and inspires self-love. All this, through the act of consumption. In the other direction, we can pursue the consumer as an addict, unable to live without self-delusions, mediated by material goods, which ultimately aggravate his or her condition. Commodities represent nothing but a daily fix. Difficult questions now confront us. Is identity a project or a consolation? Are material objects bridges to an ideal or bridges to nowhere? Does everyone deal with the problem of identity through consumption in the same way?

The ambiguities of modern consumption are such that the face of the Western consumer is open to change. Like the images we examined earlier, it is hardly surprising that the consumer as identity-seeker has the tendency to metamorphose into something else. Like them, it tends to present too monochromatic a picture of the consumer. Some of us may and do, from time to time, seek identity by browsing in front of shop windows, purchasing goods and internalizing their images. These may prove disappointing or may provide considerable support to our ego-ideals and identities. At other times, however, our identities may be built around resistance to consumption and consumerism and the subversion of the symbolism carried by objects. Defying the slogans of advertisers and sneering at the propaganda of commodities may be a sound enough base for constructing an ego-ideal as the worship of the shopping mall. Alternatively, we can pursue our projects of identity by focusing our life-narratives elsewhere. At a time, when workaholics compete with shopoholics, it seems premature to write off the work ethic. For many, work remains an arena (though of course not the only one) where identity is fashioned, as indeed is the family (single- or double-parent, extended or not) and other social networks which defy the neo-tribe soubriquet. And who would discount social class as a source of identity when practising marketers busily classify, monitor and target everyone in those terms? The organizations which we serve also nurture our ego-ideals, either by lending us some of their corporate aura (Schwartz, 1990) or by serving as objects of ridicule (Gabriel 1991, 1995).

It seems premature, therefore, to conflate the pursuit of identity or the formation of an ego-ideal with compulsive shopping, the acquisition and display of commodities and their use to adorn bodies and souls. While the ascetic ideal may be gone for good, ostentatious spending can still arouse indignation, as shown by the roasting received by the Princess of Wales in 1994, when it was revealed that her 'grooming expenses' amounted to £3,000 per week. Image purchased at too high a cost, undermines esteem.

If the conflation of identity and consumerism is premature, might the conflation of self with identity be liable to exhaustion? Before closing this chapter, we may reflect briefly on the privileged position of 'identity' in contemporary discussions of selfhood. Is it not possible that identity has become itself a fashion, used to cover a multitude of sins? It certainly has some of the marks of a fashion: universal appeal, seeming inevitability, floating signifiers, a cottage industry of media pundits and image-makers sustaining it and a stream of celebrities embodying it. One thing is certain, that the prominence of identity since the 1980s has isolated cultural studies of consumption from addressing numerous types of consumer behaviour and action which have been of central importance to people ranging from financial analysts to consumer activists, to many consumers themselves. What if for a number of us, unaffected by this suggestive apparatus, identity simply does not exist as a problem or as a project or as anything else? This is how Levi-Strauss has described his own experience of self:

> I never had, and still do not have, the perception of feeling my personal identity. I appear to myself as the place where something is going on, but there is no 'I', no 'me'. Each of us is a kind of crossroads where things happen. The crossroads is purely passive; something happens there. A different kind of thing, equally valid, happens elsewhere. There is no choice, it is just a matter of chance. (1978: 3–4)

Read as a literal and honest description, rather than as a mischievous structuralist aphorism or an Olympian utterance by a sage who stands removed from mundane matters, this statement suggests that identity may not be such a universal preoccupation, after all. It is certainly possible to think of ourselves in ways which do not depend on the output of the identity industry. Could it be that identity, like other fashions, will eventually exhaust itself, its appeal shrinking to a niche market kept alive by nostalgia? Some of us may look forward to the day when identity sheds its psychosociological identity and returns to its forensic-political roots. But what a challenge that would pose to brands!

6

The Consumer: Hedonist or Artist?

> I will offer one thousand golden pieces to any man who can show me a new pleasure.
>
> Xerxes

Pleasure lies at the heart of consumerism. It finds in consumerism a unique champion which promises to liberate it both from its bondage to sin, duty and morality as well as from its ties to faith, spirituality and redemption. Consumerism proclaims pleasure not merely as the right of every individual but also as every individual's obligation to him- or herself:

> The modern consumer, the modern citizen, cannot evade the constraint of happiness and pleasure, which in the new ethics is equivalent to the traditional constraint of labor and production. . . . He must constantly be ready to actualize all of his potential, all of his capacity for consumption. If he forgets, he will be gently reminded that he has no right not to be happy. (Baudrillard 1970/1988: 48–9)

Consumerism seeks to reclaim pleasure, not least physical, sensuous pleasure, from sanctimonious moralizing and the grim heritage of the Protestant ethic which said 'Work! Work! Work!'. It celebrates the diversity of pleasures to be obtained from commodities, proposing such pleasures as realistic, attainable goals of everyday life. Enjoying life means consuming for pleasure, not consuming for survival or for need. If we fail to enjoy life, it may be that we are failing to look after ourselves, weighed down by self-inflicted hang-ups and inhibitions. The pursuit of pleasure, untarnished by guilt or shame, becomes the bedrock of a new moral philosophy, a new image of the good life. But how well does this image match the realities of contemporary consumption? How realistic is the project of attaining pleasure through material possessions? And to what extent do we, as consumers, answer the call of consumerism to enjoy ourselves? These are some of the issues which this chapter addresses.

The world of commodities and the pursuit of pleasure

Western consumption, Bauman, Bourdieu, Baudrillard and countless others have argued, is a realm of *seduction* – alluring and glamorous. Few can escape its temptations, certainly not the poor whether they live in the First, the Second or the Third Worlds. Since the collapse of Eastern-style communism, consumerism has emerged as a global hegemonic idea, underpinning capitalist accumulation, free trade and the riotous commodification of everything (see Introduction: The Faces of the Consumer). Consumer capitalism raises commodity fetishism to heights undreamed of by Marx. As goods leave the world of production to enter the sphere of display, circulation and consumption, they become objects of fantasy and instruments of pleasure. As Abercrombie has argued:

> Not only are the denizens of modern society consumers, they are also consumer*ist*. Their lives are organized around fantasies and daydreams about consuming; they are hedonists, primarily interested in pleasure, and sensual pleasure at that; they are individualists, largely pursuing their own ends and uncaring about others. (1994: 44)

In *The Cultural Contradictions of Capitalism* (1976), Daniel Bell identified the central contradiction of late capitalism as one between the discipline, rationality and asceticism required in production and the spend-happy hedonism and waste of consumption. For Bauman (1988, 1992), a decade later, the contradiction has turned into symbiosis. Seduction becomes a mechanism of control; the consumer's pursuit of pleasure enables him or her to endure the rigours of life under the capitalist reality principle, that is, alienating work, the threat of unemployment or worse. Pleasure, for so long the enemy of the capitalist project, against which no resource of puritanical morality was spared, is now mobilized to support the project. Pleasure and reality principles are at last reconciled:

> In the present consumer phase, the capitalist system deploys the *pleasure principle* for its own perpetuation. *Producers* moved by the pleasure principle would spell disaster to a profit-guided economy. Equally, if not more disastrous, would be *consumers* who are not moved by the same principle. . . . For the consumer, reality is not the enemy of pleasure. The tragic moment has been removed from the insatiable drive to enjoyment. Reality, as the consumer experiences it, is a pursuit of pleasure. Freedom is about the choice between greater and lesser satisfactions, and rationality is about choosing the first over the second. (Bauman 1992: 50)

In *Pursuing Happiness: American Consumers in the Twentieth Century*, Stanley Lebergott argues that 'in open societies, human consumption choices share one characteristic – they are made in pursuit of happiness' (1993: 8). He then goes on to provide extensive economic documentation of the massive increases in US consumption since the end of the nineteenth century; for example, an hour's work in 1990 earned on average six times more than it did in 1900. Lebergott dismisses the notions both that consumers are manipulated into purchasing items which do not afford them pleasure and that the variety and glamour of these items represent economic inefficiency and waste. Instead he views the immense variety of commodities on display in shops as evidence that American consumers have never had it so good in terms of the quantity, quality and variety of things they consume and that American workers 'exchanged their labor hours for goods and services at a better rate than workers did in almost any other nation' (1993: 68). Aware of their privileges in comparison with the rest of the world, US consumers are both proud of their consumerist culture and capable of taking advantage of it, Lebergott says. They make expert choices, refusing to be lured by unrealistic claims, contemptuously killing countless products which do not make it in the marketplace.

Lebergott, writing in the Reaganite 1980s, is especially scathing in his criticism of Tibor Scitovsky, an economist who in the 1970s had challenged (1) the economic assumption of consumer sovereignty, that is that consumers choose whatever best satisfy their needs, and (2) the view that American consumers are either capable or willing to spend their money and even more importantly their time on things which give pleasure. Scitovsky (1976), for example, had argued that Americans are far less concerned with the taste of the food they eat than its nutritional qualities and its convenience. To Scitovsky's idea that American consumers sacrifice pleasure for comfort, Lebergott counters:

> The United States does indeed lack an official corps of tasters and chewers, to decide which dinners are 'good, representative.' But what of the vast, untidy party of amateurs who exhort and instruct in newspaper food columns? And what of the best-sellers in U.S. bookstores for decades – cookbooks? This record hardly demonstrates any 'lack of interest in the pleasures of food.' (1993: 9)

Unlike Scitovsky, Lebergott scorns to distinguish between necessities and luxuries. One of the most interesting features of his argument is that 'necessities' make as big a contribution to the consumers' pursuit of pleasure as luxuries, since they free consumers from the drudgery of housework and extend their free time. Thus convenience foods, like tinned peas, which for Scitovsky epitomize the Americans' indifference to the pleasures of the palate, are for Lebergott vehicles of pleasure – through them consumers free themselves from the drudgery of shopping for, cleaning, cutting up and preparing fresh vegetables. The greatest increases in consumer expenditure since 1900, he notes, went to those items 'that promised to extend lifetime hours of worthwhile experience', for example, labour-saving devices, cars, convenience food, heating, lighting and more recently medicine (1993: 36). He estimates that each American housewife spent 32 fewer hours weekly on meals and cleaning up between 1910 and 1975 (1993: 59).

One question which arises is how are consumers spending their 'free' time? In 'quality time' with their loved ones, in hobbies and other pleasure-imparting activities as Lebergott implies, or in increased travel times to and from work, shopping centres, and so on, or watching television, as work by Gershuny (1989), Postman (1986) and others suggests? While Lebergott builds an impressive argument on the back of the grim picture of the labour-intensive domestic chores which filled most people's (especially women's) lives at the turn of the century, he fails to establish *pleasure* as the object of contemporary consumerism. True, the burden of doing the laundry or the washing up by hand, of fetching fuel and cleaning fireplaces, of baking bread and making and mending clothes, have been lightened. But can people today be said to be either happier or more pleasure-driven than their grandparents? Discomfort avoidance, curiosity and status thirst (the first two endorsed by Scitovsky) could replace 'happiness' in Lebergott's arguments without any loss of coherence. Buying a dishwashing machine may have little to do with the pleasurable activities which one may pursue while the machine gently washes away the grime, using up fossil fuel energy and polluting the world at the same time. Instead one could see the purchase of a dishwasher as a discomfort-avoidance device, a status symbol or numerous other things.

Hedonism old and new

Like many economists, Lebergott uses a quasi-democratic argument against arbiters of taste who distinguish between high-brow and low-brow pleasures, to defend the axiom that ordinary consumers, rather than aesthetes, academics, state planners, environmentalists, consumer activists and bureaucrats, or even producers, know best what pleases them. Lebergott's hedonism is axiomatic and, as a result it adds little theoretical value, though it acts as a firm ideological support to enthusiasts of the free market. The axiom that what saves time is useful, and what is useful is pleasurable is directly attacked by Campbell (1987), who has developed one of the most advanced positions of contemporary consumption as a unique and highly elaborate form of pleasure-seeking. Campbell's account of consumerism stands out from other commentaries in numerous respects. First, Campbell refuses to separate the sphere of consumption from that of production, each characterized by its own 'ethic'. Unlike Bell and even Bauman, he argues that the same psycho-cultural forces that drive a pleasure-orientated consumption also account for the broad range of work attitudes, normally subsumed under the Protestant Ethic label. Second, Campbell, almost alone among contemporary cultural theorists, seriously explores the meaning of pleasure, both establishing its differences from utilitarian concepts like need and satisfaction and identifying different modes of constructing and deriving pleasure. Third, Campbell provides a convincing and highly detailed picture of the original qualities of contemporary hedonism, which places it apart from traditional hedonism, yet maintains the centrality of pleasure. In this way, he provides an intriguing, though controversial, way of absorbing dissatisfaction, frustration and loss into an essentially hedonistic outlook on life.

The first of several astute distinctions made by Campbell is between pleasure and utility, conflated by utilitarianism and confused by economists. Like Baudrillard (1970/1988), Campbell criticizes the concept of utility by reviewing Galbraith's (1979) arguments. But while Baudrillard goes on to distinguish between use-values and sign-values of commodities, Campbell explores utility and pleasure as distinct motivational principles, the former deriving from need, the latter aiming at pleasure (see also Doyal and Gough, 1991). Need represents the disturbance of a state of psychological equilibrium; it is based on absence, on lack, on necessity. By contrast, pleasure, argues Campbell, is 'not so much a state of being as a quality of experience' (1987: 60). Desire is triggered by the presence in one's environment of 'a recognized source of pleasure' (1987: 60). Campbell's account of the pleasure principle could hardly be more different from that of Freud (1920, 1930), who following Schopenhauer saw pleasure as essentially a negative phenomenon, a struggle to release oneself from unpleasure, pleasure being the lowering of tension which follows the gratification of an instinctual impulse. By contrast, the pursuit of pleasure, for Campbell, does not seek to restore an earlier state of disturbed equilibrium, but is a quest for a certain kind of stimulus which will bring about a pleasurable experience. Stimulation is therefore itself part of the pleasurable experience.

Both needs and desires drive consumption, though in modern societies desire assumes an ever-increasing role. Unlike Baudrillard, Campbell does not deny the continuing existence of needs or the merging of needs and desires. Hunger is paradigmatic of need; sexuality is paradigmatic of desire. The two often operate in tandem; a meal may both yield pleasure and satisfy hunger. More importantly, however, guaranteed satisfaction saps the potential for pleasure. In the presence of guaranteed satisfaction by regular meals or routine sex, the pleasure-yielding potential of eating or sexual activities are moderated. Comfort undermines pleasure.

In spite of the fact that they may merge or oppose each other, needs and desires represent very different motivational principles. Needs are far more tied to specific means of satisfaction than desires. Hunger can only be met with food. Desire, by contrast, can be stimulated by a wide variety of objects and can migrate from one experience to another. More importantly, while needs are tied to objects, desires can wander into a world of fantasy and imagination: 'whilst only reality can provide satisfaction, both illusions and delusions can supply pleasure' (1987: 61).

Campbell now draws a second crucial distinction, between traditional and modern hedonism. Traditional hedonism is a hedonism of a multitude of pleasures, a hedonism of sensations attached to the senses – taste, smell, touch, sight and hearing. Modern hedonism, on the other hand, seeks pleasure not in sensation but in emotion accompanying all kinds of experiences, including what may be called sad or painful ones. Traditional hedonism is epitomized in the lives of luxury and opulence of potentates, princes and the super-rich. Their tables are spread with an abundance of exotic foods, their palaces decorated with artistic masterpieces. Musicians, comedians and entertainers are on call to offer finer and higher pleasures; harems, jugglers and fools to gratify lower ones. But, as Xerxes's heart-rending pronouncement at the opening to this chapter makes plain, 'guaranteed satisfaction' jades the senses. Pleasure becomes the ultimate scarce commodity for the traditional hedonist. Boredom and dissatisfaction set in.

When comfort kills pleasure, pleasure may be sought in new stimuli, less predictable, less comfortable, more dangerous. Comfort must yield to adventure. Few potentates have the courage or the latitude of doing so, without risking their power, wealth and status. Some may turn to hunting or to mixing incognito with lesser mortals as a means towards greater excitement; invading Greece seemed to provide Xerxes with the ultimate thrill in 480 BC. Such pursuits are certainly not consistent with comfort, yet it is only through exposing oneself to hardships and dangers that the project of hedonism can stay on course; hence, far from being the opposite to hedonism, adventure, hardship and privation become for Campbell, its logical culmination. These 'adventurous' pursuits provide the bridge between traditional and modern hedonism. What sets modern hedonism apart from the traditional one is the emphasis on emotion and the submission of emotion to a special type of self-control which enables any emotion, including fear, pity, grief or nostalgia, to yield pleasure. This self-control disengages emotion from action and reinterprets it as a source of pleasure. Anger, for instance, can be greatly pleasurable if it can be stopped from turning into physical violence. Spectators of professional wrestling, for example, can be driven to paroxysms of rage by the orgy of evil unfolding in front of their eyes (Barthes, 1973). This is highly enjoyable for the spectators, so long as they do not join in on the melée, and even more so if the worst villains among the wrestlers meet with the most terrifying punishment. That terror itself can be highly thrilling is no more eloquently illustrated than by the successes of ever more frightening roller-coaster rides. Nearly 35,000 people were photographed screaming, during the first two months of operation of the Big One, the world's tallest and fastest roller-coaster at Blackpool Pleasure Beach in 1994.

It can now be seen how important puritanism, with its emphasis on emotional control, was in promoting modern hedonism. By blocking feeling as a motive for action and replacing it with rational calculation, puritanism did not kill feeling; instead, it made it available to support a new mechanism of pleasure, one deriving not from the senses but from experience.

> Unlike traditional hedonism, however, [pleasure] is not gained solely, or even primarily, through the manipulation of objects and events in the world, but through a degree of control over their meaning. In addition, the modern hedonist possesses the very special power to conjure up stimuli in the absence of any externally generated sensations. This control is achieved through the power of imagination, and provides infinitely greater possibilities for the maximization of pleasurable experiences than was available under traditional, realistic hedonism to even the most powerful of potentates. This derives not merely from the fact that there are virtually no restrictions upon the faculty of imagination, but also from the fact that it is completely within the hedonist's own control. It is this highly rationalized form of self-illusory hedonism which characterizes modern pleasure-seeking. (1987: 76)

Consumerism and the new hedonism

If the key to modern hedonism is the quest for pleasure through emotional experience rather than sensory stimulation, then modern consumption can be seen as an elaborate apparatus enabling individuals to *imagine* the dramas which afford them pleasure, to *dream* the scenarios which fulfil their desires. What commodities do is to act as props for the imagination, as stimulants for a reverie in which longing and fulfilment coincide.

> In modern, self-illusory hedonism, the individual is . . . an artist of the imagination, someone who takes images from memory or the existing environment, and rearranges them or otherwise improves them in his mind in such a way that they become distinctly pleasing. No longer are they 'taken as given' from past experience, but crafted into unique products, pleasure being the guiding principle. In this sense, the contemporary hedonist is a dream artist, the special skills possessed by modern man making this possible. (Campbell 1987: 79)

Consider the fashion for South American hammocks. The importation of hammocks from Peru, Bolivia and Paraguay is a curious reversal of the nineteenth century, when hammocks mass-produced from Manchester wiped out South American production (Gott, 1993). Currently, hammocks are very popular with British workaholics, who evidently imagine themselves luxuriating in the sunshine, relaxing, at peace with themselves and with the world. The hammock becomes the stimulus for a longing reverie, at once unrealistic and unrealizable, frustrating and yet strangely fulfilling. If many of the hammocks sold are rarely used, and, if when they are used they fail to yield much relaxing time (since people who daydream about hammocks are the very people unable to relax), these things hardly matter. To these people, the pleasure afforded by the hammock is at the level of fantasy, rather than as an object. The enjoyment of products as parts of fantasies and the fantasies about products are a crucial feature of modern consumerism and may explain why window shopping or looking at magazines of unaffordable items can be enjoyable.

Modern consumption, according to Campbell, is built around daydreaming, 'envisaged as an activity which mixes the pleasures of fantasy with those of reality' (1987: 85). Desire becomes itself subject to control, nurtured, encouraged, stimulated so long as it affords pleasure. Deferred gratification is no sacrifice of pleasure but a state of increased excitation, at once frustrating and enjoyable, endured in the interest of heightened pleasures ahead. Disillusionment in hedonism of this type is not the result of dulling of the senses, as it is with traditional hedonism, but the result of the fact that imagined pleasures are always greater than actual ones, that as the poet Keats said, 'heard melodies are sweet, those unheard are sweeter' (quoted in Campbell, 1987: 87). Dissatisfaction with reality, a generalized tristesse, becomes the backcloth against which the consumer as a dream artist can embroider his or her fantasies: 'Thus the contemporary hedonist not only tends to welcome deferred gratification, but may also prematurely abandon a source of pleasure, as, by doing so, he maximizes the opportunities for indulging the emotions of grief, sorrow, nostalgia, and, of course, self-pity' (1987: 88).

Campbell's account of hedonism reveals consumer culture to be a space where a wide range of emotions can be experienced, through a combination of real and imagined stimuli. A bungee jump, a visit to one of the numerous terror attractions (Madame Tussaud's, London Dungeon etc.) or watching a horror movie are all experiences in terror; a visit at the Holocaust museum in Washington, DC becomes an experience in grief; the purchase of a gift for a loved one becomes an experience in romantic love and so on. Experiences fade with repetition, hence self-illusory hedonism is always seeking novelty, uniqueness and adventure, while at all times seeking to maintain control over the intensity of stimulation, balancing endurable longing with a kaleidoscopic survey of emotions and delectable morsels of pleasure:

> The cycle of desire – acquisition – use – disillusionment – renewed desire is a general feature of modern hedonism, and applies to romantic interpersonal relationships as much as the consumption of cultural products such as clothes and records. (Campbell, 1987: 90)

This type of hedonism finds its ideal in *romanticism*, which

> had the effect of casting the individual of true virtue in the role of an opponent to 'society', whose conventions he must deny if only to secure proof of his genius and passion. At the same time, he becomes not merely a virtuoso in feeling but also in pleasure, something he must prove by creating cultural products which yield pleasure to others. Pleasure indeed becomes the crucial means of recognizing that ideal truth and beauty which imagination reveals – it is the 'grand elementary principle' in life – and thus becomes the means by which enlightenment and moral renewal can be achieved through art. (1987: 203)

Under the Romantic Ethic, the modern consumer fuses hedonism with an aesthetic attitude to life, seeking to emulate the artist in his or her pursuit of pleasures through the medium of imagination, repudiation of 'easy' pleasures or comforts in the interest of controlled stimulation and quest for a highly individual style (Ewen, 1990; Featherstone, 1991; Miller, 1987; Nixon, 1992; Simmonds, 1990; Willis, 1990). Here, Campbell joins an important tradition of consumer studies, which underlines the so-called aestheticization of everyday life, according to which everyday consumer objects are infected with aesthetic considerations, becoming signs of style and taste, and losing their functional qualities. Western consumers will spend enormous amounts of time decorating their homes, choosing their clothes, food and other goods, planning their holidays, for ever mixing ingredients, as if they were trying not merely to create works of art but to discover a uniquely individual style. To do so, commodities must appear forgetful of being use-values, and must appear exclusively as objects of pure taste. This, according to Bourdieu:

> asserts the *absolute primacy of form over function*, of the mode of representation over the object represented, [and] *categorically* demands a purely aesthetic disposition which earlier art demanded only conditionally. The demiurgic ambition of the artist, capable of applying to any object the pure intention of an artistic effort which is an end in itself, calls for unlimited repetitiveness on the part of the

aesthete capable of applying the specifically aesthetic intention to any object, whether or not it has been produced with aesthetic intention. (1984: 30)

The corollary of the aestheticization of everyday life is the de-aestheticization of art. Surrealist painting initiated the project of stripping objects of art of their transcendental qualities and mystique, either by parodying well-known masterpieces (Dali adding a moustache to the *Mona Lisa*) or by presenting everyday objects as artwork. Many museums today routinely display 'ordinary' objects of everyday life, inviting the visitor to turn them into artistic works through the use of imagination (Featherstone, 1991).

The great advantage of Campbell's account over most others highlighting the artistic qualities of modern consumption is that it keeps both pleasure and dissatisfaction in the picture, built as it is on a sophisticated theory of desire and stimulation. Tastes and aesthetic preferences are not arbitrary social constructions, but are derivative of romantic sensibilities pursuing pleasure. Trivial objects of everyday life become charged with aestheticism, not because of Veblenesque status concerns, nor because individuals are influenced by tastemakers or 'new cultural intermediaries' working in the media, design, fashion, advertising and information (Bourdieu, 1984), but because they become objects of emotion activating pleasurable reveries. Furthermore, Campbell offers strong arguments for why dissatisfaction, inextricably linked with the pursuit of pleasure, drives innovation. His hedonist-consumers are inexorably drawn to exploration and experimentation. Above all, Campbell offers one of the few plausible explanations of why consumers may be pursuing horror, fright, anger, sadness, and even pain as part of the pursuit of pleasure.

The relative weaknesses in Campbell's account of modern consumption are paradoxically linked to his success in elucidating pleasure. His account of the pleasure principle is, as we saw, rich in insights, more dynamic and in some ways more convincing than the psychoanalytic account of the same concept, which is connected to homoeostasis and the reduction of tension. Yet, where Freud saw the world conspiring against individual pleasure, Campbell sees no such limitations. For Freud, the pleasure principle must be continuously modified, compromised and deflected according to the demands of reality:

> What decides the purpose of life is simply the programme of the pleasure principle. This principle dominates the operation of the mental apparatus from the start. There can be no doubt about its efficacy, and yet its programme is at loggerheads with the whole world, with the macrocosm as much as the microcosm. There is no possibility at all of its being carried through; all the regulations of the universe run counter to it. (Freud, 1930: 76)

Unlike the psychoanalytic account of libido for ever torn between pleasure and social bonding, for ever frustrated by necessity, Campbell's pleasure principle rules supreme: Modern hedonism presents all individuals with the possibility of being their own despot, exercising total control over the stimuli they experience, and hence the pleasure they receive (1987: 76).

The main limitations on pleasure entertained by Campbell appear to be those originating in the nature of pleasure, the dulling effects of comfort and the diminishing intensity of pleasure itself. This view does not explain what happens when one individual's pleasure inhibits the pleasure of somebody else. Nor what happens when one individual's pleasure runs counter to the broader institutions of morality, religion or law. Finally, it seems that Campbell's individual can pursue his or her Quixotic adventures, oblivious to the necessities and hardships of life or any other external demands.

While much of Campbell's discussion occurs at the level of macrosocial and cultural trends across several centuries, the picture which he paints of the modern consumer is highly individualistic. The pleasure principle, as he conceives it, operates across classes, races, genders, ages and all other social and cultural distinctions. Unlike Douglas and Isherwood (1978) who view the solitary consumer as a fiction, consumers emerge from Campbell's discussions as solitary creatures, individually pursuing pleasure, absorbed in their reveries, more or less oblivious of each other. Campbell's severe criticism of Veblen, his contemptuous dismissal of Packard's (1957) thesis of consumer manipulation, his steadfast refusal to relate fantasy with escapism or substitute gratification and his indifference to the social, political and communicative dimensions of consumption all underline his uncompromising commitment to pleasure as the totalizing principle at the heart of modern consumption. His account, however, serves as a warning of some of the absurdity that one ends up with, when seeing contemporary consumption through a single prism. It would be bizarre to envisage a single mother shopping for her weekly groceries as being lost in a reverie of pleasure.

Social hedonism

To Campbell's uncompromisingly solipsistic hedonism, it is interesting to juxtapose Bourdieu's social hedonism. Bourdieu's book *Distinction: A Social Critique of the Judgement of Taste* (1984) caused quite a substantial public debate when first published in France, partly because it was seen as debunking the concept of taste (notably 'high-brow taste') by reintegrating aesthetic consumption with ordinary everyday consumption. Bourdieu combines an emphasis on hedonism with an insistence that consumption is a set of practices establishing social differences, viewing consumers both as pleasure-seeking (like Campbell) and as hungry for distinction (like Douglas and Isherwood). Tastes, according to Bourdieu, emerge at once as avenues towards pleasure and as a class phenomenon, as a form of cultural capital and as an instrument of oppression.

Bourdieu's arguments draw on two extensive surveys on consumer tastes and life-styles carried out in France in the 1960s. Judged on their own merit, these surveys are both outdated and methodologically mechanistic, suffering from all the familiar shortcomings of attempting to capture a person's life-style, tastes and meanings through standardized inflexible questions. Nevertheless, these surveys enable Bourdieu to argue that there are important differences in how different social classes, or even class fractions, derive pleasure. The food and the drinks they consume, the films and television programmes they watch, the cars they drive and the ways they furnish and decorate their homes are not merely governed by different tastes but reveal fundamentally different modes of deriving pleasure, different aesthetics, different pleasure principles.

The key to these differences is what he calls the 'Kantian aesthetic' which is central to middle-class life-styles, yet entirely absent from working class life-styles. For Kant, the aesthetic experience occupies a position between morality and sensuousness and centres on the faculty of judgement. Judgement mediates between theoretical reason and practical reason, through the feeling of pleasure; its realm is art. Aesthetic experience rejects immediate sensuous pleasures in favour of abstract appreciation of the artistic which comes through the faculty of imagination. Beauty, according to this view, is neither floating freely in an external world, nor the direct corollary of sensuous pleasure but is creatively constituted through the work of imagination. Thus beauty can be discovered in an object's form as well as in the mode of its representation, if the object can be approached in an detached, disinterested manner which completely disregards its use or material composition. Even objects which could be classed as 'ugly', can therefore become beautiful. A photograph of rotting vegetables, a painting of an ugly man or a grotesque interlude in the midst of a symphony can all afford great aesthetic pleasure if the object can be released from its bondage to both pleasure and usage and turned into a 'free' being, signifying nothing but itself, through the free play of imagination.

Bourdieu rejects the Kantian theory as a theory of aesthetic judgement (respectful parodying in the title of his book Kant's *Critique of Judgement*) but accepts it as a description of bourgeois aesthetics. He regards the detached, aloof disposition of the Kantian aesthetic not as a mental faculty, but as an orientation concomitant to the affluence of today's bourgeoisie and an instrument of social distinctions. The crux of his argument is that while the middle class embrace the Kantian aesthetic, cultivating tastes for the abstract, the working class aesthetic is that of popular culture, dictated by necessity and tied to both function and sensuous pleasure. This fundamental difference cuts across every aspect of taste. The working-class invariably seeks direct gratification while the middle class seeks 'style'.

Bourdieu provides numerous illustrations of this dichotomy, ranging from food and drink to photography, from music to home decoration. A couple of his examples will suffice. Working people like food, plentiful in protein, nutritious – what Orwell in *The Road to Wigan Pier* described as 'a little bit "tasty"' (1962: 86). Pleasure is synonymous to an 'honest' and unfussy but abundant assortment of 'strong' food, which ultimately reflects the value of virility, rooted in physical work. By contrast middle-class tastes weigh heavily towards elaborately prepared food, sauces and so on, the uses of exotic ingredients (like rare mushrooms), or, towards the extreme simplicity of nouvelle cuisine. These emphasize the 'higher and finer' qualities inherent in preparation and presentation and, in the extreme, seem to deny that food is anything quite as vulgar as nourishment.

Similar illustrations are offered by Bourdieu from music (working class prefer music with strong melodic and rhythmic content, middle class prefer avant-garde), photography (working class prefer pictures of garish sunsets or innocent children at first communion, middle class prefer pictures of dissected cabbages or car crashes) and others. In Bourdieu's account the aestheticization of everyday life is a middle-class affliction, rather than a totalizing principle of late capitalism as for some postmodern thinkers. If middle-class consumers approach their clothing, eating and home furnishing with an anti-functional, detached outlook, this is not the same for working-class life-styles: 'Nothing is more alien to working-class women than the typically bourgeois idea of making each object in the home the occasion for an aesthetic choice' (1984: 47). For Bourdieu, even where the same commodity is consumed by different social classes, its meaning will vary. Where some movie-goers watch a 'Western starring Burt Lancaster', others have watched 'the latest Sam Peckinpah'; these are vastly different ways of seeing the same film, at once reflecting different tastes, generating different pleasures and producing social distinctions (1984: 28).

Consumers' tastes, for Bourdieu, have darker, less innocent qualities than they do for Campbell or indeed economists. Aesthetic judgements act as a form of thought terrorism (a favourite term of Bourdieu's) cutting across social classes and fractions:

> Terrorism [lies] in the peremptory verdicts which, in the name of taste, condemn to ridicule, indignity, shame, silence (here one could give examples, taken from everyone's familiar universe), men and women who simply fall short, in the eyes of their judges, of the right way of being and doing; it [lies] in the symbolic violence through which the dominant groups endeavour to impose their own life-style, and which abounds in the glossy weekly magazines: 'Conforama is the Guy Lux of furniture', says *Le Nouvel Observateur*, which will never tell you that the *Nouvel Obs* is the Club Méditerranée of culture. There is terrorism in all such remarks, flashes of self-interested lucidity sparked off by class hatred and contempt. (1984: 511)

Insults rarely hurt more than when aimed at the adversary's 'taken for granted preferences'; few types of social humiliation can match the dismissal of someone's tastes. 'You like X? Oh dear, it's so passé/common!' where X can be anything from digital watches, dried tomatoes to yesterday's music idol or theories of Althusser or Baudrillard. Conversely, argues Bourdieu, a transgression of the aesthetic decrees of 'high culture' will outrage the bourgeois more effectively than the breach of a moral code. An improperly dressed person, for example, will incur more hostility than a sexual deviant. In this way, aesthetics becomes a major terrain of contest between social classes and fractions, a contest where much pleasure is derived from terrorizing the adversaries, either by passing judgements on their tastes or by violating aesthetic codes. If Campbell's hedonist-consumer is naturally driven towards the image of the consumer-explorer, Bourdieu's consumer tends to modulate from an aesthete into a snob, a sadist or a rebel, pleasure becoming linked, not to discovery and innovation, but to class violence and aggression. Bourdieu's account of the different classes' aesthetics has been criticized from both the left and the right; the left have accused him of diminishing the working class life-style to a caricature, while the right have feigned horror at his questioning of their aesthetic taboos (for an overview see Jenkins, 1992). Yet, he does not seek to evaluate these aesthetics, since he rejects any transcendental aesthetic qualities. Ultimately all tastes are socially constructed, as are their 'high' or 'low' qualities, that is distinctions between tastes. To be sure, the middle classes may sneer at the vulgarity and 'cheapness' of common culture, just as the working class may, less blatantly, belittle the airs and affectations of the high-brows. But for Bourdieu, the two represent fundamentally different aesthetics. From the two, various social fractions and intermediate or marginal groups seek to mould their own aesthetics, such as artlessly aspiring at high-brow or affectedly 'opting' for rustic simplicity. However, the mechanisms for deriving pleasure are essentially different. Working-class life-style is one of a 'realistic (but not resigned) hedonism' (1984: 49), while the middle-class life-style becomes ever more closely aligned to the Kantian aesthetic, concerned with style, form and distinction.

Bourdieu's account of consumerism is one which combines a discussion of pleasure with a class analysis of tastes and patterns of consumption. In its emphasis on class differences in consumption, it is only matched by Douglas and Isherwood's analysis. Many commentators, however, have found Bourdieu's class analysis, not only inaccurate but also patronizing. Jenkins (1992) and Douglas (1982) herself have argued that style and cultivated/inane tastes are every bit as important for working-class people as they are for the middle classes. Numerous British commentators have established the importance of style, fashion and fantasy in consumption patterns of young working-class people, whose preferred tastes in music may be as perplexing to middle-aged, middle-class people as any avant-garde may be to a working-class audience (Featherstone, 1991; Fiske, 1989; Willis, 1990). In sum, one suspects that the class dimension in Bourdieu's argument is at least outdated or more alarmingly a projection of his own middle-class presumptions.

Comparing Bourdieu's and Campbell's hedonistic accounts of modern consumption, one may be tempted to discern an equivalence between the two mechanisms of pleasure they each describe. Bourdieu's Kantian Ethic and Campbell's modern hedonism hinge on the imagination and on deferred pleasure. Bourdieu's realistic hedonism and Campbell's traditional hedonism are both associated with instant sensuous pleasure. The former present the consumer as artist or aesthete, the latter as hedonist. This similarity, however, could be somewhat misleading. For Bourdieu taste, culture and pleasure are not only class experiences but historically constructed ones. An individual *learns to enjoy* a wide range of objects and activities, from coffee to frogs' legs, from Chinese opera to heavy metal music, from jogging to foxhunting on rainy days. Many of these may appear curious to those 'uneducated' in these pleasures, yet membership of a social group and induction into its social tastes substantially determines an individual's *habitus*, which Bourdieu sees as the range of tastes from which he or she will derive a personal repertoire. This contrasts with Campbell's far more individualistic account, where individuals must discover pleasure for themselves, their aesthetic responses being a matter of individual psychohistory rather than class or group membership.

Hedonism and sadism

For all their limitations, images of consumers as hedonists or artists which emerge from Campbell's and Bourdieu's works have a compelling quality. As we stare at the clothes in a shop window, at the compact discs in a record store, at the motorboats in our leisure magazine, at the mouth-watering dishes pictured in our Sunday newspapers or at our neighbour's smart new car, we experience a feeling which can only be described as desire, a desire which is at once sweet and frustrating, a desire capable at times of convulsing our physical being as though it were purely sexual. Such objects seduce us as though they were sexual objects, sparking off strings of fantasies, which continue to prosper the longer the object remains inaccessible. As Freud (1921) realized in his theory of the relationship between sexual gratification and romantic love, the denial of consummation enhances the idealization of the inaccessible object, just as in courtly love the longing was all the sweeter, the more aloof and unresponsive was the object of the lover's languor.

The accounts which we have explored in this chapter put pleasure at the centre of modern consumption and more generally as the central ethic of Western cultures. Happiness is increasingly defined not in terms of achievement or success but in broadly hedonistic or aesthetic terms reflected in the 'quality of life' both at and outside the workplace. Happiness is seen neither as a reward for effort or virtue, nor as the result of fortune. Instead, as Rieff (1959) has brutally put it, human happiness is a question of the *management of pleasure* and, therefore, a *duty* to oneself. So long as one is not excluded from the seductive world of commodities by being dependent on the state for survival, being unhappy is inexcusable. It can only be due to one's ineptness at managing pleasure.

Neither Campbell nor Bourdieu would seek to vindicate such a position as an ethical hedonism, the true road to the good life, if such a thing exists. They both believe that consumers are deluding themselves in their espousal of the pleasure principle (in any guise), and their determination to pretend that the grey world of necessity has melted away. The very shrinking of individual women and men to the status of consumers, the willingness to define oneself and others through their standing as consumers is indicative of this self-delusion. Yet, neither Campbell nor Bourdieu are remotely willing to entertain the notion that modern hedonism, though its roots lie in delusion, is a form of compensation for the greyness of life under the reality principle or an escapist form of substitute gratification. Consumerist fantasies may be detached from reality but the pleasure they afford is real. This is a position which has been criticized with considerable eloquence by Christopher Lasch. Lasch has argued over many years that the pleasures of consumerism are not innocent, neither in their origins nor in their implications:

> Commodity production and consumerism alter perceptions not just of the self but of the world outside the self. They create a world of mirrors, insubstantial images, illusions increasingly indistinguishable from reality. The mirror effect makes the subject an object; at the same time, it makes the world of objects an extension or projection of the self. It is misleading to characterize the culture of consumption as a culture dominated by things. The consumer lives surrounded not so much by things as by fantasies. He lives in a world that has no objective or independent existence and seems to exist only to gratify or thwart his desires. (1984: 30)

At the heart of this critique lies the connection between hedonism and narcissism, a link widely discussed in psychoanalytic literature (see Gabriel, 1983, 1984b; Lasch 1980, 1984). The modern narcissist is the individual who, unable to love and unwilling to be loved, constantly seeks to derive pleasure from his or her own image. This he tries to do by embellishing his ego through the consumption of material and human objects, which become objects of fantasy and desire. Contemporary hedonism erects a massive edifice of substitute gratifications which, instead of obliterating, compounds the narcissism and lovelessness of modern life. As objects of desire, commodities and people are indistinguishable – they are objects to be used, abused and manipulated for one's personal enhancement:

> Contemporary hedonism . . . originates not in the pursuit of pleasure but in the war of all against all, in which even the most intimate encounters become a form of mutual exploitation. . . . This hedonism is a fraud; the pursuit of pleasure disguises a struggle for power. (Lasch, 1980: 65, 66)

Lasch tries to show the extent to which pleasure in our culture has become co-extensive with aggression; sex and violence become irredeemably intertwined in language, in fantasy and in reality. If individuals derive pleasure, aesthetic or otherwise, from violence or products associated with violence, this is not as Campbell might have argued because violence just happened to provide a springboard for pleasurable fantasies, in the same way that tenderness, love or romance might have done. Violence becomes one with pleasure, when pleasure becomes life's only business, detached from morality or order. If Bourdieu, following Veblen, clearly envisages the sadistic delights of both snobbery and aesthetic transgression, Lasch goes a step further. In the Marquis de Sade's explosive utopia where sexual pleasure leads to every humiliation of the other imaginable, even as far as mutilation, hacking, tearing, cutting and killing, Lasch finds both the prototype and terminus of modern hedonism, seeing no distinction between objects and people as instruments of pleasure. De Sade's message, coming at the outset of the French republican era was that uncompromised hedonism, far from leading to an emotional polytheism, can only lead to one thing, unbridled aggression. Once moral restraints have been removed, the pursuit of pleasure quickly turns into violence:

> In a society that has reduced reason to mere calculation, reason can impose no limits on the pursuit of pleasure – on the immediate gratification of every desire no matter how perverse, insane, criminal, or merely immoral. For the standards that would condemn cruelty derive from religion, compassion, or the kind of reason that rejects purely instrumental applications; and none of these outmoded forms of thought or feeling has any logical place in a society based on commodity production. (Lasch, 1980: 69)

To be sure, de Sade's vision has not become reality 200 years later. Nevertheless, aggression has assumed a central position in every aspect of Western life, including the predatory nature of personal relationships, the pitiless abuse of nature in pursuit of ever higher standards of living, the use of commodities as weapons in a Veblenesque combat for status and the savagery of modern spectacles. The fantasies of consumer culture, pleasurable though they may be, have little of the daydreaming, bitter-sweet qualities envisaged by Campbell. The material or human object's resistance to being possessed, far from heightening the delights of yearning, spawn murderous fantasies of rape, pillage and destruction. If a narcissist cannot have something, whether it be the goods in a shop window, the neighbour's car or the object of his sexual interest, far from gently dreaming of acquiring it by seduction or payment, he dreams of smashing it, breaking it or destroying it. Any residual pleasure in the object rests in its annihilation. Vandalism and destruction are the flip side of consumer hedonism, something that often goes unnoticed among those who preach both the worship of commodities and respect for human values.

Conclusion

This bleak picture contrasts sharply with the more upbeat depictions of Western consumers as pleasure-seekers. But, like them, Lasch sees individuals today as much more likely to associate happiness with pleasure than with achievement, success or virtue. They are likely to envisage pleasure as residing in those objects which attract desire, and in doing so they may treat commodities or people in a similar manner, as stimulants for fantasies. Life assumes the character of an erotic simmer, a never-ending process of seduction, maintaining a constant level of desire which migrates from object to object as they each assume the spotlight in our fantasies.

Different accounts of consumer hedonism take different views on the nature of pleasure and the extent to which it differs across social classes and other groups. Nevertheless, there is wide agreement that consumer pleasure lies not so much in physical sensation as in total emotional experience, pleasure lies in the meaning of this experience. While this experience may be fantastic or delusory, the pleasure is not delusory at all. Thus the pleasure derived from a 'designer' ashtray lies in its imaginary qualities, which lift it above the mundane realities of its function, its substance, its price or its future uses. The object is idealized in much the same way as any object of infatuation is. It seduces us in exactly the same way that a person might.

Bourdieu and Campbell go some way towards providing an explanation for the thesis that everyday reality in Western cultures becomes aestheticized, with objects and activities assuming the qualities of art and losing their functional and material bearings. Style becomes more important than utility, which acquires a vulgar, common hue. The consumer as hedonist must be able to derive pleasure from every item with which he or she comes into contact and everything must be orientated to that end.

Starting with Lasch, our view is that consumer hedonism is neither playful nor innocent. Instead it is the outcome of a culture in which the market becomes the dominant institution regulating relations among individuals and tastes reign supreme, with little restraint from loyalty, morality, duty or love. Pleasure derived from material and symbolic manipulation of people and objects entails a substantial amount of aggression and the pursuit of this type of pleasure may be ultimately futile. The consumer becomes an addict capable of inflicting any amount of pain on others in order to obtain what he or she believes will satisfy his or her desires. Consumer hedonism can lead to a complete dead end, reinforcing the very discontents which drive it. Few have expressed this idea with the force and clarity of an old militant, interviewed by Seabrook:

> People aren't satisfied, only they don't seem to know why they're not. The only chance of satisfaction we can imagine is getting more of what we've already got now. But it's what we've got now that makes everybody dissatisfied. So what will more of it do, make us more satisfied, or more dissatisfied? (1979: 132)

Whether today's consumers are locked in a vicious circle of dependency, frustration and hate or whether they enjoy in a limited but vital way the satisfactions available to them, in practice or fantasy, this remains a vital question at the heart of the debate on today's consumerism.

Hedonism is an idea which accounts for certain qualities of contemporary consumption; the thrill we get when we acquire an object we like, our insistence on what we like and what we do not like, and our ability to derive pleasure, thrills and fun out of seemingly disagreeable experiences. It also can elucidate different ways in which different social classes, including the very poorest, derive pleasure out of material objects. The underside of this is that hedonism is neither the only principle driving today's consumers, nor the liberating force celebrated by its apologists.

7

The Consumer as Victim

[C]onsumers are being manipulated, defrauded, and injured not just by marginal businesses or fly-by-night hucksters but by the US blue-chip business firms.

Ralph Nader (1968)

The idea that consumers are victims no longer enjoys quite the high profile it once did. While victimhood and empowerment are widely discussed in connection with particular social groups ranging from women to ethnic minorities or people with physical disabilities, the world of consumption is not the first to come to mind when thinking of people as seriously wronged. Is the image of the consumer as victim therefore a trifle excessive? Should it be used only for serious injustice, cases where consumption directly threatens life? We think not, although we recognize that most people think of victimhood as occurring where events are beyond their control, such as sexual harassment, political or social discrimination, and so on. Consumers cannot only be victims of blatant exploitation and fraud but may equally create themselves as victims or collude in the victimization of others.

After the publication of Vance Packard's book *The Hidden Persuaders* in the 1950s, which created a stir with its revelations of consumer manipulation by new techniques of depth psychology and mass advertising, the image of the consumer as victim occupied a central position in postwar cultural commentaries on Western consumption (Packard, 1981/1957). The consumer was seen not only as a victim of unscrupulous commercial interests but also as fodder for the sophisticated techniques of the emerging science of consumer psychology (see Introduction: The Faces of the Consumer). In *One Dimensional Man* (1964), a book that like Packard's achieved cult status, Marcuse launched a powerful attack on late capitalism as compounding the alienation of the worker by turning people into one dimensional beings solely preoccupied with consumption. This post Second World War critical tradition lost some of its glamour and momentum in the 1980s when, under the influence of postmodernism, many cultural commentators began to celebrate consumption as an active pursuit rather than a passive escapist activity. A new generation of neo-Marxist commentators represented by the journal *Marxism Today* began to argue that consumption holds not only creative but liberating potential (Hall and Jacques, 1989). In spite of attempts by Lasch (1991), Sklair (1991) and others to underline the continuing addictive qualities of contemporary consumption (see the previous two chapters), it would be fair to say that cultural studies lost interest in the notion of the consumer as victim. Instead, they have sought to present the consumer as an explorer, as a semiotic puzzle-solver, as a bricoleur, as an identity-seeker, or as we shall see in the next chapter, as a rebel.

Rejecting the view propounded by cultural theory, consumer advocates and a new wave of consumer organizations around the world have highlighted the increased vulnerabilities of consumers in the age of global consumer capitalism. In this chapter we will explore some of these arguments and some of the instances that fuelled this new critique. In Chapter 9 (The Consumer as Activist), we will place in a historical context the new type of campaigning and use of media pioneered by these organizations.

The experience of being a victim

Not so deep beneath the surface of any consumer's mind is a sense that he or she may be exploited. The act of consuming taps a deep well of experience from childhood on. Few childhoods have not experienced the excitement of the first meaningful purchase of a longed-for toy or sweet. As part of the preparation for this book, we interviewed consumer activists and employees of consumer organizations from several different countries. We asked some of them if they could remember their first significant purchase. After sometimes intense interviews discussing the complexities of consumer activism and the challenges ahead, their eyes would light up, smiles come to their faces as they told of a mother giving money to buy a sweet or some early excitement. One, brought up in an isolated, near self-sufficient community in a developing country, told of the awe of being allowed to buy a canned drink on a trip out to town, an unheard of luxury. To anticipate such pleasure on every occasion (explored in Chapter 6: The Consumer: Hedonist or Artist?) is an unrealistic expectation. One is bound to be disappointed. The excitement of the early experience of consumer power, such as buying your own toy, is counterbalanced by the bitterness or disappointment from a purchase which failed to live up to expectations. The consumer-as-victim is, in this respect, the other side of the coin of consumer as pleasure seeker.

As people get older, they often get more pleasure from giving than receiving, and few purchases maintain the sense of excitement, yet the notion of being a victim has taken psychological root. The common identification of consuming and shopping as a female preserve means that women's cultural experience of oppression transfers easily to their experience of consuming. Consuming makes one vulnerable, at risk, potential victim. It is not accidental that many of those who work in consumer organizations are women. Consuming for males, too, can be a highly charged experience. Those who are accustomed to being powerful at work, in public places, let alone the home, can easily be a victim on the high street or in the shopping mall.

Anyone who has been in the first line of contact with the public as consumers, or who trains people who deal with the public, is familiar with instances when shopping, eating at a restaurant, queuing for service, can generate situations during which tempers can fray, emotions can be raw, and social dynamics can take off in all kinds of potentially uncontrollable directions. As a result, the shop assistant, the waiter, the check-out till operator are frequently expected to exhibit extraordinary patience in dealing with the frustrations and anger of consumers who feel that their rights have been violated. Front-line staff usually only survive psychologically in their dealings with the public if they adopt one consistent style of dealing with them; this may be a style of identifying with the customer or of remaining distant, cool and professional (Pines and Aronson, 1988). Hopping from 'being solicitous to the customer' to 'frozen indifference' brings tremendous strain to the employee. Assertiveness training both for customers and staff is sometimes presented as the way of overcoming victimhood and achieving one's rights, an assumption about how to engender successful outcomes of victimhood which has been absorbed by the currently fashionable rhetoric of empowerment.

The psycho-therapeutic language of empowerment and self-assertion has close associations with the social construct of consumer-as-victim. Empowerment suggests an evolution from 'whinging' about failure, through knowing how to complain, to the pinnacle of self-assertion. The model is almost straight from Abraham Maslow (1970/1954) or Carl Rogers (1951). In effect this is not always easy for consumers to accomplish; nor is it always possible to find their rights through recourse to the state, even when the state acknowledges them. In the last decades of the twentieth century, the dominant deregulatory ideology ensured that a reference to the need for protection could be countered by a jibe about the nanny state or spoon-feeding. When the US Federal Trade Commission proposed controls on television advertising for sugared cereals for children, for instance, the *Washington Post* accused it of becoming a national nanny (Aaker and Day, 1982: 3). The notion of empowerment can be an excuse for ignoring the unequal terrain: knowledgeable company versus atomized and under-educated individual consumer and can enshrine an individualized notion of the consumer and his or her rights. Even before contemporary consumerism, the dream of Redfern (an early champion of consumers) that consumers would unite co-operatively and organize politically, had been formulated to help foster a collective consumer experience, but by the late twentieth century it had been undermined (Redfern, 1920: 55). Attempts to provide pre-shopping advice for consumers, such as the Consumer Advice Centres in the 1970s, were premised upon a welfare state notion of the relationship between consumer and the state, with the public sector acting on behalf of the consumer. These Centres were designed to instil greater self-assertion into the consumer, but in practice most of their work was dealing with consumer complaints and in mediating on behalf of consumers (Cranston, 1979). In terms the early Fabians would have applauded, but Redfern would have been wary of – the co-operative consumer movement preferring autonomous consumer action (see Thompson, 1994) – the Consumer Advice Centres were the result of demands being made of the state, both nationally and locally, to support and protect the consumer. The attempt was cut short by the election of Mrs Thatcher's government in 1979 and the reworking of the relationship between the state and both consumer and citizen (Locke, 1994a; see also Chapter 10: The Consumer as Citizen).

Political ideologies may differ in how they define and approach the consumer as victim, but they all concede that victimhood exists, a function of consumer society. No wonder, then, that consumer protection is a theme which unites all waves of consumer activist work, mainstream and fringe (Best, 1981; Nadel, 1971). The theme is built into laws and cultures world-wide for two reasons. First, even the most doctrinaire proponents of the advantages of market economics for consumers accept that there can be market failures due to the emergence of oligopolies (monopoly), imperfect information and barriers to entry. In addition, consumers can be disenfranchised due to poverty (not strictly a market failure) and poor access. To take one of these causes of market failure, monopoly, today's globalizing economy poses new challenges for consumer rights due to the emergence of hugely powerful corporations, which already have awesome market share and influence over relatively weak global institutions. As we shall see later, in the twentieth century there has been a persistent thread of individual consumer action against corporations at the national level, but the track record of concerted consumer action on an international level has yet to emerge on a routine basis (for some exceptions see Smith, 1990; and also the next two chapters – Chapter 8: The Consumer as Rebel; Chapter 9: The Consumer as Activist). As we argue in the final chapter, the ramifications of the emerging global economy suggest new patterns as well as a new volatility in consumer behaviour – what we refer to as unmanageability. Already we can note that a culture of victimization can emerge with surprising speed and vengeance. In the UK, for instance, public outcry against 'excessive' profits and high pay and share remunerations for senior managers in newly privatized public utilities emerged in the mid-1990s, only a few years after there had been hardly a warning or thought of such consumer 'injustice' when the utilities were being sold off. The sell-off went through relatively quietly, to the pleasure of market ideologues, who were left perplexed by the U-turn in public mores in such a short space of time. Even in commercial sectors famous for their market efficiency and consumer choice, such as food retailing, there can be concerns at the marginalization of large sections of consumers (see Raven and Lang, 1995). Victimization and volatility are new bedfellows.

The second reason consumer protection is so pervasive is that, as long as there have been commercial transactions, there has been the possibility of defrauding or harming the purchaser. Trading standards laws go back centuries; and in civilizations where there are no written rules, there is custom and practice to similar effect (Douglas and Isherwood, 1978; Evans-Pritchard, 1940). Today, defrauding the consumer may occur through products and in locations unimaginable even decades ago; but often the process that renders the consumer into a victim follows well-established patterns. Shopping is a complex process, involving considerable sums, let alone emotional investment, from the individual's point of view. The UK's Molony Committee, reporting in the 1960s, as the postwar consumer society got up to speed, recognized this new vulnerability for modern consumers in language which today sounds patronizing:

> Whereas the consumer of fifty years ago needed only a reasonable modicum of skill and knowledge to recognise the composition of the goods on offer and their manner of production, and to assess their quality and fitness for his particular purpose, the consumer of today finds it difficult if not impossible to do. It is only in the laboratory that the fibre content of a piece of modern cloth can be determined with certainty. The range of timbers from which furniture is made (many of them unknown to the general public twenty years ago) has increased vastly, and the methods of furniture manufacture have been materially changed in a number of ways. The uppers of shoes may be cemented, instead of sewn to the soles, which in turn may be made of synthetic materials instead of leather. Properly utilised, these and a hundred other new materials and manufacturing method may be of great advantage; employed without regard to their limitations or placed in the hands of an ill-informed purchaser, they may prove worthless. (Board of Trade, 1962: para 41)

You buy a car, and find it was stolen; a food sold as pure turns out to be adulterated or contaminated; a washing machine advertised as a best buy breaks down; a medicine turns out to have hidden side-effects; a quiet package holiday in the Mediterranean turns out to be a noisy nightmare next to a disco; a warranty that turns out to exclude most eventualities in the small print; and so on. The legal profession as well as media consumer programmes prosper on the back of such daily victimization (Ramsay, 1989).

Herrmann has argued that consumer movements since the late nineteenth century have emerged always in reaction to 'three persisting problem areas: (1) ill-considered applications of new technology which result in dangerous or unreliable products, (2) changing conceptions of the social responsibilities of business, and (3) the operations of a dishonest fringe and the occasional lapses of others in the business community' (Herrmann, 1982: 31). Organized consumer activism is thus often a reactive social force (see Chapter 9: The Consumer as Activist). Consumers are thus inevitably on the defensive; they respond and react to events and changed circumstances where other interests dominate, whatever the rhetoric of the market. Specialist consumer research, as well as coverage of consumer affairs in the media, reinforces this view repeatedly. Consumer experience incorporates widespread victimhood, not just in faulty goods, but also service. The European Union's Consumer Policy Service, for instance, commissioned a study of after-sales service and consumer guarantees. This study explored 800 consumer complaints in Germany, Spain, France, Italy, Greece, Ireland,the Netherlands and Portugal and found that national laws gave consumers weak rights of redress if there was poor after-sales service (BEUC, 1994). Complaints included failure to get replacement goods if they were faulty, failure to accept guarantees and responsibility being passed from the retailer to manufacturers, and so on.

Mark Nadel's study of the political negotiations in Congress over US consumer protection suggests that often, but by no means always, new law has been introduced or tightened up only after a scandal, a whistle blowing or an expose, broken by a watchdog organization or journalist (Nadel, 1971: 143). Two of his three case studies were famous scandals – the thalidomide tragedy led to amendments to US food and drug law, as did the shoddy treatment of Ralph Nader, the consumer advocate, after he exposed General Motors on the safety of one of its models. The mass media thrive on such stories which provide a perfect combination of personal interest, collective experience and the victim's humiliation or suffering. The story is often crowned with a happy outcome, if the programme researchers have done their work and can force a recalcitrant firm or official or institution to make amends while they are in turn publicly humiliated. Readers and viewers sigh to themselves 'there but for the grace of God, go I'. This makes for perfect television, but hardly changes the ground rules of consuming experience; if anything, it can accentuate the worry and victimization for consumers.

Companies are increasingly sophisticated in how to respond to such media exposé. The sugar still gets put into babies drinks, and rots teeth, but a new 'sugar-free' drink is brought to the market. In this way, a victim story has helped create a new niche product. It also places the responsibility on the consumer by making it his or her choice whether to purchase the old product. Blame is now placed squarely on the victim: 'If you care about your children's teeth, why did you not purchase our sugar-free brand?'

This pattern of exposé, followed by public outrage, legal intervention, modification by case law and cultural acceptance, has been witnessed in most affluent consumer societies. The attention and glamour in consumer circles centres on the exposé rather than the follow-up, which is where commerce can erode the gain, or side-step the motive behind the new legislation, setting up the conditions for new exposés, and so on. This dynamic has been common in most main product markets, from houses to cars to food. US legislation and public interest in food quality has been invigorated by endless best selling books, since the publication of exposés like Upton Sinclair's *The Jungle* in the 1900s and Kallett and Schlink's *100,000,000 Guinea Pigs* in the 1930s. Such exposés appeal to all social classes and fractions. In Britain, the struggle for consumer protection through legislation can be traced still further back. Frederick Accum prefaced his famous exposé of systematic food adulteration in 1820 with the observation that the practice of adulteration affected all classes, all people. The appeal to consensus did Accum little good, as he was ultimately hounded out of Britain, on a trumped up charge of overdue books at the British Library (Paulus, 1974).

In most mature capitalist societies by the mid twentieth century a platform of consumer protection laws and services were in place. There is no shortage of provisions aimed at protecting the consumer, yet the effectiveness of these provisions at the structural level is highly variable. Why is this? Because of the individualized nature of modern consumption which makes the individual consumer's plight his or her problem alone. Enabling consumers to apply their weight collectively is a challenge of Atlas-like proportions for the consumer movement. While one consumer may feel sympathy for another's plight, as shown on television, he or she is not likely to take up cudgels on their behalf unless there are exceptional circumstances. A major scandal, for example, broke out in the 1990s over the British pension industry; millions of consumers had been encouraged to opt out of established state, relatively secure, schemes which the Government wanted to phase out, and to take out private pensions. There was little support from those unaffected when these private schemes did not live up to the promise. Whose responsibility was this? A report on private pensions in the UK by the Securities and Investment Board (SIB) in 1994 detailed the poor state of control over the self-regulated private pensions sales system (SIB, 1993). On the other hand, there were those who argued that this was state abuse, the state actively promoting a deal to advance its financial position and not protecting people when others offered them a poor deal. Those who had remained in the state scheme were understandably smug and felt those who had opted out had received their come-uppance. Consumers of financial services had been beautifully divided.

One occasion when public tolerance of the status quo was overcome and consumers were united was the international campaign to remove the residues of a particular pesticide from apple juice and apples in 1989. A combination of environmentalists and media stars formed alliances like Mothers and Others for Safe Food in the US and Parents for Safe Food in the UK and Australia and forced the withdrawal of the product almost everywhere in the world (Taylor and Taylor, 1990: 7–9).

Dimensions of victimhood and globalization

There is a qualitative difference between the harm done to individual consumers by inadequate or dangerous goods and the generalized damage inflicted on future generations and the planet by the wanton consumerism and pollution of their forebears. These represent different forms of victimhood. One is individual, the other is collective; one is short-term, the other is long-term. Nor do the problems confronted by consumers in the Third World, where old-style adulteration of food and the sale of products which have been banned in other countries pose extra hazards, and those of the First World necessarily coincide. The problems of consumers in all three dimensions – personal/collective; present/future; First World/ Third World

– are exacerbated by the globalization of capital and the virtual impossibility of regulating across international borders.

Until recently, in affluent economies, first, legal provisions in what the consumer can expect from a commercial transaction and second, fear of media exposé have curbed the worst excesses. Today, however, the mechanisms for legislation to counteract global fraud and the systematic long-term damage to the interests of consumers or the environment across national boundaries are vague or non-existent. Not only redress for individual victims, but collective measures to protect consumers internationally and the future are severely hampered. The new globalized economy constrains justice for consumers to the individual level, when often what is needed is action at the collective level. The failure of the Bank of Credit and Commerce International (BCCI), a bank with heavy investments and drawings by ethnic minorities in both the USA and UK, illustrated the shortcomings of consumer protection across national boundaries (Bingham, 1992). National systems of financial scrutiny were not up to the task of monitoring complex international financial transactions. As a result, the shortcoming of regulatory controls and the inadequacies of consumer protection were exposed. Indeed, the standard consumer movement position on competition policy (see John, 1994; Locke, 1994b) which includes seeking better representation on regulatory, monitoring and advisory bodies (Whitworth, 1994) is probably inadequate for dealing with problems posed by the power and speed of global transactions in the new world order. In a global production and distribution system, the trader, rather than the consumer is sovereign. The International Organization of Consumers Unions (formerly IOCU, now known as Consumers International) for instance, having taken a favourable line towards the market-orientated General Agreement on Tariffs and Trade (GATT) (Davidson, A.,1992; IOCU, 1993; National Consumers Council, 1993), now correctly recognizes that it 'has strengthened the hand of the transnational corporation' in competition policy (Evans, 1994: 96).

Dissatisfaction, victimization and consumer protection

In marketing terms, the notion of being a victim does not exist. When things go wrong, there is the language of consumer irrationality. Business is rational, its customers unpredictable. The marketing task, therefore, is to plot the predictability of the unpredictable, and to lay down the rules of how to handle what might seem random (O'Shaughnessy, 1987: 83 ff.). Shopping is an irrational pursuit which the business framework or home economist or consumer activist has to rationalize. To the marketer, there are just pre- and post-purchase satisfaction and dissatisfaction ratings. The entire model can be seen as elitist (Andreasen, 1982), but there is nothing callous about this categorization; far from it. The good firm knows that if it can get its dissatisfaction rating down, a repeat purchase is on the cards. Retaining the customer generally is a cheap, but none-too-easy form of marketing, which is why in the USA car manufacturers await the Power Report, a regularly updated ranking of makes and models by users, with some trepidation. Power polls 30,000 consumers to compile a Consumer Satisfaction Index (Loudon and Della Bitta, 1993).

Those marketing texts which review 'postdecision regret' (Engel et al., 1990: 544) tend to rely upon a psychological model of the consumer as suffering from cognitive dissonance, a disequilibrium of attitude. More recently, marketing textbooks have adopted the language of risk-assessment, whereby every purchase can be assessed for the risk it carries. Risk assessment is being used by today's corporations, particularly in high profile areas such as agrochemicals and nuclear industries, to counter consumer claims that they have been turned into unwitting victims. They claim that every form of consumption carries a risk. It quickly follows that consumers ought to be prepared to carry some risk. Risk assessment to today's management serves the same function that many psychological models from the 1950s did; it allows the enterprise to decide what is good (or bad) for the consumer while at the same time blaming the victim whenever things go wrong. It thus become easy to scorn the consumer who rejects an infinitesimal risk. Writing in the business magazine *Fortune*, Guzzardi scoffed at the 'mindless pursuit of safety':

> Now ascending among the many blessings that the citizenry expects of government in our society is that flower, safety. Popular demand for this latest entitlement has become practically a national frenzy, and the rush is on to give us full protection from those former-friends-turned-enemies, the myriad products and conveniences and adornments of the industrial age. (Guzzardi, 1982: 365)

Guzzardi argued that the pursuit of safety is itself dangerous and launched an attack on the US Food and Drug Administration and the Federal Trade Commission. Rigid standards can be bad for business, if imposed from outside and to unrealizable degrees, he argued, an appeal reiterated in defence of market power over the decades.

To the consumer, satisfaction and dissatisfaction are at two ends of a continuum measuring outcome compared with expectation. Yet whether people complain, and how they complain is not easily predicted from psychological models. They may be more or less passive, more or less direct to the maker and seller. Singh (1990) produced a typology of dissatisfaction response: passives, irates, voicers and activists. Complainers in the USA, as everywhere, tend to be people from higher socioeconomic classes.

From the marketing perspective, publicized complaints are bad for brand image, but equally, retailers may use 'money back if dissatisfied' promises as an active part of their marketing strategy. Since brands add extra value to a product, complaints are tarnish, so the seller or maker is generally encouraged to clarify and tighten up procedures on the following: information to customers, guarantees, after-sales service and assistance, speed of response to complaints, and so on (Loudon and Della Bitta, 1993: 575–82). But for the consumer, the welter of warranties can itself become an additional burden. In the UK, for instance, 200,000 home-owners annually are the victims of unscrupulous installation and repair tradesmen, according to one survey by a trade guarantee firm (Cole, 1994). Another survey found that only one in five house repair guarantees are actually backed by insurance. So is the solution to take a warranty for house repair work only if it is backed by an insured scheme? One might think so, but both the Consumers Association (CA) and the Office of Fair Trading (OFT) think otherwise, arguing that guarantee companies themselves do not have to register as insurance companies. The consumer, in short, might even be duped when thinking she or he is doing the sensible thing. Both the CA and OFT argued that the law gave the consumer stronger rights than such guarantees anyway. Such mazes add the risks and traps in the path of every consumer, making it hard for the individualized consumer to know what the best course of action is.

In UK law, consumers are protected when buying goods by the Sale of Goods Act 1979, which is elegant and simple. It says that goods must be 'of satisfactory quality', that is, free from defects unless the purchasers have been informed about them (e.g. the good is shop-soiled); be 'fit for the purpose', that is, the computer purchased was actually a computer not a toy; and 'as described', for example, if the shirt was advertised or labelled as cotton, it should be just that. The law requires goods to be free from even minor defects and of an appearance and finish reasonably to be expected. For services, the law states that they should be done with reasonable care and skill, within a reasonable time and at a reasonable charge, if no price was fixed in advance (Office of Fair Trading, 1994: 4–10). Other laws add to and strengthen this basic provision. The Supply of Goods and Services Act 1982, for instance, would give a consumer who had poor building repairs done more rights than a guarantee backed by insurance. For the complainant, however, to have to take recourse to law is an additional burden, and as was evidenced by the reviews of the Consumer Advice Centres operating in the 1970s, consumer grievance action was and is an overwhelmingly middle-class pursuit. The key issue here, note, is the difficulty any consumer would have to define what is or is not reasonable. No wonder many consumers feel that choosing a builder to repair their roof or a garage to fix their car or a plumber to unblock their drains is akin to entering a minefield.

US protection

One of the paradoxes of contemporary consumer activism is that it appeals to the middle-classes individually, but can only be effective if practised collectively by a broad alliance of forces. As Nadel, the author of an important study of US consumer protection, has argued, the success of legislative pressure has depended on how well organized the forces are across public interest groups, the Executive and Congress. US consumer protection has its roots in social processes which began after the Civil War, and patterns were set then that persist to this day (Nadel, 1971: 5–6). Farmers and railroad companies had united to promote 150 laws to facilitate railways between 1868 and 1887, but abuses such as discriminatory pricing and excessive rates led to a backlash and an Interstate Commerce Act of 1887 was enacted to ban such practices, becoming a landmark bill in 'the development of [US] consumer protection'. The passage of the Pure Food and Drug Act of 1906, following the publication of Sinclair's book *The Jungle*, symbolizes the beginnings of the emergence of consumers as a political force in the USA. This legislative advance came after years of campaigning for firmer consumer protection, as Nadel shows, from inside the state machinery by people like Dr Harvey Wiley, chief chemist for the US Department of Agriculture (a role later filled by Rexford Tugwell, Assistant Secretary at the USDA).

Sinclair's book, often and justly cited, in fact brought to a head years of bubbling and poorly articulated discontent (Tiemstra, 1992). Herrmann shows that the 1906 Pure Food and Drug Act was enacted only after years of effort before it and strong pressure from a powerful President Theodore Roosevelt. Sinclair's book was the final catalyst (Herrmann, 1982). The new law enshrined the case for inspectors to act in the interests of consumers, implicitly acknowledging the principle that individual consumers need protecting and that the market alone did not offer adequate safeguards. This principle has been severely undermined at the end of the twentieth century under the onslaught of the New Right which successfully promoted the argument that self-regulation and the market mechanism effectively ruled out the need for state intervention to protect the consumer, although still recognizing the case for anti-fraud laws. In general, the Right has argued, consumers can protect themselves through the market (Nadel, 1971: 6–13). The culture to come was flagged by the then Governor Reagan of California in the late 1960s when he advised consumers to rely on manufacturers' handbooks rather than the report of consumer organizations to guide their purchasing (Nadel, 1971: 238).

Consumer protection in the USA was thus a meeting point – Nadel calls it 'the lowest common denominator' – between different classes of people (Nadel, 1971: 15). As Reich argued, it came in three waves: 1887–1914, 1927–39 and 1962–1978 (Reich, 1981). Tiemstra argues that in every instance, these waves of regulation were driven by a 'long-standing and uniquely American suspicion of large, powerful institutions, whether economic or political', the belief that the little guy can be crushed (1992: 3). If the first regulation was promoted at the turn of the century by the Progressives, the middle phase was identified with Roosevelt's New Deal. This period instituted not inspectors but Boards and Councils. Roosevelt created the Consumers' Advisory Board in the 1930s with the best intentions of protecting the consumer, but its purpose was undermined by the lack of any significant organized consumer movement to give it bite. The state processes and structures were well in advance of an effective, organized, articulate movement's capacity to use them, just as in the area of labour legislation, Roosevelt's Wagner Act was ahead of the labour movement's ability to take full advantage of its provisions (Gabriel, 1984a; Millis and Brown, 1950).

By the 1960s, Nader and his Raiders argued that these state provisions had atrophied to such an extent that they criticized them as morally corrupt and against the citizen's interest (Gorey, 1975). The third new regulatory phase

> grew from a view that there was a need to redress the imbalance in the marketplace between buyer and seller. It was manifested in John Kennedy's 1962 statement of consumer rights . . .; it was symbolized by the behavior of the nation's largest corporation (General Motors) toward an individual (Ralph Nader) sharply critical of that firm.
>
> Conditions were right for the [consumer] movement. The increased complexity of products, the broadening of service channels and depersonalization of shopping, the growth of consumer services (of which consumers have more difficulty in judging quality), the broader availability of the 'material things of life' to those with newly expanded discretionary buying power; and other factors – all combined to create strong 'consumer demand' for ideas and action that would help the public obtain a better deal in the marketplace. (Bloom and Greyser, 1981: 4)

Business, however, took a very different view of state provisions, especially of the most recent regulatory wave initiated in response to pressure from Nader and other consumer organizations. It argued that these provisions amounted to an infringement of its liberty to make and sell as it wanted. Fernstrom called this transition of US regulatory policy an evolution from *caveat emptor* (buyer beware) to *caveat vendor* (seller beware), and suggested that the evolution went to a point where business leaders felt 'government had totally usurped the consumer's responsibility to think for or protect himself' (Fernstrom, 1984: 1–3)

What, then, has been the effect of these phases of regulation designed to protect the consumer from falling into victimhood? Nadel's assessment is clear. In general, to be effective in preventing consumers becoming victims, there needs to be a combination of forces, inside and outside the legislature: well-briefed, 'on-side' journalists, individualists in Congress, public good-will and well-researched activists (see Chapter 9: The Consumer as Activist). Nadel found occasions when such combinations occurred, but often pioneering work was done despite the absence of this combination. The picture he paints for the USA is of consumers en masse as too disparate, too individualized; consumer professionals too small in number; and Congress more of a follower than an initiator. While 17 Acts were initiated in the period 1962–8 which he studied, most were the fruits of determined individuals in and out of Congress. Nadel's analysis is sobering. Consumer protection is not so much a forward march halted, as a halting march forward.

Can the law prevent victims or is the market enough?

Experience suggests that in complex markets consumers find themselves in constant danger of becoming victims to unscrupulous traders. Two questions follow. First, is it possible for the consumers to be victims even if the traders stay within the limits of the law? Second, can any law by itself offer adequate protection to consumers? In developed countries, protection relies upon a combination of statutes and competition in the market. The crucial issue, as we have suggested throughout this book, is the balance of forces between consumer, state and companies. Reviews of the value of the law seem agreed that the law, however strong or weak in relation to consumers, cannot cover the infinite diversity of eventualities facing consumers in the marketplace (Best, 1981; Cranston, 1984: 399–407).

Legislative bodies have always been ambivalent on whether to offer protection to consumers or whether to allow the market mechanism itself to obviate all but the worst excesses. According to the latter view, the markets sooner or later will eliminate inferior, uncompetitive or inefficient traders who offer less good value for money to consumers. The European Union, for instance, did not take a stance on consumer protection until the Paris summit of 1972, when it set up the first consumer protection services, housed with both nuclear and environmental protection services. For a decade or so, these services attempted to institute common rules and standards to little effect, for instance spending years trying to determine a common position on food additives and the composition of jam. With the Single European Act 1986 which ushered in the end of barriers to trade between the then 12 member states, the European Commission took an entirely different tack, which combined a permissive approach to business with a minimalist aim of 'the removal of fear' for consumers, designed to remove unnecessary risks (Lawlor, 1988). By this time, Europe was placing its faith increasingly on the market mechanism.

Ross Cranston, author of the classic treatise on UK consumer law, is scathing about this kind of approach. 'It is difficult to take seriously the argument that the market will further consumer protection', he concluded (Cranston, 1984: 399). He argued that consumer protection is too easily a rhetorical afterthought, and that consumers' interests need to be built into the regulatory framework from the start. Echoing Nadel's findings about the US, we could note that no law on its own can fully protect consumers; it takes a culture. For Cranston, what was needed is a half-way house between total market laissez-faire, with its deregulation and lack of consumer protection, and total state *dirigisme*, with its heavy hand and inflexibility. While expressing opposition to deregulation at the hands of free traders, Cranston felt that some self-regulation in the form of codes of conduct can be useful, and to include these in law in every case would be cumbersome (1984: 40–1). The problems stem from those codes which patently do not work or which are highly contentious, such as the codes on advertising practice. Emotions run high when children are concerned, almost always. In these cases, Cranston argued, legal statute is a better alternative: clearer, enforceable and transparent (1984: 55–9).

Not all commentators agree with Cranston. Penz, for example, while recognizing that consumers are vulnerable in the marketplace, seeks to attribute this vulnerability to their own needs, wants and inadequate self-knowledge. Protection is therefore limited from the start, though consumer grievances may be exacerbated by factors like market inefficiencies, the power of the corporations and techniques of mass manipulation such as advertising (Penz, 1986: 79). Margolius (1982) has highlighted another factor which adds to consumer grievances in complex markets. Consumers are burdened by both not having enough information and having information over-load. Echoing Baudrillard, he argues that they are bombarded with information from morning to night and face considerable difficulty in discriminating between stimuli, between fact and fiction. A good illustration of the confusion caused by the modern media is the current use of so-called advertorials and infomercials, where the boundary between news and advertising or commercial propaganda is dissolved; sometimes this is made clear to the reader, for instance by the magazine writing 'Promotion' at the top of the page; sometimes not. The editorial process thereby becomes less an expression of the journalists' views or an account of facts than the painting of a company or a product in favourable light. This is now beginning to cause some concern, even among media enthusiasts (Parsons and Rotfeld, 1990).

Best conducted a review of 2,419 unsatisfactory consumer purchases, 132 of those studied in detail, for Nader's Center for Study of Responsive Law in the USA. His assessment started cryptically: 'Do Americans get value in the marketplace? Sometimes' (Best, 1981: 3). In extreme cases, consumers were indeed victims, having been blatantly swindled, but even then Best had difficulty in ascertaining the facts. This was more pronounced when the problem was poor goods or services. He found that many consumers were very reluctant to report instances of victimization (1981: 31). This suggests that many consumers do not want to appear unstreet-wise or foolish and therefore take the blame for bad service or goods on themselves; victimization is thus internalized. Ironically, while British commentators like Pirie, head of the Adam Smith Institute, see American consumers as highly vociferous in defence of their rights (Pirie, 1991), Americans too have been criticized for 'accepting low quality and unfair prices' and one commentator quoted by Best looked fondly towards Europe, arguing that it harboured a healthier culture of bargaining, comparing and seeking the best brand (Best, 1981: 32)!

Best's research, however, goes well beyond the consumers' blaming themselves. He found cases of intimidation, retaliation by sellers, poor access to the law, and a lack of support for consumer victims for which he put the responsibility firmly at business, at a legal system more interested in its own strictures than justice, and at a culture of victim blaming. This latter feature is a 'common business technique for rejecting consumer complaints' (1981: 74) and is commonly employed from humble transactions to serious matters of life and death. Best cites a man whose expensive shirts were lost by a laundry being told that he should not have sent such good ones to it, and this classic: 'They cut the legs off my new sofa when they came to deliver it. They should have measured the front door better' (Best, 1981: 5).

Blaming the victim is a convenient smoke-screen for industry to distract attention from responsibility for its own actions and occurs overtly and covertly (Crawford, 1977). The former occurs, for example, when food poisoning or a national epidemic is blamed on poor hygiene by consumers in their own homes. Covert victim blaming occurs when an explanation or even an apology offered by a company insinuates that the consumer played a part in his or her own downfall. Despite such processes of passing the buck, which inevitably leads to apprehension about the market and business, one much-quoted study found that consumers did not expect to get everything their own way, nor did they want business to be on the defensive; they wanted a balance of forces. Consumers generally operated a 'buyer beware' approach, learned from the 1960s and 1970s consumer activist campaigns, without becoming excessively paranoid (Greyser and Diamond, 1983).

All in all, therefore, most consumers are realistic that they can expect only a modest amount of protection from the law or the mechanism of the market, and that victimhood looms at every turn of consumption. This is a far cry from the position of the free marketers of the Chicago School, criticized by Cranston as failing 'to take adequate account of the severe deficiencies in the operation of the market and common law system. Based on questionable premises, the [Chicago School's] conclusions are demonstrably false' (1984: 23). He argues that the effectiveness of the law depends crucially on consumers' knowledge of it and their capacity to resort to agencies with teeth, but unfortunately, this is far from the case. Consumers are often ignorant of their rights, enduring their victimhood and writing off their losses. Often they do not even know that they are subsidizing business by accepting substandard goods, or by making early payments, or accepting allowances which round off figures to the seller's advantage. Overcharging a small amount on a systematic basis can amount to significant extra profit. In spite of all these reservations, Cranston still proposes that 'social engineering within the system is worthwhile and can be achieved' (1984: 8). The function of the law is to lay out the framework of rules and obligations, sanctions and rights. This it may do admirably, but unless consumers know their rights, are prepared to fight for them, and have suitable institutional backing, the law by itself can achieve little.

Consumers across national boundaries

Cranston argues that there are two clusters of factors affecting consumer protection: structural ones such as the law or government policy and individual factors such as information, income and position in the world. Third World consumers are particularly at risk from structural forces. To them, the market mechanism offers virtually no protection and their own governments almost as little. He cites the massive international campaign to restrict the sale of powdered milk for babies in developing countries and points out that Papua New Guinea was a rare instance where legislative action was taken prohibiting advertisements which encouraged bottle feeding in 1977. The moral of the tale was that only national governments can control the actions of transnational corporations, yet they rarely do (Cranston, 1984: 9–10). Another study examining the position of consumers in the Third World reinforces this assessment, arguing that those consumers are especially at risk from pressures to consume such as advertising associated with the life-style of developed countries (James, 1983: 159 ff.). They also suffer additional victimization when companies and states in developed countries act with double standards, setting tough rules for the home market but not for export. In this way produce of uncertain standard is kept out, while hazardous products, such as pesticides, banned at home continue to be exported abroad (Bull, 1982; Dinham, 1993: 11–37). Ironically, consumers in the developed countries may then get back residues of the pesticides when eating imported food (Weir and Schapiro, 1981).

The case of pesticides underlines how the protection of the individual as a consumer (and therefore eater of hazardous products), as a producer (and therefore a worker with hazardous products) and as an inhabitant of an environment (where hazardous products are dumped) are overlapping issues (Lang and Clutterbuck, 1991). The ill-effects of pesticide application are disproportionately suffered by rural inhabitants of the South. In 1990, the World Health Organization estimated that there are a minimum of 3 million acute cases of pesticide poisoning and 20,000 unintentional deaths a year, mostly in Third World countries (United Nations and UNEP, 1990). Many more millions suffer as a result of pesticide use each year (Jeyararat-nam, 1990).

Consumer protection measures vary from country to country, as does the overall culture regarding consumer rights. In Sweden, there has been a long tradition of the state siding with the consumers, on the basis that producers were strong enough to look after their own interests (Johansson, 1982). Sweden developed one of the most sophisticated systems of consumer protection laws and agencies, ranging from a Public Complaints Office to a National Price and Cartel Office, as well as the celebrated Scandinavian phenomenon of the Ombudsman. The role of these officials, initially meant to investigate citizen's complaints against the government, has now been expanded to investigating consumer grievances and to assisting in achievement of fair settlements. The Scandinavian model of consumer protection is probably the most divergent from the laissez-faire model which has prevailed in the USA and UK in the 1980s and 1990s. A statement such as the following is inconceivable within a culture of consumer choice:

> If a particular brand of product X is judged as the one which best meets the real needs of the consumer it is unnecessary to have alternative brands on the market, particularly since they must be inferior. To paraphrase, if Volvos are best everyone who wants a car should drive a Volvo. (Johansson, 1982)

Strange as this Swedish quote may seem to contemporary Anglo-Saxon eyes, the notion of restricting choice as a measure for protecting the consumer is not far-fetched. The Seikatsu Clubs, a highly successful system of consumer co-operatives in Japan, offer their members a product range of around 600 goods, on the argument that if they are the best products and meet consumers' needs, why offer a range of 15,000 as do supermarket chains?

Self help?

Both of the above examples seek to undo the effects of individualization by restoring the principle of co-operation among consumers. The sacrifice of personal choice is aimed at increasing trust as well as economic muscle. Instead of every consumer setting out to beat a path through the marketplace jungle by themselves, they draw on the judgement of a trusted representative who can advise them reliably and point out obvious dangers. As soon as consumers act collectively, it is no longer necessary for each and every one of them to duplicate the Herculean task of acquiring knowledge on all market options. In this way, contemporary consumers are rediscovering the principle of co-operation developed in the nineteenth century (see Chapter 9: The Consumer as Activist). The Mountain Equipment Co-op in Canada is an interesting half-way house between the conventional firm and a fully-fledged worker co-operative. It is a retail consumer co-operative, member owned and directed, has half a million members and a (Canadian) $64 million annual turnover. To purchase from its good range of products – in the outdoor clothes and pursuits market – the buyer has to sign up to become, in effect, a co-op owner by paying $5 for life-time membership. You have to be a member to buy the company's products and this entitles the consumer to vote for the Board (MEC, 1994).

However, acting co-operatively appears to run contrary to the entire ethos of contemporary Western consumption. As every previous chapter of this book has shown, whether as chooser or as identity-seeker, whether as communicator or as aesthete, today's consumer accords the highest value to the right to be individual. So long as this ethic persists, consumers will continue to be vulnerable and the muscle that they can exercise in the marketplace will be limited.

What practical measures can consumers resort to when things go wrong? A system of small claims courts, first advocated in the USA in 1913 by Roscoe Pound, were in place in 8 states and 12 cities by the 1930s (Best, 1981: 167). Their purpose was to simplify and reduce the cost of consumer complaints, yet their effectiveness was limited. Despite this, similar courts were introduced in the UK in 1970 after a government report *Justice Out of Reach* (Cranston, 1984: 88–9). After decades of experience the consumer potential to benefit from small claims courts has been tempered by experience. It can be argued that they have been usefully colonized by business as a cheap way of collecting business debts; and they are not particularly consumer-friendly, a problem exacerbated in England by their being 'bolted on' to the County Court, with no separate rules. Small claims may often still not be worth pursuing because the cost and inconvenience of getting the award can outweigh the sum at stake; in these cases, there is often no effective sanction against malpractice. A 1980 study of 2,000 complaints found that none had used the small claims procedures against a shop or supplier (National Consumer Council, 1981) By contrast, in Denmark and Norway, for many years, there have been consumer arbitration and conciliation tribunals which are relatively simple and informal and do not require expensive lawyers.

Another measure to support the wronged consumer is a system of advice, like the Consumer Advice Centres, described earlier in this chapter. Not surprisingly, their effectiveness was found to vary enormously across socio-economic classes, the heaviest use being by middle-class consumers, pursuing complaints; there was little use by lower socioeconomic classes, and 'at-risk groups such as the elderly, divorced, widowed and separated' (National Consumer Council, 1977: 26). Yet the study found that the average cost of handling was a very modest £3 (1977: 21).

In contrast to both the British and Scandinavian approaches which have sought pragmatic, reasonable, conciliatory measures to resolve the conflict between consumer and producer, a popular US handbook in the early 1970s with the memorable title *Sue the Bastards* advocated a high conflict approach (Matthews, 1973). Through the demand for punitive compensation from recalcitrant firms, the object is to deter bad practice and to keep firms on their toes, redressing the inequality of power in favour of consumers. Echoing Voltaire, in *Candide*, it punishes one to 'encourage the others'. In spite of some spectacular awards, consumer supporters on both sides of the Atlantic have expressed deep reservations about the effectiveness of this approach on the mass of the consumers (Best, 1981: 182–193; Cranston, 1984: 402).

Generalized hypochondria?

But do consumers need supporters at all? Is it not the case that billions of consumers go out into marketplaces daily and enjoy the fruits of consumerism, hardly ever coming to grief? A few instances of victimization in consumption are surely inevitable, as they are in every walk of life. There is no need to blow them out of all proportion. It makes gripping television, just like crime, and like crime it creates unnecessary fear in the minds of the populace. Such criticisms are the hallmark of the free market ideologues and fly in the face of evidence of the courts and of law enforcement agencies. Moreover, these criticisms disregard the fact that if the market is to function as a chastising mechanism, disadvantaging unprincipled or inefficient suppliers, it requires the activities of consumer activists, testing organizations and other bodies which disseminate information and ensure that the worst excesses will be brought to light. If these checks did not exist, the market mechanism would lose its effectiveness.

Furthermore, it is thanks to the tireless activity of campaigning consumer organizations, that firms have had to accept minimum standards of service, information and quality which they would not have had to concede otherwise. Many companies themselves now welcome regulation on both environmental and consumer protection grounds, if only as safeguards of their own reputation. So long as they can appear to abide by these independent standards and as long as they are independently monitored, they can counter criticisms levelled at them. If it were not for the existence of consumer supporters inside and outside the state machinery, the market mechanism would be no more effective as a protective mechanism than the jungle in protecting the interests of the turkeys who wandered into it.

The view that consumers suffer from a kind of generalized hypochondria, where the slightest threat to their health or well-being is magnified out of all proportion, is, if anything, evidence of the overwhelming powerlessness that consumers can feel when confronted by the might and sophistication of vast organizations whose resources and techniques they cannot match. Complaints registered by the UK's Office of Fair Trading have not abated significantly in recent decades, yet as we saw earlier, consumers in advanced capitalist societies tend to give corporations the benefit of the doubt, unless major infringements are exposed (Greyser and Diamond, 1983). If anything, as consumer advocates the world over lament, consumers tend to be too pliant and can too easily be fobbed off by excuses and rationalizations offered by the Public Relations and the image-making machinery of corporations (Barnet and Cavanagh, 1994).

A more serious limitation of the image of the consumer as victim could be raised on the basis of the current fashion for 'quality' and 'service' as core business values. At least since the publication of Peters and Waterman's *In Search of Excellence* (1982), few ideas have held as powerful a grip in management thinking. Businesses devote huge sums of money each year to train their staff and to raise product safety and to improve their environmental records, in order to keep the loyalty of their customers and to outperform their competitors. A single, well-publicized case of a dissatisfied customer, a dangerous or substandard product or one environmental disaster can be enough to undo the hard work of years of product development and image-making. From this perspective, what more protection can consumers require than the one that companies themselves so assiduously offer them? The company's self-interest, rather than any guarantee from a nanny state or a self-appointed consumer busybody, is the safest base for consumer protection.

These arguments which carry resonances of Adam Smith's butcher, brewer and baker (see Introduction: The Faces of the Consumer), ignore the difference between a company's image and the reality of its products, service and methods. Of course, companies are concerned to present a smiling face to their customer. Of course, they train their staff to give the impression that the customer is sovereign. But for all the outpourings on quality and corporate culture, profit remains the overpowering objective of most companies. Why else are they in business? Necessary as customers are to ensure profits, the need to cut costs and corners, increase prices and reduce service poses a constant threat to consumers. Besides, the entire rhetoric of corporate culture and values was terminally tarnished by the early 1990s recession (Gabriel, 1991, 1995) which established that when it was a question of staying afloat, neither the employees' jobs nor the overall product quality mattered as much as the maintenance of an effective image and an intensified public relations exercise to keep the confidence of shareholders and fund managers.

Systematic victimhood?

A criticism from a different political quarter would argue that consumer activists have been incorporated into consumer capitalism; they merely oil its wheels. They have become agents of a system, reformists, concentrating their fire on extreme and untypical cases of victimhood and disregard the massive and systematic alienation of modern consumerism. They have allowed themselves to be sucked into the relative triviality of product quality and environmental hazards, when the key issue is the inequalities of power and the endless dissatisfaction that Western consumerism fosters. Western consumers, according to this charge, are victims not only when they get a dud deal from a corporation or inadequate information from a government body, but also every time that they place their hopes for a better future in this commodity or that. Here, we rejoin the Marcusean critique of consumer capitalism where the consumer as victim actively colludes in his or her own oppression. By wanting goods and by having such high expectations of them, life is impoverished. People become slaves to the goods, still more to ensuring that they get the best deal (Winward, 1993). In the very act of trying to improve our lives by consuming, we submit ourselves to the forces which exacerbate our alienation.

The above bleak and uncompromising view can lead to patronizing and arrogant attitudes where intellectuals or organizations pontificate to the public about what is good for them. It also may play into the hands of the New Right which seeks to flatter consumers rather than paralyse them with tales of woe. Finally, this view may underestimate the extent to which consumers can turn the tables on victimhood by becoming rebels. This is the focus of the next chapter.

8

The Consumer as Rebel

People never rebel just because they have to carry a heavy load or because of exploitation. They don't know life without exploitation, they don't even know that such a life exists. How can they desire what they cannot imagine? The people will rebel only when, in a single movement, someone tries to throw a second burden, a second heavy bag onto their backs. The peasant will fall face down in the mud – and then spring up and grab an ax. He'll grab an ax, my gracious sir, not simply because he can't sustain this new burden – he could carry it – he will rise because he feels that, in throwing the second burden onto his back suddenly and stealthily, you have tried to cheat him, you have treated him like an unthinking animal, you have trampled what remains of his already strangled dignity, taken him for an idiot who doesn't see, feel, or understand. A man doesn't seize an ax in defence of his wallet, but in defence of his dignity.

Kapuscinski (1983: 97)

The image of the consumer as rebel flies in the face of the age-old wisdom, summed up in Juvenal's dismissive view of the populace:

They are only seriously bothered about two things – bread and circuses. (*Satires* x, i, 80)

It is commonplace to regard food, drink and spectacle as the true opiates of the people, perpetuating their quietude and dependence, undermining the desire and the will to challenge an existing order. Before the arrival of postmodernism, a whole generation of social critics in the 1960s and 1970s battled against consumerism, which they blamed for the disappearance of revolutionary ardour among the working classes of Western societies. Consumerism, as the bourgeois ideology of material possessions, was readily absorbed within the Marxist view of alienated consciousness, a consciousness alienated not only in the course of commodity production but equally by the state, the machinery of mass media and other ideological apparatuses. For Marcuse consumerism penetrates into the unconscious mental structures, becoming the basis for a 'biological' second nature

The so-called consumer society and the politics of corporate capitalism have created a second nature of man which ties him libidinally and aggressively to the commodity form. The need for possessing, consuming, handling, and constantly renewing the gadgets, devices, instruments, engines, offered to and imposed upon the people, for using these wares even at the danger of one's own destruction, has become a 'biological' need . . . The second nature of man thus militates against any change that would disrupt and perhaps even abolish this dependence of man on a market ever more densely filled with merchandise – abolish his existence as a consumer consuming himself in buying and selling. The needs generated by this system are thus eminently stabilizing, conservative needs: the counter-revolution anchored in the instinctual structure. (1969: 11)

That generation of social critics would have found images of the consumer prevalent in the 1980s highly problematic. For them consumers were massively manipulated, passive hostages to the capitalist logic of production; mass consumption was frequently seen (as in the quote above) as a smoke-screen, a euphemism for mass production and mass alienation (see also Williams, 1976: 68–70).

Throughout the 1980s, an entirely new set of images of the consumer started to appear; these images grew out of a rejection of earlier critiques of modern consumption and all its paraphernalia, its luxuries and absurdities, its emphasis on style, its seeming unconcern with the origins of the commodities on offer, its obsession with difference and its domination by mass advertising and marketing. In place of the managed, manipulated and duped images of consumers of old, the new images became brighter, more active, more creative. Heroic qualities started to creep into images of consumers as explorers of new worlds or as artists. No image, however, captures these heroic qualities as vividly as that of the consumer-rebel.

Symbols of rebellion

The view that social groups can find and express oppositional meanings in particular activities or objects is hardly new or original. Smoking, for example, can be a gesture of defiance:

> Smoking is not an addiction, but a form of rebellion – and much preferable to lobbing missiles at Heathrow. This has always been clearest in the case of women. From the beginning, smoke issuing from a lipstick-painted mouth was taken as a sign of sluthood. Thus millions of women took up the habit in solidarity with sluts and in hopes of being mistaken for one. . . . The other great smoking rebels are, of course, blue-collar males. Once smoking was a bonding ritual performed by men of all classes, but when the suits turned to Perrier and jogging, it became a mark of proletarian pride . . . [and] defiance. Confronted with the capitalists' homicidal abuses of the indoor and outdoor environment, who would not prefer to die gallantly by one's own hand? (Ehrenreich, 1994)

Particular ways of looking, talking or walking, hair-styles, Camel cigarettes, Harley Davidson motorbikes, bleached jeans, Doc Martens shoes, can all function as icons of disaffection and defiance. It may be argued that the adoption of branded commodities by the alienated or the rebellious to convey rejection of the system has little to do with the consumer-as-rebel. Such groups do not rebel *against* commodities, but use commodities to express protest. According to this view, Doc Martens, tough looks apart, are not even an instrument of rebellion (like the axe in the hands of Kapuscinski's rebel) but a symbol, which incidentally happens to be a branded commodity. In similar ways, punks, used safety pins and razor blades as jewellery, signalling their protest through the use of cheap and unbranded items of everyday life.

Symbols of disaffection, whether expensive branded items or cheap everyday ones, may be dismissed as tokens of youthful rebelliousness accompanied by submission to the rule of commodities. This view has been challenged lately, in a series of arguments which suggest that not only disaffected young people but many if not all consumers in industrialized societies of the North use commodities to rebel against the commoditization of everyday life. What unites safety pins as ear-rings with Camels as symbols of defiance is the discovery of *uses* for objects distinctly different from those assigned to them by manufacturers and merchandisers. This constitutes a rebellion against

> the authority of the producer [which] lies in the capacity to define the meaning of that which is consumed. Producers have more authority to the extent that the meaning or value of an object or service is defined by how the producer understands, interprets, [and] judges it. (Abercrombie, 1994: 51)

According to this view, unorthodox uses of standardized objects are not seen merely as semiotic games (see Chapter 4: The Consumer as Explorer), but genuine acts of rebellion against the authority of the producer.

This is the starting point in Michel de Certeau's *The Practice of Everyday Life* (1984), which seeks to loosen the connection between a commodity and its sign-value, defined by some omnipotent Baudrillardian code. It is wrong, argues de Certeau, to equate consumption with the purchase of a particular item, its physical expenditure or the appropriation of its (given) sign-value. Instead he argues that consumers can resist the dominant economic order even as they consume its outputs, its commodities and its images. This is done not by active resistance (such as consumer boycotts, discussed later) or by passively refusing to buy its products and images, but by using them in ways which are foreign or antagonistic to those intended by manufacturers, advertisers and so on. In this way, consumers may challenge the hegemonic order by rejecting the legitimacy of its claims, even if they do not reject its products.

Two inter-related metaphors are central to de Certeau's thinking-anti-colonization and guerrilla warfare. Native Americans resisted the religious, political and legal practices and representations imposed on them by Spanish colonialism, 'not by rejecting them or transforming them (though that occurred as well), but by many different ways of using them in the service of rules, customs or convictions foreign to the colonization which they could not escape' (1984: 32). Like those native Americans, consumers operate in an occupied territory; like the native Americans, they appear to accept passively what they receive. Yet in practice, they transform it, distort it, undermine it, twist it, and laugh at it. De Certeau uses the Lévi-Straussian idea of 'bricolage', a mixture of creative makeshift, improvisation, cunning and guileful ruses, to describe how consumers experiment with latent symbolic properties of commodities and images, fashioning new and unexpected entities out of mass marketed components.

De Certeau criticizes those radical and conservative critics of consumption who regard the consumer as victim or at least passive recipient of standardized, glamorized products:

> In reality, a rationalized, expansionist, centralist, spectacular and clamorous production is confronted by an entirely different kind of production, called 'consumption' and characterized by its ruses, its fragmentation (the result of the circumstances), its poaching, its clandestine nature, its tireless but quiet activity, in short its quasi-invisibility, since it shows itself not in its own products (where would it place them?) but in an art of using products imposed on it. (1984: 31)

In this conception, consumption emerges as guerrilla fighting in an occupied territory. The powerful define and construct 'places' like shopping streets and malls, houses, cars, schools and factories which they seek to control and rule, using strategies and plans. The weak, for their part, are forced to operate in these places, but are constantly seeking to convert them into their own 'spaces', using ruse, guile and deception and relying on suddenness and surprise. To the strategies of the powerful, the weak proffer tactics, operating in isolated actions, for ever discovering cracks in the system and opportunities for gain. The joy of consumption, then, comes not from the temporary sating of an addiction or from the fulfilment of greed, but from outwitting a more powerful opponent who has stacked the cards:

> Innumerable ways of playing and foiling the other's game, that is, the space instituted by others, characterize the subtle, stubborn, resistant activity of groups which, since they lack their own space, have to get along in a network of already established forces and representations. People have to make do with what they have. In these combatants' stratagems, there is a certain art of placing one's blows, a pleasure in getting around the rules of a constraining space. We see tactical and joyful dexterity of the mastery of a technique. Scapin and Figaro are only literary echoes of this art. (de Certeau, 1984: 18)

Torn jeans

Fiske takes de Certeau's arguments a step further, arguing that 'consumption is a tactical raid on the system' (1989: 35). Consumption is neither passive nor purely individual, but is part of a 'popular culture [which] is made by the people, not by the culture industry. All the culture industries can do is produce a repertoire of texts or cultural resources for the various formations of the people to use or reject in the ongoing process of producing their popular culture' (1989: 24). Meanings and pleasures, argues Fiske, are not conjured up by merchandisers of culture, trend-setters and other hirelings of capital; nor do meanings and pleasures reside in the texts themselves, whether they be television programmes (Fiske, 1987), shopping malls, designer clothes or advertisements. Instead, the meaning and the pleasure emerge from consumers' active engagement with such texts and frequent attempts to undermine them and subvert them. Fiske does not deny that today's cultural commodities

> bear the forces that we can call centralizing, disciplinary, hegemonic, massifying, commodifying. Opposing these forces, however, are the cultural needs of the people, this shifting matrix of social allegiances that transgress categories of the individual, or class or gender or race or any category that is stable within the social order. These popular forces transform the cultural commodity into a cultural resource, pluralize the meanings and pleasures it offers, evade or resist its disciplinary efforts, fracture its homogeneity and coherence, raid or poach upon its terrain. All popular culture is a process of struggle, of struggle over the meanings of social experience, of one's personhood and its relations to the social order and of the texts and commodities of that order. (1989: 28)

In contrast to de Certeau's consumer-guerrillas who, judging by the examples he provides in the latter parts of his book, seem engaged in rather timid and esoteric practices, Fiske's consumer-guerrillas sneer, jeer and shout. They despoil the landscapes of capital, with graffiti, rubbish and noise; they tear, they break, they steal (or 'shop-lift'). They challenge ceaselessly capital's attempts to define the meanings of things and discover pleasure in destroying the pleasures which capital ostentatiously offers. In this argument, Fiske taps an important tradition within Anglo-American criminology, which through a series of studies of working-class youth culture generated the idea that what mainline sociology defined as deviance amounted to symbolic rebellion. (See Matza, 1964; Robins and Cohen, 1978; Taylor, et al., 1973; Willis, 1977). A dominant theme of this tradition was that what seemed like hoodlum or nihilism was in fact a statement, at times poorly and at times well articulated, against the values of respectable society, including those of respectable working class.

Fiske transposes some of these ideas from the area of crime to the area of consumption. His discussion the 'Jeaning of America', highlights the force of these arguments. Far from lamenting the hegemony of blue-jeans in American campuses as a sign of students willingly putting themselves in mass uniforms, while deluding themselves with images of youthful vigour and glamour (as Marcuse might have done), Fiske sees jeans as a cultural resource on which students set busily to work. Blue-jeans are a text on which students can write and read their own meanings. By disfiguring their jeans in particular ways, such as by bleaching them, tie-dying them or, especially, tearing them, students can express oppositional meanings to those intended by manufacturers and advertisers. Thus, wearing torn jeans is 'an example of a user not simply consuming a commodity but reworking it, treating it not as a completed object to be accepted passively, but as a cultural resource to be used (Fiske, 1989: 10). This is no idle fiddling, but 'a refusal of commodification and an assertion of one's right to generate one's own culture' (1989: 15).

Unlike de Certeau's cheerful bricoleurs, Fiske's rebels are angry, conscious and self-conscious; their tactics are not limited to semiotic games, jokes and fantasies but extend into action. In Fiske's view, shop-lifting is true guerrilla infiltration into enemy terrain. It affords the thrill and excitement of rebelling against a system in which everything has to be paid for, and, when successfully accomplished, it marks a temporary victory of cunning against the strategies of capital, its electronic eyes and surveillance apparatuses.

> Shop-lifting is not a guerrilla raid just upon the store owners themselves, but upon the power block in general. The store owners are merely metonyms for their allies in power – parents, teachers, security guards, the legal system, and all agents of social discipline or repression. (Fiske, 1989: 39)

In recent years, earthquakes, power-cuts and civil disturbances have unleashed massive property plunder leading some commentators to describe the 1992 Los Angeles riots, following the acquital of the police officers accused of the Rodney King beating, as orgies of consumerism. From this perspective, if individual shop-lifters may be seen as free-shooters or guerrilla snipers at consumer capitalism, urban rioters represent mass consumer rebellion. Television screens saturated with images of people plundering electrical stores and super-markets may be an indication that consumption is once again becoming the focal point of social struggle and rebellion, as it was at the time of the food riots of two centuries ago (Rudé, 1959; Thompson, 1993/1971).

Tactics of consumer rebellion

Perhaps the quintessence of images of consumer-as-rebels is the joy-rider, who steals a smart car, drives it at tremendous speed, performs outrageous manoeuvres, causes as much havoc along the way as possible, and outsmarts attempts by police to stop him or her. Such figures are celebrated, becoming quasi-folk heroes, in spite of the havoc they wreak and the real suffering which they cause when their escapades take them in the path of pedestrians. Joy-riders are daring as they are unpredictable. They can enjoy the ultimate offering of consumer society, the fast car, not only without paying for it, but without being restrained by the responsibilities and burdens that such cars impose on their legitimate owners; alternatively, they may choose slow, ugly and battered old cars to pit against the police, before wrecking them or torching them. In all cases they literally take over a piece of the road, rebelling against and rewriting its rules and meanings (Light et al., 1993; McCarney, 1981; Parker, 1974;). To be sure, their victories may be short-lived as are those of most rebels, but they are none the sweeter for it. They also create victims out of other consumers.

Another tactic of consumer rebellion has been given the name ram-raid. A powerful vehicle drives at speed into the window of a shop, usually late at night; the raiders empty as many of the contents of the shop into the van as they can and leave, while bystanders idly watch the spectacle or even cheer the ram-raiders. At one ram-raid in genteel Bath, the bystanders physically stopped a policeman who tried in vain to arrest a group of ram-raiders (Ryle,

1992). Since then ram-raids have generated a moral panic for some in that city (local newspaper headline: 'A City Centre Held to Ransom'), whereas for others they have become a weekly spectator sport (Pook, 1993). Ram-raiders seem to take literally the advertisers' message 'Come and get me', ignoring, as advertisers do, the other part of the bargain, the obligation to pay. Like joy-rides and shop-lifting, ram-raids feed middle-class paranoia and become demonized by respectable society, which endlessly seeks to criminalize and control them. Yet, the difficulty of controlling such guerrilla tactics reveals how well the tactics are chosen both to highlight the weakest points of the system and to take advantage of them.

A rather different type of rebellion against commodities is described by Susie Orbach. For her not only fat and over-eating but also anorexia and related eating 'disorders' are forms of protest against consumer society; both over-eating and starving are rejections of the social roles which define women in industrialized societies (Orbach, 1978, 1986). If fat is a rebellion against being an object of adornment and pleasure, anorexia is a symbolic rejection of the fruit of consumer society, a refusal of the poisoned chalice. Anorexia, like a hunger strike, is a political gesture, observes Orbach. Like shop-lifting, joy-riding and ram-raiding, eating disorders can be interpreted as rebellions against the edicts of consumerism, rebellions which do not always seek to destroy the objects of consumption but to redefine them, reclaim them and re-appropriate them.

One tactic of rebellion which deserves to be mentioned has been given the name 'subvertising'. It can take the form of adding graffiti to existing advertisements to subvert their meaning and destroy their appeal as consumerist icons (ECRA, 1994: 20–21). Occasionally it can assume organized forms as in the campaign to disfigure sexist advertisements of Panda cars in the 1980s and the Australian campaign BUGA-UP (Billboard Utilizing Graffitists Against Unhealthy Promotions) set up by a group of health professionals who systematically disfigured cigarette advertisements (Chesterfield Evans, 1987). When such tactics assume organized forms, they are referred to as demarketing, as when campaign groups sponsor advertisements calling on consumer not to consume a specific product, most notably used by anti-fur and animal welfare campaigners (Matsu, 1994).

Rebels?

It would be easy but short-sighted to dismiss such rebellions as marginal or inconsequential. This is precisely what the strategies of hegemony would dictate, just as occupying forces dismiss every act of resistance, sabotage and vandalism against their rule as the product of a few trouble-makers and agitators. In the United Kingdom, 1.2 million customers as well as 28,000 shop staff were apprehended in connection with shoplifting in 1993, for a total of 2.1 million criminal incidents. This hardly represents a small proportion of the population, given that most shoplifting incidents go unnoticed. The British Retail Consortium which represents 90 per cent of British retailers estimated that shop-lifting cost retailers a total of £2 billion annually (Buckley, 1994; Frean, 1994; Young, 1994). Enormous resources in money (£370 million per year according to one estimate (Buckley, 1994)), equipment, manpower, systems, plans and strategies are devoted to its curtailment and control (see Murphy, 1986; Walsh 1978).

Yet, in a paradoxical way the tactical raids on the system reinforce the rule of commodities and consumerism; for they are primarily rebellions against a system which denies its bounty to those who cannot afford it, but they seldom challenge the value of the bounty or the companies that produce it. On the contrary, the ram-raiders who display a preference for Benneton, just like the joy-rider who favours BMWs, reinforce the iconic allure of these products.

Similarly, the adoption of particular brands as symbols of oppositional ideologies reinforces the rule of brands. To be sure, torn jeans, unfiltered Camels and Harley Davidsons may act as potent signs of nihilistic dissaffection, but offer only a limited challenge to those in power. Rave parties, ram-raids, joy-rides and even shoplifting ultimately are tactics of symbolic protest, causing annoyance and paranoia, but are hardly likely to cause the merest tremor in the world's stock exchanges. On the contrary, many rebellious tactics merely fuel new areas of commodity production. This is not only manifested in the burgeoning growth of the security industry, but equally in the appropriation and subsequent emasculation by manufacturers of the symbols of rebellion. Do manufacturers care if youngsters bleach their jeans, if they want different brands or celebrate multicultural diversity, so long as they keep buying the products (Rieff, 1993)?

No sooner does a product become an icon of opposition than manufacturers seek to capitalize on it, by mass-producing it, raising its price or discovering a niche for it. The experience of jeans, discussed by Fiske, is instructive. As soon as manufacturers discovered that jeans were no longer a uniform icon of youth, independence and freedom, they adapted their products accordingly. Macy's, the large US department store, eagerly started selling jeans which are already shrunk, bleached or torn. In this way, the big retailing outlet affects to become an accomplice to rebel-images of disfigured jeans, thereby compromising them and neutralizing them. To be sure, as Fiske argues, new marks and new distinctions are produced by consumers, for example, between 'really rugged jeans' and 'mock rugged' jeans. Yet, one suspects that rebellions which end up consumed with such minutiae, only reinforce a system which prospers on diversity and difference. These rebels, whether joyful or angry, may divert themselves and others with their creative bricolage and occasional raids on the system. They may be celebrated as triumphant tricksters who poke fun at the system, but ultimately they lack the moral indignation, the single-mindedness and the destructive fury of true rebels.

Rebels with causes

A system which can institutionalize rebelliousness by channelling it into unorthodox uses of its staples, blue jeans, motorbikes or cigarettes, it could be argued, commodifies rebelliousness itself. As Vance Packard (1957) first noted, consumer capitalism has an extraordinary capacity to take what first directly threatens it and, after a deep intake of breath, convert it into a marketing opportunity. Instead of destruction and retribution, rebels vent their anger and frustration into commodities, buying them, stealing them, disfiguring them and investing them with meaning. In such ways, they become entrapped in the very mechanism from which they seek to escape.

Consumer boycotts

Not all forms of consumer rebellion are quite as easily accommodated. If the tearing of jeans leaves the power block largely untroubled, the mere suggestion of consumer boycotts or sabotage of its products can seriously damage company's stock and cause executives sleepless nights. The term 'vigilante consumer' has been coined to describe the activities of those organized or semi-organized consumers who take a serious interest in companies' ethical and environmental standards and lead public opinion against those companies which are found wanting (Dickenson, 1993). The *Ethical Consumer* (January 1994) listed over 50 consumer boycotts going on in Great Britain at the time. These ranged from boycotts against banks for their involvement in Third World debt to supermarkets for building on green-field sites to cosmetic manufacturers for animal testing to chemical companies for continuing production of CFC gases. Entire countries have been singled out for boycotts – Norwegian products are boycotted because of that country's commercial whaling, Barbados is boycotted as a tourist destination for the export of monkeys for animal experimentation, Taiwan for continuing to import rhino horn.

Many of these boycotts attract limited media attention, though they may be significant enough to affect corporate policies. (Garrett, 1987; Smith, 1990). The journal *Ethical Consumer* (e.g. 1994) routinely monitors consumer boycotts and reports on the company reactions. Neutrogena, manufacturers of the Norwegian Formula hand cream, moved its production to France and declared that it was 'adamantly opposed to whaling'. All major supermarket chains in Britain have either stopped buying Faroese fish or declare its origin on the label, in response to a campaign to protect the pilot whale. The cosmetics manufacturer L'Oreal succeeded in having a consumer boycott of its products lifted, by signing an agreement with PETA, a US animal rights organization, to stop animal testing on its products.

Consumer boycotts, it could be argued, are too numerous, too parochial and too restricted to the fringes of consumption to have a serious effect. The majority of consumers, overloaded by moral causes and saturated by information, signs and messages, ends up confused and impotent. The latest boycott, fuses with numerous other messages and images, and vanishes as meaningless noise rather than as a significant call to action. Yet, neither companies nor the masses of consumers can ignore the critical commentary on commodities sustained by continuing, mutating and merging consumer boycotts. Baudrillard's flying signifiers (1970/1988: 45) do not merely migrate from commodity to commodity as objects of desire but also as objects of rejection and avoidance. So it does not matter particularly what countries, companies or commodities are objects of current boycotts, as that a succession of boycotts constantly mobilize consumers to remind manufacturers, merchandisers and retailers that they have moral and environmental responsibilities. The boycott tactic invites consumers to act in their individual capacity to a broader social end. Their effectiveness depends crucially on how well organized they are and how much media coverage they generate (Friedman, 1985; Herrmann, 1993; Smith, 1990), issues which we shall pick up in the next chapter.

'Alternative' consumption – pop festivals

If consumer boycotts and vigilante consumers express a concern for the environment and ethics, they hardly undermine the deeper foundation of consumerism, that good life is synonymous to rising living standards, better and bigger consumption. Alternative forms of consumption represent a different type of rebellion, one which repudiates products and practices of big capital, not because they happen to be ethically questionable and environmentally damaging, but because they are products and practices of a system which is ethically moribund and environmentally calamitous. Such rebellions are not expressed in unorthodox uses of products (though this may be part of it) nor in the rejection of targeted products as in boycotts. These rebellions reject all Western-style consumption and seek to supplant it with a radically different type of consumption, which encompasses a number of principles:

1 Consume less.
2 Consume local products.
3 Avoid products produced and merchandised by big capital.
4 Avoid cash and use alternative modes of economic transactions.

The last two of three of these principles are graphically portrayed by Hetherington in his description of the Stonehenge pop festivals and New Age travellers, who have sought to recreate in the 1990s something of the ethos of the 1960s hippies:

> Almost anything could be bought at Stonehenge: drugs, New Age paraphernalia, health remedies, old bits of tat, scrap, vehicle parts, food, services; one person used to provide hot baths in an old tub in the middle of the field (surrounded by a screen), somebody even had the enterprising idea of selling people breakfast in

bed, strawberries and Champagne if it was your birthday, otherwise fried-egg sandwiches! . . . Consumption at Stonehenge when related to festival is highly ambivalent. It is both spontaneous and organized, monetary but with a strong emphasis on gift exchange; it is removed from all associations with rational consumption (licensed, taxed and regulated) but the sense of reciprocity is strong. (1992: 85, 86–7)

Hetherington provides vivid descriptions of consumer-rebels who take over the places of the powerful and at least temporarily make them their own. What could be more symbolic that taking over Stonehenge, the archetypical heritage site turned consumerist theme park, and reducing it to a no-go area for respectable visitors, police and big capital. In this way, it becomes a shrine of alternative consumption, waste and excess. Noisy, extravagant, unrestrained pop festivals represent one challenge to the strategies of modern consumerism. They too, however, can be compromised and hijacked by the cash nexus, as was illustrated when the recreation of Woodstock free festival in 1994, 25 years after the original, turned into an all-ticket consumerist orgy.

LETS

There are, however, more quiet, organized and down-to-earth challenges to consumer capitalism. One such challenge is the LETS or Local Exchange Trading System. This is a form of cashless local economy in which people trade with each other on a bartering basis. LETS provides a network of members, often computerized, who offer their services and goods in exchange for units of a notional currency. This notional currency is not convertible to cash, but can be used to buy goods and services from other LETS members. The services range widely from gardening and baby-sitting to legal advice and car maintenance, from music lessons to accountancy, and from leasing of equipment (computers, lawn-mowers, washing machines) to architectural design. The first LETS experiments took place in a cash-starved area of British Columbia in 1982; since then the system has spread into the USA, New Zealand, Australia and elsewhere. In Great Britain by 1994, there are over 200 local currency systems, most of which were formed since 1991, when LETSLINK, a national development agency was set up. The membership of individual LETS may vary from about 10 (the number required to set up a new system) to 500 and interest in the scheme increased rapidly as a response to structural unemployment.

LETS is not merely a trading system, at the margins of mainstream economy, devoid of ideology or a sense of mission. On the contrary, many of their members regard it as a way of strengthening community links undermined by the cash nexus, and of regenerating local economies without relying on conventional capital. LETSLINK declares:

Capital flight deprives an area of a means to trade within itself. Many low-income areas, however, still possess skills, human energy and potential, and all kinds of material resources. All the components of real wealth are there, locked away, alongside a myriad of unmet needs. All that is missing, essentially, is a medium of exchange. We simply need a communications system, linking supply and demand. (LETSLINK, 1994: 1)

LETS enables those with limited cash resources to become involved actively in their local economies and communities. Everyone, including the poorest person, has something to offer; everyone, including the richest, has a need to be met. Many of those who joined LETS report that they joined for ideological reasons, but they discover that it makes good economic sense, especially in a period of recession, when the number of transactions increases considerably if payment is accepted in the local LETS currency. Some local traders, like grocers, opticians or clothing stores, have opted to accept part of the payment in cash and part in local currency and have reported much increased trade (Kellaway, 1993).

One issue which divides LETS schemes is whether their members should all charge the same basic unit for their time or whether they should be allowed to charge depending on the demand for their products and services. Some local economies uphold two LETS schemes, one in each category. Predictably, this has a divisive effect, since higher-status occupations tend to favour the differential system, while lower-status occupations favour the uniform rate. At the moment, it is not clear which system will predominate or whether the two can co-exist side by side. In any case, LETS systems have provided a radical alternative to conventional consumption, in several different ways. First, they focus on unbranded, unadvertised and un-mediated goods and services. (Advertising is limited to internal bulletins.) They reaffirm the value of hand-made, home-made products and regenerate arts and crafts, ranging from organic farming to woodland management, cheese-making, spinning and weaving, which are swept aside by big capital. Second, they bring together the person as a producer and seller of goods and services with the person as buyer and consumer. In this way they replace an impersonal cash nexus with a visible, personal relationship between consumer and producer. Third, they enable individuals and groups whose lack of cash would exclude them both from the local economy and from involvement in the community. Fourth, they bring together people of different social classes in relations of mutuality, which cross social bound-aries and encourage accountability and responsibility. Fifth, they keep capital local. Finally, they find a legitimate way of generating economic activity which avoids taxation and by-passes the legislative and other apparatuses of the state.

The ultimate consumer-rebel: 'Consume less'

In all these ways, LETS represent a highly organized and promising alternative to mainstream consumption, challenging its ethos and breaking some of its taboos. It is a mild rebellion, a well-tempered rebellion. It even goes as far as to challenge the ultimate taboo against which few dare to express themselves – the equation of better life with more consumption

(Durning, 1992). The ascetic line, once such a prominent element of the Protestant ethic and later a central value of hippie life-styles, seems to have disappeared from the public discourses of the mass media and mainstream political debate. Television, press, magazines, dependent as they are on advertising revenue, have warmly espoused the concerns of activist-consumers or even ethical consumers, but they shy away from any direct assault on the premise of consumerism. It is only in the last 20 years that some progressive environmental and ethical consumer groups have started to discuss seriously a frontal assault on the religion of 'Shop 'til you drop, spend 'til the end, buy 'til you die'. In the words of Ignacio Peon Escalante, a Mexican consumer/citizen activist:

> Our vision is that we should live a more austere life, but also a better quality life; less quantity and more quality. Mexicans believe that if they want to be modern, they must imitate the Americans, aspire to their living standards. They confuse development with materialism, they think that being 'modern' means having instead of being. Consumerism is an absurd form of materialism; this is true of the Third World as well as of the First World. (Interview with the authors, 1994)

'Consume less' is the focal point of these discussions – is it a recipe for political suicide, as the British Greens discovered when they seriously raised the issue as part of their electoral campaign in 1992, or is it an outlandish slogan today which will emerge as the common sense of the future? Calls to consume less are all too frequently ridiculed, especially if those who make them can be seen sporting anything more ostentatious than sackcloth and ashes (Lansley, 1994: 205–9). Yet, the earth's finite resources and its finite tolerance for abuse and neglect are no longer what Lasch called the 'forbidden topic' (1991: 22). While the Northern countries maintain their 'riotous consumption standards', they have no moral authority to pontificate to the ravished and exploited countries of the Third World on the needs to respect the environment and to preserve the earth's natural resources.

'Consume less' may become the final frontier of the consumer-rebel, the consumer who does not merely seek living space within the present system or use the products of the system to express disaffection and protest, but decides that 'enough is enough', anything less than a frontal assault on the core assumption of consumerism is inadequate. Such an assault would, of course, transcend the limits of rebellion and would amount to a major moral and political challenge to capitalist hegemony. As Sklair (1991) has eloquently argued, capitalism throughout the world has become so dependent on consumerism for its legitimation and reproduction, that any threat to the equation of 'more' with 'better' would be deeply subversive:

> The control of ideas in the interests of consumerism is almost total. The ideas that are antagonistic to the global capitalist project can be reduced to one central counter-hegemonic idea, the rejection of the culture-ideology of consumerism itself. Without consumerism, the rationale for continuous capitalist accumulation dissolves. It is the capacity to commodify all ideas and material products in which they adhere, television images, advertisements, newsprint, books, tapes, films and so on, not the ideas themselves, that capitalism strives to appropriate. (1991: 82)

Beyond rebellion

Images of consumers as rebels which started to emerge in the 1980s grew out of a rejection of images of consumers as passive objects of manipulation, as victims. Yet, these are precisely the images which have fuelled the anger but also the tireless activity of self-confessed consumer advocates over the last two centuries (see Chapter 9: The Consumer as Activist). In this chapter, two different forms of rebellion have emerged. On the one hand, we examined the rebellion of those consumers who challenge the authority of producers, not by completely rejecting their wares but by rejecting, first, the meanings assigned to them; second, the methods of acquiring them; third, the methods of using them; fourth, the methods and costs, cultural and environmental, of their production. On the other hand, we have looked at the rebellion of those who reject everything about consumption in the First World, its products, its meanings, its suppliers and its glamorizers and who are beginning to map out a radical new vision:

> We are reaching the end of the line in terms of that kind of existence, materialism and consumerism. People have not enough time in their lives to live. They work for long hours for less pay. How do we move beyond consumerism and materialism? It is not enough to preach and critique.
>
> The only way away from materialism and consumerism is an alternative economic and social framework with which people can identify. People will have less time at work and more on alternative things. What do you do the rest of the time? You can spend it sitting in front of a TV and get packaged entertainment and remain a bloated consumer society, or there is a possibility that we can entice each other to become part of what I call the intimate society. This is a volunteer economy, in which there are no market coercive relationships which transform people into things, but on service and gift giving. The bottom line is that the more people identify themselves with a serving capacity or a stewardship capacity, the less they define themselves by the material things. I know that people who volunteer for work have less and less time for their possessions and are less possessed by their possessions. They are serving, they are giving, they are participating in a real way. Having said that, I realize that you cannot have true participatory democracy in a market economy. Worker-run companies have absolutely no way of invigorating principles of democracy based on volunteer work, so long as they have to survive in a market economy. (Jeremy Rifkin in an interview with the authors, 1994)

The future of consumption, according to this vision, lies neither in rebellion, nor in activism limited to the area of consumption. The consumer must act beyond his or her interests as consumer, in short he or she must once again act as a citizen, taking responsibility for the future.

Conclusion

How convincing are images of consumers as rebels? As a corrective to images of consumers as infinitely malleable, seducible and manageable, the phenomena studied in this chapter are of considerable importance. De Certeau, Fiske, Abercrombie, Herrmann and others have drawn attention to the unexpected, creative and unmanageable aspects of modern consumption. Their contributions parallel arguments concerning the resistance of workers to management's strategies of control. Just as organizations may contain an unmanaged terrain in which individuals evade management controls through play, jokes, stories and fantasies (Gabriel, 1995), contemporary consumption entails a large unmanaged dimension, vividly portrayed by these writers. The unmanaged dimensions of consumption lie, not so much in the rejection of consumer products, let alone in the rejection of consumption itself, but in unorthodox appropriation and uses of these products, especially in ways which express protest.

Finding heroic qualities in these activities seems more problematic. Teenagers enjoying fast rides in stolen cars may be romantically envisioned as rebels against a system which denies each man his own fast car. Anorectic women can be seen as hunger strikers, heroic in their defiance and self-sacrifice. Shop-lifters may be conjured as tricksters scoring victories at the expense of omnipresent electronic eyes. Young people piercing or tattooing their skins or (more temperately) disfiguring their blue-jeans may be seen as revolting against the values of respectable society. Yet, such constructions may reveal more about the omnipotence of consumerism than challenges to it. Not only does consumer rebellion become automatically channelled into the world of commodities where it can be compromised and appropriated, but it automatically becomes commodified itself. Far from rejecting consumerism, one can become a rebel (and appropriate the heroic qualities of this image) simply by engaging in the appropriate type of consumption. Why pick up an axe (like Kapuscinski's rebel) when you can be a rebel merely by tearing up your blue-jeans or having a stud passed through your nose? Camus was one of the first to signal that rebellion can quickly degenerate into style, the rebel turning into a dandy or an aesthete:

> Romanticism demonstrates, in fact, that rebellion is part and parcel of dandyism: one of its objectives is outward appearances. . . . Dandyism inaugurates an aesthetic which is still valid in our world, an aesthetic of solitary creators, who are obstinate rivals of a God they condemn. (1971: 49)

Camus was not reluctant to castigate the sterility of this attitude which accommodates, eviscerates and commodifies rebellion. By comparison with aesthetic rebels of this genre, who denounce the god of consumerism without denying him, the rebels who preach alternative consumption, organize consumer boycotts or set up a local LETS are far less romantic figures. Hollywood makes no films about them and postmodern theorists seem not to notice them at all. Their tireless and largely unpaid work goes mostly unnoticed, unless they can rouse enough people against the building of a nuclear power station or the sale of powdered milk to the Third World so as to put a spanner in the plans of capital. Yet, it is these largely invisible rebels who may in the long run provide the greater, if not the only, challenge to consumerism. By saying 'No', they may force a questioning of the core assumptions of consumerism and open up a range of choices that are currently invisible.

9

The Consumer as Activist

Consumption and leisure are not substitutes for power.

Lester Thurow (1993: 121)

In previous chapters, we have looked at different expressions of consumerism, as a set of values, a way of life or a political ideology. The term has also got a very distinct meaning as 'the process of advancing the cause of consumers – members of the public in their role as purchasers and users of goods and services – and listening to what they have to say' (Locke, 1994a: 174).

Even benign definitions of the consumer interest pay homage to the need for consumer advocates who promote the consumer's interest (Forbes, 1987). Yet, as Winward suggests, consumer activism 'has always been under-theorised' (1993: 77). The consumer movement tends to analyse its own work in private, leaving the theoretical analysis to academics or practitioners who have tended to underplay the importance of activism. The dearth of good analyses of activism is surprising because it is plain to even cursory reviews of the consumer scene that there are – and always have been – considerable tensions within the consumer movement about how to define the consumer and where his or her interests lie. These arguments over consumer philosophy are by no means marginal issues inside the consumer movement. The Consumers Union of the USA, the largest consumer organization in the world, for instance, was born out of a long and bitter struggle in the 1930s in another organization, Consumer Research Inc. The fight was over attitudes to organized labour and over internal management styles (Herrmann, 1993). Another heated debate occurred within, without and between consumer organizations over the threats and advantages for consumers of trade deregulation in the late twentieth century (Lang and Hines, 1993: 108–11; Nader, 1991).

Consumer activism has always functioned within a moral context. The US non-importation movement of 1764–76 was America's first consumer revolt, inspiring people to boycott British goods (Witkowski, 1989). Like all such revolts, it was more than a rejection of colonial tax laws; it was also an expression of cultural independence, an assertion of the local over the global, echoed in anti-colonial struggles elsewhere, notably by Gandhi's independence movement in India. By stopping the flow of imported goods, the non-importation movement hoped to inflict damage on British traders, who in turn would pressurize British politicians to alter taxes on American colonialists. By signing a declaration in public that they would stop purchasing British goods, the adherents also espoused, de facto, a pledge to live more frugally and from local resources in an assertion of community values. The movement was politically successful, but Witkowski concludes that there is little evidence that it altered consumer preferences and consumption patterns in the long run (1989: 222).

The social historian E.P.Thompson showed how the emergence of the new corn markets in eighteenth century England – manifestations of Adam Smith's free market ideas – were 'disinfested of intrusive moral imperatives' (1993: 202). The morality of Smith's new political economy had to be imposed on British society, and a new culture was made in the process. People's expectations and life assumptions had to be remoulded, in a process which was messy and at times bloody. The process is indeed still continuing. In his celebrated essay on 'The Moral Economy of the English Crowd in the Eighteenth Century', Thompson showed how the food riots of that century were the expression of people taking direct action against the imposition of the new free market in grain because they were hungry. More importantly, however, they were reacting to changed food prices which they saw rightly as higher because of a shift away from the paternalism of Tudor economics with its notions of responsibility to the amorality of Smith's market forces. Food rioting crowds were diverse, but 'in times of high prices and of hardship, the crowd might enforce, with a robust direct action, protective market-control and the regulation of prices' (1993: 261). This thesis is echoed in Rudé's (1959) classic study of the crowd in the French Revolution. For Forbes, contemporary consumerism is but a version of the same principle, namely the 'organised reaction of individuals to inadequacies, perceived or real, of marketers, the marketplace, market mechanisms, government, government services, and consumer policy' (1987: 4).

Consumers as activists have always been, and still are, morally driven people. This chapter examines the forms that consumer activism has taken and how they articulate different consumer concerns. Unlike consumer as rebels, many of whom have acted as individuals, consumers activists have always emphasized that collective organization is necessary to improve the lot of consumers. We identify four waves of Western consumer activism, each one of which augured, not only new forms of organizing, but also different ways of looking at consumption. All of these waves have left traces which are still visible in the world of consumer organizations today throughout the world.

First wave: co-operative consumers

The first widespread, organized consumer movement, the pioneer of them all, began as a working-class reaction to excessive prices and poor quality goods, food in particular. The Co-operative Movement took off in its modern form in Rochdale, in North West England, in 1844, at the height of the industrialization process. The first co-operatives in fact date from even earlier and were co-operative corn mills established by skilled artisans. These were set up in opposition to local monopolies who in the words of one Co-op historian 'had conspired to supply that most basic of commodities, bread, at very high prices' (Birchall, 1994: 4). At Woolwich and Chatham, just to the south east of London, in the 1760s, not only were there co-operative mills but bakeries too. The Woolwich co-op mill was burned down, and the other local bakers were accused of the arson.

Drawing on such experiences and the example of utopians such as Robert Owen whose thoughts and practices had developed at New Lanark Mills in Scotland, the movement developed its creed. As Dr William King, one of the key early thinkers said: 'These evils may be cured: and the remedy is in our own hands. The remedy is co-operation' (Birchall, 1994: 9). By 1832 there were 500 local co-operative societies, but the movement collapsed in 1834 in the face of outright repression of working-class movements and internal weaknesses such as lack of legal status. In some cases such as Brighton's 1830s co-op, the success was such that its members were lured into selling their shares for cash (Birchall, 1994: 31).

Nevertheless, not only had an idea been born and fleshed out, but there was some practical proof that consumers could exercise power over production. Co-operation rather than Adam Smith's self-interest could function as the basis for meeting consumer needs. The Rochdale co-op built on this idea by setting up a shop – now a museum – to sell goods to those who joined up. Profits, instead of being allowed to accumulate and ploughed back into manufacture, as in Owen's model, were divided among the co-operators (Redfern, 1913: 1–11).

The principle of this new movement, which was extraordinarily successful both in business and ideological terms, was 'self-help by the people'. No distinction was made between people as consumers and as producers. Business, co-operators argued, divided producers from the output of their own hands. Co-operation was the great social alternative to the capitalists' economic armoury which merely divided and ruled the mass of working people (Thompson, 1994). This principle was admirably expressed by Redfern in 1920:

> In our common everyday needs the great industries of the world take their rise. We – the mass of common men and women in all countries – also compose the world's market. To sell to us is the ultimate aim of the world's business. Hence it is ourselves as consumers who stand in a central relation to all the economies of the world, like the king in his kingdom. As producers we go unto a particular factory, farm or mine, but as consumers we are set by nature thus to give leadership, aim and purpose to the whole economic world. That we are not kings, but serfs in the mass, is due to our failure to think and act together as consumers and so to realise our true position and power. (1920: 12)

Co-operation offered a richer, more fulfilled social existence, a chance for working people to build a better world. To allow this mass to participate, a new civic society had to be created, and vice versa. It was a subversive combination of theory and practice, means and ends, which was and still is deeply threatening to prevailing market theory. The co-operator Holyoake parodied the movement's detractors as follows:

> The working class are not considered to be very rich in the quality of self-trust, or mutual trust. The business habit is not thought to be their forte. The art of creating a large concern, and governing all its complications, is not usually supposed to belong to them. (1872: 1)

The movement prospered and proved these Jeremiahs wrong. The Rochdale Pioneers, for instance, had within six years their own corn mill. The practice of local co-ops spread like wildfire – and continues to this day (Thompson, 1994). Co-operation from below, rather than Owen's benign vision of production for mutual benefit, put the consumer in charge, probably for the only time ever. Today, the distance between producer and consumer is wider than ever, in part due to the international division of labour, and in part due to economic concentration and specialization. In the mid-nineteenth century, the co-operative movement grew with hundreds of societies being formed, but as those began to merge in the next century, the mutuality principle weakened, becoming more like a distant and tiny share-holding at the point of sale. Indeed, for most British people in the second half of the twentieth century, co-operation meant a retail store where the customer received a coupon with the bill at the check-out counter – the famous 'divi' or dividend, which before its demise in the 1960s had become a rather weak parallel to the nakedly capitalist savings stamps schemes run by the rival private or stock-holder retailers. The practice of consumer co-operation for mutual benefit had become a trading stamp.

A century and a half after its foundation, the Co-operative movement has spread throughout the world. One in three citizens of the USA is a member of a co-operative; co-ops are the largest dairy in Denmark; are huge and growing concerns in Italy; are pioneers of modern forms of retailing in Spain; handle most of Canada's wheat sales; include one of the top ten investment houses of world finance – the farmers' insurance co-op Zen-kyoren, with assets of more than $132 billion; and are important players in both Japanese retailing and Latin America. There are 700 million co-operators in the world in just over 100 countries, with 442 million co-op members in Asia alone, and 1.8 million employees in Europe (Co-op Union, 1994). The progeny of the Rochdale Pioneers, an amalgam of many societies, is Britain's largest farmer and one of its largest retailers and supermarket chains, with nine per cent of the total food retail market in 1994 and 4,000 shops throughout the UK (Co-op Union, 1994; Myers, 1993).

Banks, factories and insurance companies all reside under the Co-op movement umbrella, although the UK movement began to sell off huge parts of its food industrial empire in the 1990s. Vertical integration, owning everything from land to point of sale, for so long a strength of the movement, had by the end of the twentieth century become an economic weight round its neck. This was now the era of flexible contracts, a far cry from the co-operators' dream of an autonomous empire with everything kept within the co-op family. With time and scale of operations, the direct control of consumers has slipped away. The Co-operative Wholesale Society or any of the hundred plus UK co-ops descended from the Pioneers are overwhelmingly large concerns – only a few fiercely independent societies are still single town or village based. The pressure on the movement is to merge societies, in order to be able to compete with the supermarket giants, but this further undermines the co-operative principle.

The most dynamic element in the Co-operative movement is today best exemplified either in the new small food co-operatives linking (usually small) farmers practising biological husbandry techniques with networks of consumers (Booth, 1994) or on a grander scale by the Japanese Seikatsu Clubs, one of a network of 700 consumer co-ops that have prospered from the 1960s (New Consumer, 1991; Nelson, 1991). The Seikatsu club movement was started in 1965 by a Tokyo housewife to buy milk more cheaply in bulk. When members join the Seikatsu Club, they make an initial investment of 1,000 yen, and pay a similar sum every month. The Clubs believe they have a duty to be harmonious with nature by 'taking action from the home' (Gussow, 1991: 101–3). It was a message that obviously resonated, for by the 1990s there were 25,000 local groups turning over an annual £260 million (Ekins, 1992). Seikatsu clubs are not, however, the only new forms of consumer co-operatives. Others which have begun to expand in the US, Japan and Europe are direct farmer-consumer links under which the consumer pays a fixed sum to the grower and in return gets a box of fresh food, whatever is in season (Festing, 1993).

Active on the world consumer scene and fiercely independent, the Japanese consumer co-op movement is well organized, prosperous and proud to defend its cultural traditions – as it had to over the GATT world trade talks (Lang and Hines, 1993). The Japanese movement was active in resisting its government's desire to import US grain and rice and to break the cultural tradition of rice and meat self-sufficiency. It lost, but made the point that consumer pressure is a political force to be reckoned with.

Like many social movements, the success of the co-operative movement has led to a dilution of the ideals of its founders. The hard work, zeal and commitment of the pioneers who built the local societies, who saved and invested in new shops, factories and land to serve working people, all this brought good quality goods and services to those who hitherto had lacked them. But as the movement has grown in size and influence and its affairs have inevitably come to be conducted by professional managers, its vision has become more pragmatic, though it has never collapsed into quite the ethos of other retail organizations. Despite these limitations, the idea retains its potency even if today's global markets and the international division of labour make it hard to realize.

In recent years, consumer co-operatives have emerged in a slightly different guise. While retaining the emphasis on affordable goods and services, they have incorporated an environmental dimension and have experimented with replacing cash with local forms of currency. Two strands in this movement are discernible. One is predominantly middle class, and ranges from wholefood co-operatives (Hines, 1976) to LETS (see Chapter 8: The Consumer as Rebel). The other is more directly working class, spawned by the re-emergence of structural unemployment and the long-term poverty that accompanies it. With the arrival of modern hypermarkets and the gradual disappearance of local retail outlets, large numbers of low income consumers in inner city areas have found themselves poorly serviced (Raven and Lang, 1995: 31–5). In order to obviate the detrimental effect on their diet and health, a number of local authorities in Britain began to foster food co-operatives. The best known of these and the largest network grew in Glasgow, Scotland and by the mid-1990s there were 40 such consumer co-ops across the region, with up to 500 members each. In these new generation co-operatives, something of the Rochdale pioneering spirit has been recovered, which might have been lost in the larger and more successful co-ops.

Second wave: value-for-money consumers

The second wave of the consumer movement, often wrongly regarded as the sole consumer movement, took its modern form in the 1930s, but built upon tentative US consumer initiatives in the late nineteenth and early twentieth centuries.

A Consumers League was formed in New York in 1891. In 1898, the National Consumers League was formed from local groups, and by 1903 had 64 branches in 20 states. The movement took off after a celebrated exposé of wide scale food adulteration and bad trade (see Chapter 7: The Consumer as Victim). Upton Sinclair, a radical journalist, was sent to write newspaper articles on the insanitary condition at the Chicago stockyards and the meat packing plants, and wrote *The Jungle*, a novel published in 1906. A socialist, he hoped to proselytize with the political message that market forces served neither worker nor consumer; he hoped to bring down US capitalism, instead he changed US food law. 'I aimed at the public's heart and by accident hit it in the stomach', he wrote, anticipating many a single issue consumer campaign which launches a simple message, from which it generalizes. As a result of the reaction to Sinclair's book, legislation was rushed through Congress, the Pure Food and Drug Act of 1906 and the Meat Inspection Act of the same year, an extraordinary impact for a book, but not the only exposé to have such an effect, as we have already seen (see Chapter 7: The Consumer as Victim) (Forbes, 1987: 4). The Federal Trade Commission and a variety of anti-monopoly laws were also set up at the turn of the century.

These early US consumer groups placed heavy emphasis on the containment of the emergent powerful corporations. Their writings were full of concerns about the power of the new combines over individuals, both as workers and as consumers. Unlike the first wave of consumerism, these groups were concerned about the threat posed to consumers by increasing concentration and monopoly capital. In the roaring 1920s with its unprecedented explosion of consumption, a best selling book, *Your Money's Worth* (1927), tried to show how consumers were being exploited even as they were first tasting the fruits of mass production. A year later, one of the authors, Schlink, founded Consumers Research Inc. to carry out consumer product testing on a large scale, its purpose to provide research and information to consumers. This was the first time that consumer activism saw itself as enabling consumers to take best advantage of the market, rather than trying to undermine the market through co-operative action or political agitation and lobbying. In 1936, following a bitter confrontation over Schlink's authoritarian management, a group from Consumers Research Inc. split to form the Consumers Union. Consumers Union is now a huge organization with around 5 million subscribers to its magazine *Consumer Reports*, which epitomizes the principle of second wave consumerism, namely enabling its members to get best value for money by offering authoritative information. The principle of value-for-money took root in the consumer movement and reached its heyday in President John F. Kennedy's 1962 Consumer Message to Congress (see Introduction: The Faces of the Consumer) (Forbes, 1987: 37).

Some value-for-money organizations have grown into very substantial operations. The UK Consumers' Association's *Which?* had a 700,000 subscriber list by the mid-1990s (down from a million at the start of the decade), while the Dutch Konsumenten Bond had 660,000, the highest membership for any consumer movement in the West proportionate to national population, and the Belgian Test Achats, whose own subscriber list is 320,000, has considerable extra weight due to its formal link up with similar Spanish, Portuguese and Italian groups who have 230,000, 150,000 and 350,000 subscribers respectively. Smaller organizations with the same ethos and publishing a regular magazine can be found in many other countries, such as Germany, Belgium, Denmark, Australia, New Zealand, and even the newly independent Slovenia. These magazines test products for safety, ease of use, price, durability, task effectiveness, in short overall value-for-money. Readers are informed about the 'Best Buy' and warned about cons and bad buys. Large sums of money are spent testing the products, usually in the consumer organization's own laboratories or test benches.

Unlike the co-operative movement, this second wave of consumer organizations has no pretensions of offering a radically different vision for society. Its adherents see their role as ameliorative, to make the market-place more efficient and to champion the interests of the consumer within it. Their aim is to inform and educate the consumer about the features which will enable them to act effectively as consumers (John, 1994). The value-for-money model places considerable stress on rights to information and labelling and the right of redress if something goes wrong. John Winward, Director of Research at the Consumers' Association, conceives of these non-profit organizations as 'information co-operatives' (1993: 76–7). Currently, second wave consumerism is facing a number of difficulties. On the one hand, post-Fordism and the proliferation of niche markets undermine the possibility of meaningful comparisons between broadly similar products (Winward, 1993: 76–7); on the other hand, the number of subscribers to these organizations has dropped as a result of the early 1990s recession. But most important of all, second wave consumerism has addressed consumers as individuals. This has been both its strength and its weakness. As John Beishon, a former Chief Executive of the Consumers' Association, has suggested, the 'main difficulty is that there is no strong commonality of interest among consumers. . . . Another serious difficulty lies in raising the revenue to support a powerful, independent consumer body' (1994: 5). This is a candid admission of the limitations of second wave consumerism, coming as it does from one of the richest consumer organizations in the world, and coinciding with some critical assessments of that organization's outlook (Barker, 1994; Nicholson-Lord, 1994).

The main criticisms raised of second wave consumerism have been that it fails to address longer-term environmental and social issues; that it has an overwhelmingly middle-class orientation based on the assumption of ever-increasing standards of living; that it disregards the plight of poorer consumers; and that it has an inappropriately conservative approach to consumption. Second wave consumerism has:

> rarely questioned the fundamental premise on which American industrialism is based: the desirability of technical efficiency and of technological and economic growth. Instead, consumerism has focused most of its attention on such problems as the lack of product safety or of adequate consumer information. (Bloom and Stern, 1978)

These criticisms apply to second wave consumerism everywhere, not just in the USA. However, they should not obscure the constraining effect that second wave groups have had on business. Their independence, their unwillingness to accept advertising revenue and their sometimes religious obsession with accuracy has given them an authority which companies and governments can only disregard at their cost.

Third wave: Naderism

The third wave of consumer activism, like the second, emerged in the USA. Its figurehead, Ralph Nader, has become one of the most admired US citizens in national polls for years. Nader shot into prominence with the publication in 1965 of his expose of the car industry, *Unsafe at any Speed* (Nader, 1991/1966). The book argued that one automobile model in particular, the Chevrolet Corvair, and automobiles in general were poorly designed and had built-in safety short-cuts. The industry had resisted giving priority to safety, Nader alleged, a policy which according to Nader resulted in an annual slaughter of Americans – 51,000 in 1965. Highway accidents cost $8.3 billion in property damage, medical expenses, lost wages and insurance overhead expenses (1991: cii). Relying on independent tests, Nader showed how the Corvair easily went out of control at 22 miles per hour, contrasting with its advertising claims of 'easy handling', being 'a family sedan' and a car that 'purrs for the girls' (1991: 27). Yet the car's road-handling on corners meant that it demanded 'more driving skill in order to avoid collision than any other American automobile'. As though that was not bad enough, he catalogued how General Motors had failed to come clean on the Corvair's design faults. In consumer movement terms, what marked Nader's approach as special was that he not only generalized from the particular, documenting how the Corvair may have been an extreme case of consumer safety being a low priority, but that he spelt out at great length how the case was only the tip of an iceberg.

Nader, a Harvard educated lawyer, set up the Center for Study of Responsive Law and the Project for Corporate Responsibility in 1969. By the end of the 1970s he had spawned a series of organizations, staffed by young professionals, 'Nader's Raiders', often lawyers like himself. By the 1990s there were 29 organizations with combined revenues of $75–80 million (Brimelow and Spencer, 1990). The common themes of these organizations were a distrust of corporations, a defence of the individual against the giants, a demand that the state protect its citizens and above all, an appeal for Americans to be citizens, not just consumers. Naderism assumed that the consumer is relatively powerless in a world dominated by corporate giants, whether these be automobile or insurance companies, the health sector or the government-industry complex. The nature of commerce is stacked against the customer, unless regulations or standards of conduct are fought for. This is a hard fight, so the consumer organizations have to be tough, well briefed, well organized and able to make optimum use of the mass media.

Nader brought a new punch to consumer politics and tapped a deep well of public unease about the power of large corporations vis à vis the individual customer. He saw the role of consumer organizations as going beyond getting the consumer the best deal in the market, to confronting the market itself. Writing about the US food industry in 1970, Nader made a number of charges about what it will do if left to its own devices:

> Making food appear what it is not is an integral part of the $125 billion food industry. The deception ranges from the surface packaging to the integrity of the food products' quality to the very shaping of food tastes. . . . In fact, very often the degradation of these standards proceeds from the cosmetic treatment of food or is its direct cost by-product. . . . For too long there has been an overwhelmingly dominant channel of distorted information from the food industry to the consumer. . . . Company economy very often was the consumer's cost and hazard. As a result, competition became a way of beating one's competitor by racing for the lowest permissible common denominator. (1970: v)

The role of the state, in the absence of consumer pressure, is to collude with this downward spiral, which disadvantages good businesses. The consumer activist's role was and is to confront, to expose, to stand up for public rights, to be a citizen. A persistent theme is to bring the corporate state under the control of democratic forces, and away from the grip of big business (Krebs, 1992: 440–3).

Like the second wave of the consumer movement, Naderism is adamant on the role of information and that information should be free and fair. The second wave sees its own role as that of providing information for the consumer to be able to operate more effectively in the marketplace. Naderism, on the other hand, places more emphasis on information from consumer bodies as debunking the misinformation systematically disseminated by companies. Nader has described the situation thus: 'It is time for consumers to have information that will provide them with an effective understanding of the secrecy-clouded situation' (Nader, 1970: vii). Freedom of Information – rather than product information or mere labelling on a packet – has been a persistent theme for Nader. Indeed, he helped inspire the UK Campaign for Freedom of Information in its uphill task to reform the British state's reflex for secrecy. For Nader, secrecy is often a collusion between state and commercial interests, and it is the duty of the consumer activist to break that collusion, or else she or he becomes an accomplice to it. Only vigilant consumers can break the pact, said Nader:

> Major corporations like their consumers to remain without a capacity for group purchasing action, group legal action, group participating action before regulatory agencies. . . . The possibility that consumers banding together can muster their organised intelligence to play a major role in shaping economic policy and the future of our political economy is an unsettling one for the mega corporations that play much of the world's economy. So too would be an organised consumer initiative to assess the hazards of technology or forestall the marketing of products which use consumers as test subjects or guinea pigs. (quoted in Beishon, 1994: 9)

Nader's views have fed on the deep apprehension of American consumers, and the public in general, towards anything big and unfettered, corporate power in particular. Unlike second wave organizations, Nader and his colleagues believe that only active involvement by citizens at the local level can counteract these forces. Whereas second wave groups are reformist and 'top-down' in their strategies, preferring lobbies to rallies, Naderism has been equally content to lobby and rally, priding itself upon building up grassroots citizens action. In the marketplace, the message is to be frugal, to get wise in 'the vital art of self-defence' to 'protect yourself in the marketplace', whether buying a car, health insurance, food or a house (Nader and Smith, 1992). These are terms which echo the early American non-importation movement (Witkowski, 1989).

Unlike second wave consumerism, Naderism, though admired, has not easily been grafted onto the consumer cultures of other countries. Neither the political culture nor the legal system nor the scale of consumption in other countries has until recently favoured the growth of Nader-like organizations. But with global deregulation in the 1990s, and the emergence of regional trade blocs such as the European Union and the North American Free Trade Agreement (NAFTA), Naderism's persistent charge at the collusion of big business and the state has found new allies. These have included environmental groups, animal welfare groups, trades unions, as well as other consumer groups (Lang and Hines, 1993).

The globalization of consumer activism

Consumer International, formerly the International Organization of Consumers' Unions (IOCU), is a global network founded in 1960, which has over a hundred affiliated organizations from over 80 countries. Prominent among them is a group of organizations from developing countries. Developing countries have produced a new generation of consumer activists such as Anwar Fazal, Martin Khor, and others, who have not only applied the lessons of Naderism in their own countries but have taken on corporations outside their national boundaries. Developing countries, they argue, are particularly vulnerable to the globalization of capital, equally for the well-being of their consumers, as for their workers. The stress on citizen is particularly appealing to them; justice, poverty and equality are more important concerns than value for money in the strict sense. In the words of Khor:

> The main consumer issues in Malaysia are firstly, satisfaction of people's basic needs for food and clothes; secondly, protection of the environment; and thirdly, protection of consumers of Third World from exploitation by First World. The main difficulties we face arise from the unequal distribution of income; the rich indulge in excessive consumption while poor in Third World have barely enough to survive.
>
> Traditional value for money consumerism (what brand of washing machine to buy) is not important for the Third World. What is important is pollution, world resources, what products should be promoted and what products should be banned. Should we have washing machines at all?
>
> The most important changes required are changes in mentality about happiness and pleasure. But this can only happen if the developed countries offer an example here, because they disseminate their culture to the developing countries. So massive change in consumption patterns, in motivation and in the meaning of life itself are very important. But that can only come about if we can change the distribution of commercial and therefore political power world-wide, between countries and within countries, so that the local communities can have their fair share of resources, so that they can vote in the marketplace or in their communities on how to fulfil their needs. (Interview with authors, January 1994)

By the late 1980s, IOCU/Consumers International could state that 'the overriding concern of IOCU and its members is to promote social justice and fairness in the marketplace' (IOCU, 1987). This is evidenced in Consumers International/IOCU's emphasis, not only on consumer rights, but also on consumer responsibilities. According to its Statement, consumer responsibilities include:

> *Solidarity*: The responsibility to organize together as consumers to develop the strength and influence to promote and protect our interests.
> *Critical Awareness*: The responsibility to be more alert and questioning about the price and quality of goods and services we use.

Action: The responsibility to assert ourselves and act to ensure that we get a fair deal. As long as we remain passive consumers we will continue to be exploited.
Social Concern: The responsibility to be aware of the impact of our consumption on other citizens, especially disadvantaged or powerless groups whether in the local, national or international community.
Environmental Awareness: The responsibility to understand the environmental consequences of our consumption. We should recognize our individual and social responsibility to conserve natural resources and protect the earth for future generations. (IOCU, 1987)

Equally, Consumers International/IOCU's conception of consumer rights goes well beyond a narrow utilitarian definition to embrace what might be seen as overall rights of citizens:

Basic Needs: The right to basic goods and services which guarantee survival: adequate food, clothing, shelter, health care, education and sanitation.
Safety: The right to be protected against the marketing of goods or the provision of services that are hazardous to health and life.
Information: The right to be protected against dishonest or misleading advertising or labelling. And the right to be given the facts and information needed to make an informed choice.
Choice: The right to choose products and services at competitive prices with an assurance of satisfactory quality.
Representation: The right to express consumer interests in the making and execution of government policy.
Redress: The right to be compensated for misrepresentation, shoddy goods or unsatisfactory services.
Consumer Education: The right to acquire the knowledge and skills necessary to be an informed consumer.
Healthy Environment: The right to live and work in an environment which is neither threatening nor dangerous and which permits a life of dignity and well-being. (IOCU, 1987)

In spite of these lofty ideals, their realization across national boundaries and in the face of overwhelming odds, is a Promethean task.

Fourth wave: alternative consumers

A new wave of consumer organizations emerged slowly in the 1970s and accelerated in the 1980s, and which might be usefully called 'alternative consumerism'. The movement has many elements: green, ethical, Third World solidarity and fair trade organizations. Initially, the most influential of these was green consumerism which introduced the argument that the consumer should play a leading part in protecting the environment in a number of ways, from purchasing more environmentally-friendly products to resisting consumption altogether. For the first time since the early Co-operative movement, consumers were given a direct productionist message: buy this rather than that product and you can help good producers to out-compete bad producers. 'Good' and 'bad' were defined in environmental terms. Suddenly, the environment movement shifted from being oppositional to staking a claim in the marketplace. The impact has been significant, although some argue that it is temporary (Cairncross, 1991: 153).

Green consumerism

The green consumer movement began in Europe and spread west to North America. As Cairncross noted 'the sheer speed with which green consumerism erupted in some countries will also leave its mark' (1991: 189) Seemingly overnight, aerosols with CFCs and apples with pesticide residues became no-go areas in the supermarket. The green consumer movement forced companies to listen to them and spawned new ranges of products such as phosphate-free detergents and cars with recyclable components which gave consumers the option of choosing 'green'. Often these products, however, remained at the margins of mainline consumption. Perhaps the more important role of green consumerism was to question market supremacy that had dominated the 1980s. Green consumerism represented a significant shift from the rampant individualism, short-termism and venality of the Reagan-Thatcher years, assuming the role of primary opposition to the New Right.

One effect of pressure from green consumer groups was that companies started to undertake environmental audits as a way of gaining competitive advantage over their competitors, and fending off criticism. One branch of green consumer activism monitored companies and pursued an approach akin to that of second wave consumerism by comparing products for their environmental soundness and the green credentials of the company that produced (Elkington and Hailes, 1988). Its fundamental message now is less apocalyptic than it was in the early 1970s. 'Consume carefully' it proclaims rather than 'don't consume' or 'consume less'. This has generated a whole new category of green businesses and green product ranges from cosmetics to electrical goods and even cars, leading to a green producer-consumer nexus, where environmentalists act as referees of corporate behaviour. There has been a proliferation of green business consultancies built to service this nexus.

A study of 75 radical, green and ethical businesses in the North of Britain explored the 'convergence between consumers and entrepreneurs' (Kennedy, 1994: 4). For Kennedy, these alternative businesses – some large and some community-oriented – have fostered a new type of relationship with their customers, encouraging activity rather than passivity. He argues that:

> an increasing number of consumers are striving to re-define their role away from one of relative passivity where they exercise a certain post-modern 'free' choice in their personal selection of pre-determined signifiers from an array of market-researched products but have little say in the way goods are actually produced, packaged and presented or in the initial construction of symbolic values. . . . it can be argued, a growing minority of consumers – and perhaps a majority to some extent – are engaged in developing an active, demanding and participatory role as agents or co-determinants in the various stages of the economic decision-making

process, and not just in the spheres of production and consumption but also in the disposal of post consumer and industrial wastes. (Kennedy, 1994: 1)

Recycling is another central theme of green consumerism. No wonder; the figures are startling. An average American family dumps about 100 lb of trash every week (NRDC Earth Works Group, 1989: 9). In Britain, about £10 of every £65 a family spends on food weekly goes to packaging and is thrown away immediately. Waste is the direct result of the throw-away culture. Soft drinks used to be sold in returnable bottles, and still are in less developed countries, where a bottle is still regarded as an object of value. In Hungary, following the collapse of the old regime, the national habit of returning used bottles disintegrated within weeks of the arrival of a Western disposable carton company, partly financed by the World Bank (Fairlie, 1992). Yet consumers even in the West do not need a strong inducement to enter a recycling ethos. In Sweden a deposit scheme of only 5p on a PET (plastic) drinks bottle achieved rates of return of up to 70 per cent. In America, however, in 1989 fewer than half of the states recycled more than 5 per cent of their waste (Cairncross, 1991: 212–13).

The 1990s appeared to have established green concerns as part of the consumer landscape. A MORI poll in Britain, for instance, suggested that half the country's adult consumers had made at least one purchase where the product was chosen rather than another because of its environment-friendly packaging, formulation or advertising (Elkington and Hailes, 1988: 3). Less than four years later, reservations were being expressed about the depth of this consciousness in the light of the recession, yet there was evidence that green consciousness has remained, even if purchases of green products, which are often more expensive, have suffered (Worcester, 1994).

Perhaps a more lasting effect of the recession has been to bring into the open an internal argument between the reformists and radicals. In one camp, lay the proponents of a more caring, considerate capitalism. In the other, those who argued that the thrust of green consumers should be to consume less altogether (Irvine, 1989). In some respects, the first camp was charged by the latter with coming to the rescue of consumer capitalism and giving it new opportunities for niche products, at the very moment when traditional markets were being saturated. The Confederation of British Industry estimated that the world-wide market for environment-friendly products and technologies was £100–150 billion in 1989, a figure which has since been revised heavily upwards (Irvine, 1989: 11). This was yet another instance where consumer capitalism has proven itself equal to the task of incorporating arguments of its critics and of capitalizing on them (Packard, 1981/1957: 217–18) (see also Chapter 7: The Consumer as Victim).

Like earlier generations of reformers, green activists have been victims of their own success, a process recognized by activists themselves, many of whom have harboured no illusions about the limitations of green activism when restricted to consumption. As a result, radical segments within the movement have advocated the case for more structural change (Irvine,

1989). Helena Norberg-Hodge, the author of a study of the cultural devastation wrought by consumerism on Ladakh, in Northern India (1991) has commented:

> Consumerism is the result of the breakdown of community and meaning in our lives. This has led to a need to be recognized, to be seen, to be respected, to be somebody; this need now fuels the need to consume. People feel that if they get that flash new car, that fine new house, they will earn the respect of others. It is an attempt to link up with other people which tragically ends up in a vicious separation from them.
>
> Increased consumption has no benefit whatever for the consumer. Increased consumption means another plastic wrapper around the tomato, you buy. The consumer did not ask 'Give me a wrapper around each tomato'.
>
> I personally believe that the consumer is not aware of the ways he is being manipulated; hence I am interested in consumer education, not just token actions of recycling. The consumer has sensed that these are pretty meaningless, they don't make a dent on the system. These are the limits of green consumerism. What we need is a shortening of the chain between producers and consumers, increased real power for the consumer. (Interview with authors, January 1994)

Ethical consumerism

Another strand in the new alternative consumer movement sees consumption in ethical terms. It seeks to reaffirm the moral dimension of consumer choice. The US Council on Economic Priorities introduced a guide which rated 1,300 US brands thus: 'Every time you step up to a cash register, you vote. When you switch from one brand to another, companies hear you clearly. You can help make America's companies socially responsible by using this guide' (Will et al. 1989: 143). Like the reformist strand within the green consumer movement, some ethical consumer activists see their task essentially as the rating of companies' overall ethical stance. Both the US Council and its UK counterparts, New Consumer and Ethical Consumer Research Association, grade products and companies on a number of criteria: donations to charity, women's advancement, minority advancement, military contracts, animal testing, disclosure of information, community outreach, nuclear power, South Africa (prior to the fall of apartheid), records on the environment and land rights, donations to political parties and trades union relations, and so on (Ethical Consumer, 1993; Adams et al., 1991)

When the Ethical Consumer Research Association was founded in Manchester, close to Rochdale of pioneer fame, in the late 1980s, it was advised not to use the word 'consumer' in its title 'because the word is too narrow a definition of what people do' (Rob Harrison, personal interview with the authors, February 1994). The word consumer places an emphasis on only one aspect of people's behaviour, one which tends to deny the political and moral goals the organization had come into existence to promote. By the mid-1990s, Rob Harrison of Ethical Consumer argued that the organization's goal is really to change culture and to promote a consumer awareness of the global implications of Western consumption. Issues such as fair trade, aid and exploitation of Third World workers far from being marginal to the ethics and politics of Western consumption lie at its very heart (Wells and Jetter, 1991). Globally aware consumers, argued Anwar Fazal of IOCU Asia Office, 'cannot ignore the conditions under which products are made – the environmental impact and working conditions. We are linked to them and we have a responsibility for them' (quoted in Wells and Jetter, 1991: 3).

The fair trade movement has sought to encourage links between producers and workers of the South and consumers of the North, by delivering products from developing countries directly to rich consumer markets. It asks consumers to buy these products partly because they return more money to the original producer than does conventional trade and partly as a way of supporting non-exploitative firms operating in the South. In this way they hope to revitalize the old co-operators' goal of bringing the consumer and producer into closer relationship (Barratt Brown, 1993: 184–6). One particularly successful product in Europe, for instance, has been a coffee branded as Cafédirect in the UK and as Max Havelaar in the Netherlands, named after a famous Dutch novel of the same name, published in 1860, which denounced the use of slaves in the coffee trade, an early appeal to consumers (Mulatuli, 1987/1860). This coffee was adopted by the European Parliament as its official brand. The Cafédirect brand sold its millionth packet in 1994, just two years after its launch.

If such sales are the positive face of ethical consumerism, the new wave of consumer activism has often taken recourse to the more traditional tactic of the boycott (Friedman, 1985). Boycotts, named after Captain Boycott, an Irish land agent, date from the 1880s, though solidarity action against particular products were known before, as Witowski's (1989) study of the American non-importation movement in the late eighteenth century shows. In the twentieth century, Gandhi's *ahimsa* or non-violent direct action included the organization of consumer boycotts of British cloth and salt. Boycotts vary from local to global in their scope and vary enormously in the degree to which they are organized. A celebrated consumer boycott of Californian grapes was organized by the Mexican farm workers in the USA from the mid-1960s in protest at poor labour rates and safety conditions. Its effects went on for decades, as a way of bringing more farmers to the negotiating table.

How effective are consumer boycotts? Smith argues that their effectiveness depends on their visibility and that business will always try to get round this, as when Argentinian corned beef was reputedly repackaged and labelled as Brazilian to sell it in Britain during the Falklands-Malvinas 1982 War (1990: 227). Smith also argues that consumer boycotts against food products tend to be more effective because food is a perishable good and consumed daily. One major study of the effectiveness of consumer boycotts found that about a quarter were successful in the USA between 1970 and 1980 (Friedman, 1985). Another study, however, found that when stock prices of the target firms are taken into the reckoning, then boycotts are considerably more effective (White and Kare, 1990). Herrmann (1993) reports that in 1992 as many as 16 per cent of grocery shoppers in the USA had joined a boycott as compared with 8 per cent in 1984.

In sum, consumer boycotts, if well organized, can have an effect on both public consciousness and corporate policies, at least in the short term. In his review of consumer boycotts, Smith argues that they are a 'high risk strategy' for consumer groups, which may explain why they are favoured by fourth wave consumer organizations and generally eschewed by more traditional consumer bodies who prefer the 'quieter route' of 'committee work'. (1990: 230). Smith considers boycotts to be 'moral acts by consumers' (1990: 255), a rare harnessing of consumer sovereignty.

Single issue campaigns

The strengths and the limitations of the boycott tactic are made plain by the experience of one of the best organized and longest-lasting boycotts in recent years, over baby milk. This has been led by women opposed to companies undermining breast feeding for babies and selling breast milk substitutes to women, especially in developing countries. The International Baby Foods Action Network has targeted one company, Nestlé, and set up a global network monitoring the company's actions and lobbying world bodies such as UNICEF and the World Health Organization. Set up in the 1970s, the campaign had considerable success in restricting the sales of breast milk substitutes by the early 1980s. However, it had to be reactivated at the end of the decade claiming that the company was infringing world agreements (Allain, 1991). Allain attributes the persistence and single-mindedness of the action to the fact that it is almost exclusively run by women and appealing to women. Has it worked? This is Allain's assessment:

> The good news . . . is that activist campaigns and boycotts will make industry sit up and listen. The bad news is that after listening, they will not act to remove the source of the problem. Instead, they will seek to eliminate or contain the problem by making a minimum of changes and strengthening their links with the 'government system'. (1991: 210)

Consumer activism, she argues, can only succeed if it takes a long view: 'The effects of 50 years' promotion of bottle feeding cannot be wiped out in five or even ten years and new products and practices appear before there is a chance for legislation.' (1991: 213). This extraordinarily sober assessment raises a number of questions. Is the consumer as activist doomed to struggle endlessly against the odds, only achieving 'success' if it is narrowly defined? A few cents or pence on or off a share price here; a dent in a company's market share there? If, as both Allain and Harrison suggest, the ultimate goal is to redirect consumer culture, this is an enormous task and surely way beyond any consumer organization, however rich, however well staffed.

The new wave of consumer activists undoubtedly contain people of considerable skill and vision. As morally and politically driven people, they work hard, long hours, often for low pay. Their rewards are a strange pleasure, from most consumers' or workers' point of view; it is a job satisfaction of meaning, rather than utility of the pay-packet. From the point of view of the activist, effectiveness is usually most easily measured only in single issue campaigns. A victory in the short-term can be a government or company acknowledgement about an error, or the introduction of a sought-after piece of legislation. To the outsider, the reaction might be 'so what?'; to the activist, this is an occasion for some cheer, a reassertion of moral right. This certainty maintains the effort.

Single issue campaigns are both the most visible, because the media take an interest in them, and the most effective ones, because they can mobilize public sentiment without overt political connotations. They are most conspicuous when targeted at the introduction of new technologies (such as the milk-inducing hormone BST in cows) whose use is dictated by the market interests of sections of business, rather than the needs of consumers (Brunner, 1988; Gussow, 1991; Rifkin, 1992; Webb and Lang, 1990). Their effectiveness is often out of all proportion to their paid-up membership, which is always far smaller than that of second wave organizations. The Food Irradiation Campaign, set up in 1985, became a classic single issue campaign. It is a campaigners' maxim that good campaigns are only *for* something, never *against*; yet here was a campaign that set out to stop governments, big food manufacturers, some international United Nations bodies, not to mention the nuclear industry from introducing a technique based on soft nuclear technology. Food irradiation was promoted by its adherents as the answer to food poisoning. Poultry in many developed countries contain unnecessary amounts of food bacteria such as salmonella. If a chicken, after slaughter, is irradiated, these bacteria can be destroyed. Why the problem? The activists argued that first, irradiation destroys good features in the food, such as vitamins; second, that it is a method of covering up bad standards before the consumer buys the poultry; third and most importantly, that it wasn't needed. Here was the campaigners' sting: arguing *against* the technique was turned upside down into arguing *for* good food, hence the slogans: 'good food does not need irradiating' and 'if a food has been irradiated, you need to ask what was wrong with it'. The proponents of irradiation were thus forced on the defensive and to address many awkward questions, such as over vitamin loss and over the possibility that irradiation, by destroying 'good' bacteria when a food was vacuum-sealed, could lead to more serious dangers such those caused by *clostridium botulinum* (Webb and Lang 1990: 91–4).

The campaign maintained a high profile for seven years in many different countries, where the issue of food irradiation seemed to tap a public concern about food quality. Even though it failed to stop the legalization of food irradiation in some countries, including the UK and the USA, it still counts as one of the great single issue successes of recent years. Why? Because the campaigners produced and publicized such an effective array of arguments that almost no food retailer or processor would use it, since this would be seen as a tacit acknowledgement that they had taken short-cuts with their food hygiene. A coalition of interests emerged world-wide which ensured that even if governments were too timid to ban the technique, self-interested capitalists were not. Over this period, a network of activists was built up around the world, proving that a single issue campaign rightly pitched and properly argued could unite consumers across vast cultural and geographical distances and differences. As one of the present authors (TL), who was centrally involved in this campaign, explains:

> I knew our message was hitting home when three things happened. First, we called a meeting on food irradiation for women's media journalists and the room was full. We got nothing but favourable coverage for years afterwards in all the women's magazines, that ordinary people read; nothing political or 'heavy'. Second, I got into a London taxi once and was lectured by the driver on how stupid and iniquitous this 'new' idea of irradiation was. Good food didn't need irradiation, he told me, not knowing who I was. I sat in the back seat, agreeing (and smiling). And the third occasion was when I went into my corner grocery shop and saw a box of mushrooms, inscribed in loud letters 'Not irradiated'. I thought then that even if we lost the battle over legalizing the process, as we did, food culture had been altered in a small way; we had taken the political high ground which is what mattered in everyday consumer life. It helped that the campaign had never pitched its hopes or strategy on the legal battle anyway. The mass consciousness was always going to be more important.

The consumer as activist struggles daily to redefine the notion of progress and quality of life, to pursue happiness by consumption and to promote or create debate. Crucially, it is the consumer as activist who confronts consumption, explicitly seeking to alter its meaning and to redefine the cultural dynamic of goods by reintroducing the validity of the idea of needs and wants. Few movements apart from the feminist and gay movements have had a discernible effect in truly remoulding culture. And yet the consumer as activist seems to be the great absentee from many celebrations of contemporary consumer culture. This absence has left discussions on the subject seriously impoverished.

Conclusion

In this chapter we have looked at four waves of consumer activism. Each wave set out to make a contribution to the well-being of consumers. Each wave has also offered a new way of looking at the consumer, highlighting different dimensions of consumption and pointing to some of the hazards that line the paths of consumers. All four waves have left traces, ranging from little landmarks to important monuments which are scattered in the landscape of modern consumption.

The effectiveness of different consumer campaigns has varied. Reich (1981) has argued that moves to protect the consumer are sparked off by periods of business mergers, new systems of production and new consumer products. Tiemstra accounts for this by arguing that these are periods when business legitimacy suffers and concerns about its political accountability generate a suitable climate for campaigning. It is then that consumer activists can be most influential by articulating people's concerns and worries about business and government.

> When business legitimacy is at a low ebb, the agenda of the consumer movement has a great deal of popular political appeal, and politicians can enhance their personal popularity by identifying themselves with the movement's agenda. However, during times when business legitimacy is high, politicians can safely ignore or even oppose the consumerist agenda. (Tiemstra, 1992: 14)

Tiemstra argues that no consumer organization has been 'large enough, rich enough or even persuasive enough' to affect by itself the landscape of modern consumption. 'Their influence is always due to their ability to identify issues with mass political appeal' (Tiemstra, 1992: 8).

Tiemstra's attempt to reintroduce the consumer movement into the study of contemporary consumption is exceptional. He notes that the movement has been written out of consumer history and economic theory, a view which we endorse. The contribution of consumer activists in defining the consumer has been neither fully appreciated nor adequately analysed, although Nader as an individual phenomenon has attracted considerable attention in the USA (Bloom and Greyser, 1981; Gorey, 1975). Consumer activism has been singularly left out of virtually all cultural discussions of modern consumption; it has been addressed in mechanistic terms by economist analysts using terms like information cartels, monopsony and disregarding its cultural and political dimensions. Sociologists have shied away from exploring its standing as a social movement within late capitalism, as they have done with, say, feminism or gay liberation. Yet, the panorama, or, as some would say, the discourse of contemporary consumption would be very different without the contribution of consumer activists, who in their different ways have sought to remould the consciousness of consumers, to break away from the narrow conception of consumer interests, to redefine the meaning of the word information and to articulate and generate moral indignation against the worst excesses of the market. Above all, consumer activism has sought to define consumption as an area of human action which need not be individualistic, but can be organized, at least in a certain measure, according to collective principles. In all these ways, the influence of consumer activists is every bit as important as that of consumer-rebels, in establishing that consumption is an area of moral and political behaviour, not only in its implications but also in its motivation.

Consumer-activists, however, go far beyond the rebel both in the extent to which they are able to articulate their moral indignation and in the way they are able to channel it into organized action. Their efforts and their limited but significant successes, constitute a stubborn rejection of the anarchism of the market, by persistently stressing that right and wrong, damaging and beneficial, useless and useful, needs and wants are concepts which cannot be written out of consumption. The vast majority of consumers recognize in these terms their everyday experience much as postmodernists would like to deny them.

Yet, as we saw earlier, many activists acknowledge that consumer capitalism can redefine itself in ways which accommodate many of their demands. This may take the form of creating niche markets (for ethical or green products) or by accepting a degree of regulation as a necessity for its continuing legitimation. Some consumer-activists recognize this as an inevitable limitation of much reformist activity, which in no way annihilates its value or undermines its objectives. Their contribution lies in acting as the moral conscience of the existing system. Others, however, have moved beyond this, viewing reform as inadequate in stopping the ruinous path which consumer capitalism is pursuing. For them, the concept of the consumer must now be overcome itself, having become fatally flawed and compromised. Only by redefining themselves as citizens rather than as consumers and by acting accordingly, can individuals today individually and collectively recover some of the control which they have lost to the organizations and objects which now dominate their lives and through which they express themselves. Only by acting as citizens they can overcome the psychological dead-end to which consumerism, as the global ideology of the power block has led them.

Unlike the practices of activists engaged in day-to-day campaigning, often on single issues or local causes, the idea that today's consumer must be destroyed in order to be transcended by the citizen has not entered the general discourse on consumption yet. It is an idea, which strikes at the very heart of commodification; should it enter the general political and social discourse, consumer capitalism may not find it easy to accommodate, certainly not as easy as the demands for green, ethical or responsible consumption. Is the time not imminent when we may say farewell to the consumer at least as a figure of popular discourse, if not of academic discussions? In the past other figures (the peasant, the proletarian) came to prominence eventually to bow out of public discourse in the West. Is it possible that the consumer may be preparing him – or herself for a final bow? If the consumer is, in the UK National Consumer Council's definition, 'everybody in society in one part of their life: that is, as the purchaser or user of goods and services, whether privately or publicly supplied' (Whitworth, 1994: 16) now so ubiquitous that to talk of consumers doesn't add very much to understanding? If so, perhaps the consumer as a useful notion is already withering. Or is it possible that the consumer is about to metamorphose into a citizen? Or is this notion too about to disappear, submerged into the consumer?

10

The Consumer as Citizen

We are witnessing the swift debasement of the concept of 'citizen' – the person who actively participates in shaping society's destiny – to that of 'consumer', whose franchise has become his or her purchasing decisions.

Stuart Ewen (1992: 23)

In recent years, there has been a surprising re-emergence of interest in the idea of the citizen. Previously, the term had a rather quaint, old-fashioned ring to it; citizenship was what liberal political theorists referred to, civics was what children were taught in class. It is ironic, then, that just when the triumph of consumerism and the omnipotence of markets seemed destined to consign the notion of citizenship to the history textbooks, it found itself the object of a heated debate. The failure of liberalism or socialism to stage any effective opposition to the New Right agenda throughout the 1980s led groups of progressive intellectuals and commentators to return to the notion of citizenship as the joint basis for an effective, new platform of opposition (Andrews, 1990; Coote, 1992; Rustin, 1992). Many consumer activists, as we saw in the previous chapter, have also sought to proclaim the ideal of citizenship in contradistinction to the notion of the consumer, which they saw as too individualistic, restrictive, in short irrecoverably hijacked by the political Right. In this way, they have resurrected an older idea propounded by the founder of the UK's Consumers' Association and National Consumer Council, Michael Young, who had envisaged organized consumers as a new third force for the citizenry, alongside organized labour and organized capital and management. Even earlier in 1920, the co-operative theorist, Percy Redfern, had called on consumers to unite to

build a new social order – an order which may restore the primitive social unity, but now upon a world scale instead of within the narrow circle of the township and village. (1920: 42)

In the past the consumer has paid. In the future he and she together must live and act as citizens in the commonwealth of man. (1920: 57)

Yet almost as soon as the idea of citizenship re-emerged as the focus for progressive opposition in the late 1980s, attracting to it demands for freedom of information, written constitutional rights, electoral reform, and so on, the idea was seized by the New Right (Pirie, 1991) as a life-line to keep the Thatcherite project on course, even as it was beginning to come apart.

In this chapter, we examine the chronic tension which has existed between the idea of the consumer and that of the citizen, and assess whether the two represent conflicting tendencies or whether they can be brought closer together. We also examine whether one of them can usurp the other, or whether there remains a place for both of them in contemporary culture. Finally, we provide a provisional assessment on whether the concept of the citizen can form the basis of a co-ordinated opposition to consumer capitalism. We will see that the idea of citizenship is itself often commodified and corrupted by consumer capitalism and the political and ideological powers which underpin it. Yet, we shall also note that whenever a vocabulary of opposition and defiance is required it is as likely as not to proceed from the ideal of the citizen.

Citizens and consumers

We have no serious difficulty thinking of ourselves as consumers. Thinking of ourselves as citizens is more problematic, even for those of us who spent our childhood saluting the flag daily: 'In this society, citizenship is an archaic term. It is not part of the language of everyday life. Its value for understanding this life is not evident either' (Wexler, 1990: 166). Demands for citizenship and the right to vote might be high on the popular agenda in a country engaged in mass struggle for enfranchisement, such as South Africa during the five apartheid decades, but in the so-called mature democracies like the USA and Great Britain, the right to vote, let alone broader notions of citizenship have atrophied.

The idea of citizen implies mutuality and control as well as a balance of rights and duties which is neither evident nor especially attractive to us. Citizens are active members of communities, at once listened to, but also prepared to defer to the will of the majority. Citizens have to argue their views and engage with the views of others. In as much as they can make choices, citizens have a sense of superior responsibility. Choosing as a citizen leads to a very different evaluation of alternatives from choosing as a consumer. As a citizen, one must confront the implications of one's choices, their meaning and their moral value. The notion of citizenship has at its core a 'bond', as T.H. Marshall noted, 'a direct sense of community membership based on loyalty to a civilization which is a common possession' (Wexler, 1990: 169).

Consumers, on the other hand, need not be members of a community, nor do they have to act on its behalf. Consumers operate in impersonal markets, where they can make choices unburdened by guilt or social obligations. Both Marx and Simmel remarked on how the cash nexus dissolves social bonds, the former to criticize it as the root of alienation under capitalism, the latter to praise it as the liberation from the fetters of the gift economy (Marx, 1867/1967, 1972; Simmel, 1978).

The two ideas have very different pedigrees. The citizen, the foundation of Athenian democracy and reinvented and expanded by the American and French revolutions, implies an equality among citizens, even if it denies it to others, slaves, immigrants or refugees. It is essentially a political concept, defining individuals standing within a state and a community, according them rights and responsibilities. The citizen is an impersonation of what Philip Rieff called 'political man', the cultural ideal based on the notion that the good life, justice and happiness can be attained through political action, rather than through religious faith; the latter had been the recipe for salvation of political man's predecessor, the 'religious man' (Rieff, 1959, 1966). Common to both religious and political ideals was the presupposition that each individual is an organic part of a whole, unable to achieve full individuality and happiness except as a member of that whole. Where the ideal of the citizen dramatically deviated from that of the religious believer was in the inalienable rights of citizens to hold their own opinions and views. One can be a citizen while disagreeing and criticizing the government; this was a new form of freedom.

The consumer, on the other hand, originates in a very different ideal, referred to by Rieff as economic man, who seeks the good life in markets. Few variants of this ideal are as clear-cut as the Protestant Work Ethic, or, in the twentieth century, what we refer to as the Fordist deal (see Chapter 1: The Emergence of Contemporary Consumerism). Here individuals act as atoms, unencumbered by social responsibilities and duties, free of the obligation to account for their preferences and choices. They are never required to endure sacrifices for a superior goal, nor do their actions represent anybody other than themselves. They need not defer to any collective majority.

The idea of the citizen can become easily idealized, becoming the focus of nostalgia for a time when individuals were meant to be active members of political communities, and when economies where conceived as having national boundaries, when a vote created a political assembly which could control a national economy. However, if such a notion of citizenship implies control, commitment and bonding, it also carries since its earliest origins disturbing resonances of exclusion and discrimination. Non-citizens, stateless persons, immigrants, refugees, exiles, people without official papers and fixed addresses, vagrants, these are people who may be legitimately harassed, exploited and discriminated against in most so-cieties, especially those which place a high premium of citizenship. The outsider can be used as a mechanism of social division. Consumers, on the other hand, generally face no such discrimination, so long as they can afford to pay. Through money they may acquire a wide variety of things, including in many cases 'citizenship', the right to participate in a way of life, a dream.

How then is it possible that two ideas so different as citizen and consumer can become part of the same discourse? Two main avenues have led to this convergence. The Left, having lost faith in the consumer as the hero of right-wing economics has sought to enlarge the consumer into a responsible consumer, a socially-aware consumer, a consumer who thinks ahead and tempers his or her desires by social awareness, a consumer whose actions must be morally defensible and who must occasionally be prepared to sacrifice personal pleasure to communal well-being. In other words, the Left has stretched the idea of consumer in the direction of citizen. The organization Public Citizen and all the other organizations started by Nader have been prolific in campaigning and promoting the idea of the citizen and of consumers as citizens. So concerned was his team about the decline of meaningful US citizenship by the early 1990s that it produced a civics package for use in schools (Isaac, 1992). This profiled a number of key citizens' movements representing the rights of women, minorities, consumers, unions and environment. More importantly, the civics package took students through the options a citizen has for participating in civil society: whistle-blowing, pamphleteering, getting organized, arranging meetings, conducting research, legal action, direct action, becoming a shareholder activist, and so on. The book, to some extent, was a 'how to' and 'what' summary of much of Third and Fourth Wave consumer activism and was a classic statement, as Nader wrote in the Foreword, of 'practicing civics, becoming a skilled citizen, using one's skills to overcome apathy, ignorance, greed or abuses of power in society at all levels'. The message was that the only route to rebuilding citizenship from a consumer starting point was involvement with others.

The Right, on the other hand, has sought to incorporate the citizen into its image of the consumer by using the spurious concept of 'votes' and ballots. According to this argument, consumers vote in the marketplace in exactly the same way as citizens voted in the Athenian agora of old. The marketplace becomes a surrogate for political discourse or, in their view, incorporates political discourse rendering it redundant. The citizen is being redefined as a purchaser whose 'ballots . . . help create and maintain the trading areas, shopping centres, products, stores, and the like' (Dickinson and Hollander, 1991: 12). Buying becomes tantamount to voting, market surveys the nearest we have to a collective will (Ewen 1992:23). In this way, the more wealth or purchasing power the consumer has, the more 'votes' she or he gets.

So, when the idea of the citizen crops up in discussions of consumption, it assumes different meanings. Nowhere is this more clear than in discussions of television. Market enthusiasts want unregulated television where individuals choose to watch what ever they want. If they do not like a programme, they vote by switching to a different channel or by switching off. Public service advocates, on the other hand, believe that if individuals act merely as consumers, they end up with a profusion of virtually indistinct channels appealing to the lowest common denominator. Their choice is narrowed to minutiae (Brown, 1991). If, on the other hand, they act as citizens, they seek to control and regulate what is shown on their screens, voting for a particular range of options and stopping others. Ultimately, the citizens do not take markets as given but will seek to regulate them, control them and tame them. They seek to do so either through direct action and active participation, or indirectly, through the state. And this is where the state comes into discussions of citizens and contemporary consumption.

The dilution of the citizen? or resurrection?

The nature of the state, however, is furiously contested. On the Left, critics have long seen the state as the club of the ruling class, a mechanism for facilitating the interests of capital and oiling the wheels of commerce (Miliband, 1969; O'Connor, 1973; Poulantzas, 1975). Social democrats and liberals have taken a more accommodating position, arguing that the state can be used to ameliorate the conditions of the poor, notably through welfare, educational and health provisions (Beveridge, 1942). Conservatives of the older paternalist school did not deviate much from the idea of the state as safety-net, though they would draw a line between those deserving assistance and those not:

> [Conservatism] regards it as the duty of the modern State to ensure to the subject pure air and water, to see that his food is unadulterated, and to assist him to maintain himself and his family in sickness and old age. It lays it down as a cardinal principle that every citizen shall have a right, so far as is humanly possible, to a good education, open spaces, and healthy conditions of life. The modern State is the assurance company which assures these benefits to its citizens. (Bryant, 1929: 17)

Under the New Right, the state disowns such responsibilities. Throughout the 1980s (the Thatcher-Reagan years), they set out, first, to dismantle the welfare philosophy through privatization and contracting services to independent firms, and more recently, they have sought to redefine it (Osborne and Gaebler, 1992; Pirie, 1991), explicitly turning citizens into consumers (HM Government, 1991). According to this view, it is up to citizens as consumers to decide whether they want a service from the state, and what quality they are prepared to pay for. In simple terms, why bother voting for politicians to provide public parks and clean air, if the Chicago futures market will trade pollution permits and if parks can be supplied by Disneyland and others? Public space, from parks to pavements, is seen as an opportunity to sell, not to commune; it becomes a marketplace, not a social place (Worpole, 1992: 25–49, 104–7).

Twenty years into the New Right project, its critics draw upon three strands of analysis, broadly, sociological, economic and political. One strand argues that government has been taken over by totally unaccountable forces which corrupt the possibility of anyone having control, whether termed consumer or citizen (Greider, 1992). For both citizens and consumers, rights have become dependent upon wealth. For Bauman, the poor have been made to look like failed citizens who mishandled their exercise of choice and are now forced to accept the state's choices on their behalf (1988: 73). As Golding has said, 'to be poor is to endure conditional citizenship' (Lister, 1990: vii). The second strand of criticism asserts that the very idea that consumers or market forces can govern affairs of state is absurd and that a public sector, distinct from the private sector, has to be retained.

> The analogy between government and firms doesn't hold water. Since the public sector is not driven by the same profit motive – citizens' priorities are different

from stockholders' – it has no inherent reason to price its services more expensively. (Lynch and Makusen, 1993: 128)

The third strand has set out to reclaim the notion of citizenship from the clutches of the Right (Coote, 1992; Lister, 1990; Lynch and Makusen, 1993; Rustin, 1992; van Vucht Tijssen). This strand argues that the modern Anglo-American 'hands off' state with its individualistic and pro-business orientation marks the nadir of true citizenship. David Rieff views the US citizen as no more than a supermarket cultural browser: 'For better or worse (probably both), ours is a culture of consumerism and spectacle, of things and *not* ideas' (1993: 63).

Where does the consumer movement stand in all this? The consumer movement has been divided by the Right's attempt to redefine the citizen as consumer. The second wave value-for-money organizations generally support initiatives like John Major's *Citizen's Charter* and privatization with minor reservations (National Consumer Council, 1991). They believe that such moves will offer a better deal for consumers, raising the quality of service and widening the range of options available to them. Few can argue that before the wave of privatization, nationalized industries were perfect models of responsiveness, efficiency or consideration for the needs of their customers. In doing so, second wave organizations have implicitly acknowledged the argument of the New Right that the state is unable to conduct economic activity effectively, whether this amounts to running a transport network, a health service or an automobile manufacture (see, for example, Winward, 1994).

The third and fourth waves of consumer organizations, on the other hand, have been dismissive of both privatization and performance targets for the state sector (Lang, 1991). Privatization is seen as accelerating the dilution of citizenship, accentuating social equality and making social services contingent on the ability to pay. If the ideological principle of progressive taxation is on the verge of extinction, the idea that all citizens are entitled to certain services on an equal basis is also going by the board. Many third and fourth wave thinkers are disparaging of the New Right's efforts to resurrect an ideal of citizen, even as it fosters inequalities and divisions among the citizenry. These efforts are even more visible when seen against the tone of political and cultural discourse set by the mass media. The days of the agora, of reasoned debate and personal involvement have long been overtaken by the politics of the sound-bite, the image, the simulation and the passive evaluation of policies and politicians after the manner of soap-powders. Even governments genuinely committed to the ideal of citizenship, would find it hard to take independent political or economic action in an age of free trade, capital globalization and transnational institutions (Lang and Hines, 1993: 49; Nader, 1991).

The rest of this chapter explores further the arguments above through three important arenas, which are currently at the centre of political debate: privatization and sub-contracting of public services, information and advice, and the environmental impact of consumption.

Privatization and subcontracting

The privatization of state industries is one of the central arenas in which these arguments are currently being fought over. State industries were targeted by Thatcherism as inefficient, failing to give value for money to the customer and ripe for market discipline. Prior to that, certain consumer bodies had already argued the case for increased competition in public services (National Consumer Council, 1978, 1979). They found themselves overtaken by the Thatcher government, which went well beyond their recommendations and, in a wave of spectacular privatizations, sold off water, telephone, electricity, gas, the state airline and even public transport all to the private sector. The main opposition to these moves, outside party politics, came from unions and, occasionally, environmental groups which took a broader citizen's approach, expressing a series of concerns regarding standards, public health and safety implications, increased costs for low-income groups and lack of democratic accountability.

The consumer might in the short term benefit from competition, smarter packaging, greater choice, but even the consumer bodies expressed reservations about monitoring by independent regulators, financial redress, and so on (Locke, 1994a, 1994b). The citizen, on the other hand, stood to lose massively from these moves. Not only were a number of national assets taken away from them, but, subject to the market mechanism, unprofitable operations were run down. More importantly, these moves symbolized the ideological triumph of the Thatcherite creed that only free enterprise could run business efficiently and that all state-run enterprise was doomed to dip endlessly into the tax-payer's pocket. A service or a commodity which did not attract purchasers in the market, according to the Thatcherite logic, could be dispensed with. A wedge had been driven between citizen and consumer. Under the rhetoric of a share-owning democracy, the concept of the citizen was itself being privatized.

Another prong of the strategy to reduce citizens into consumers consisted of the introduction of compulsory competitive tendering for local authority services. Services such as street cleaning, school meals and direct labour organizations in building maintenance were all contracted out in the early 1980s (Whitfield, 1983). Subsequently in the 1990s, middle-class professional services such as architects, legal services and residential care homes were all contracted out too. What had previously been a nexus of national and local services regarded as integral parts of the state's support structure for the citizen, became markets. Integrated services were now internally split into purchasers and providers; as was seen in Chapter 2 (The Consumer as Chooser), this did not on the whole lead to an automatic shift of power in favour of the consumer, but the citizen was certainly lessened.

The introduction of a new language of 'empowerment', 'internal markets' and 'mixed economy of care' into public service organizations is significant. A service becomes a commodity, even as a hollow vocabulary of empowerment, choice and quality is rehearsed to justify it (Mather, 1991; Pirie,

1991). What the rhetoric of the consumer achieved beyond doubt was to put business in the driving seat, while constantly undermining the idea of citizens with rights and obligations. The buzz-word of empowerment, hijacked from minority right movements, was to provide both the coup de grace to the old notion of citizen and its banalization in the *Citizen's Charter*, a government initiative launched in 1991 promising certain 'rights' for customers of state services (HM Government, 1991). This was a misnomer and might have been more accurately described as a customers' charter for public services about to be privatized. Academic critics viewed it as 'an exercise in improving supplier responsiveness to customers but unaccompanied by any real shift in power to consumers' (Hambleton and Hoggett, 1993). Utilities were made to promise targets such as the length of delay before answering a phone, the percentage of trains arriving within a few minutes of the promised arrival time, the number of crime enquiries completed, and so on. Needless to say that these measures quickly became items of some scepticism with the public, the majority of whom have remained doubtful of the overall benefits from further privatization and contracting out.

Advice and information

The second issue which has highlighted the distance between older traditions of citizenship and its reinvention by the New Right has been the information required to operate effectively as a consumer in a marketplace. Consumer advocates are in agreement on this one. Since the earliest days of the consumer movement, they have argued for the value of information, notably product information and labelling, on the one hand, and general consumer education on areas like nutrition and health which then enables them to discriminate between products and to make good use of labelling information, on the other hand. As was seen in the previous chapter (see Chapter 9: The Consumer as Activist), one of their earliest arguments was that markets cannot operate as effective mechanisms against unscrupulous or inefficient suppliers, unless consumers have the requisite information. All strands of consumer activism have also been in agreement that it is essential for consumers to know their rights in front of the law (Cranston, 1984). In the UK, a national system of law centres, offering legal advice to consumers on a collective basis, started in the 1970s, borrowing heavily from the US experience, and proposed by the Society of Labour Lawyers (1968). The aim was to offer everybody access to the law, irrespective of their means to pay.

A separate scheme aimed at giving consumers information and advice emerged in the 1970s, the Consumers Advice Centres. These had been pioneered by the Consumers' Association, based on experience elsewhere in Europe. The aims of the centres were to offer pre-shopping advice to help people decide which product to purchase, as well as to assist them with complaints when purchases had gone wrong. In practice, people did not use the pre-shopping advice that much, but they did make extensive use of the complaint support schemes (National Consumer Council, 1977: 18–21). Some of the centres handled as many as 40,000 enquiries a year, no mean index of interest at a local level. By 1975 there were 75 in the country and they processed half a million complaints in a year. By 1977 there were 120 centres, 79 of which had been set up without central government help (Fulop, 1977: 22–3) Better evidence of consumers' thirst for support and information cannot be supplied than the success of this scheme. Yet one of the very first things that the new Thatcher Government did was to cut central government funds to the Consumers Advice Centres!

And what of information? Capitalist societies are not all the same. They have starkly contrasting cultures and notions of rights, community and individualism, in short, of citizenship (Hampden-Turner and Trompenaars, 1994). Freedom of information is a right in the USA, but not the UK (Delbridge and Smith, 1982: 28–39). Yet consumer activists have insisted that unless there is information about goods and services, inadequate goods will be left on the market, when with due information, they would not survive. The market alone cannot be left to discriminate between safe and unsafe products, such as medical drugs or food additives. Information, in the form of independent findings, is an essential prerequisite for consumer and citizen safety. And what was the solution of Thatcherism to this? To commodify information and advice, just as it encouraged the commodification of public services and of the idea of the citizen itself. If consumers want advice, was the argument, let them pay for it individually; there is no need for government to supply such information. Companies, watchdogs and, not least, consumer organizations themselves can do this very effectively. Consumer activists, on the other hand, argued that in the light of the massive resources devoted to advertising by capitalist organizations, state involvement and some funding is vitally needed to counter the vast inequality in resources companies put behind sales information for products (through advertising, marketing, and so on), compared with the resources available for consumer information and education (Loudon and Della Bitta, 1993: 29–78; Perry, 1994). The debate had become increasingly academic by the 1990s, when the last vestiges of consumer education in schools, in the form of domestic science teaching, was removed from the national curriculum in the 1994 (Lang and Baker, 1993).

Citizens, consumers and the environment

The environment is another key location from which to explore the differing outlooks between consumer and citizen. It also is a litmus test for distinguishing between the citizen as a mechanism for self-discipline and control, and the citizen as a vehicle for seeking to re-establish a deeper spirit of community and general welfare. The consumer's role in either damaging or protecting the environment is an issue which has generated considerable

rancour within the organized consumer movement, sections of which did not
see the environment as a consumer issue at all. Some of them went as far as
seeing environmental regulations as anti-consumer, a back door into
protectionism and, therefore, higher prices in the shops. 'The environment
is not a consumer issue' is a position which occasionally appears in consumer
circles. The older waves of the consumer movement were slow to integrate
even weak environmental criteria into their value-for-money assessments of
consumer goods.

Environmentalists, for their part, have since the late 1960s urged retailers
to cut down on packaging and shoppers to recycle or re-use where possible.
As a result, appeals to consumers to clean up their own backyard and use
their purchasing power to force industry to clean up its act have become part
of the cultural landscape. Jay Hair, then President of the National Wildlife
Federation, urged Americans to take ten practical steps if they wish to act as
citizens rather than consumers (Hair, 1989). These included actions such as
cutting down on trash, using cloth diapers (nappies), not leaving water
running needlessly, re-using grocery bags, planting a tree and using public
transport or car pools. Such encouragements to act responsibly, to consume
wisely and to think of the eco-sphere as one consumes seek to reintroduce a
citizen's ethic of social responsibility, which goes beyond the consumer's
narrow self-interest, countering the ethos of a throw-away society. What this
vision of planet-Earth citizenship lacks, however, is any wider notion of
social solidarity, civic debate, co-ordinated action or sacrifice. It individual-
izes the idea of citizenship, as if becoming a citizen is a matter of individual
choice alone. In this way, citizenship becomes a life-style, however
praiseworthy and necessary, which can easily degenerate into tokenism and
is hardly likely to alter the politics of consumption.

A more collective appeal to consumers as citizens resorts to communal
citizens' action to restrain the free market and introduce 'green' measures
through legislation or taxation, at international, national or local levels.
European environmental groups have turned to the European Union as the
state forum in which campaigns for the protection of the environment and
individual consumers could be debated and acted upon. It was at this forum
that measures such as the setting of standards for controlling pesticide
residues and the pollution of European beaches, as well as access to
environmental information and eco-labelling (such as labelling washing
machines or refrigerators for their energy efficiency) were debated. Some of
these debates went in the environmentalists' favour and some went against.
However, the significant matter is that European institutions emerged as an
important new terrain for citizenship.

Citizenship, at a local level, can go beyond choosing as an individual
whether to recycle the aluminium can of your soft drink or beer into acting in
concert with other citizens. In the German town of Kassel, citizens forced
the authorities to institute a local tax charged on fast food packaging, against
bitter legal opposition from well-known fast food companies and canned-
drink dispenser machine companies. The tax dramatically altered consumer

behaviour and also led to a reduction in packaging. Its success encouraged 500 other towns to follow suit (Tomforde, 1994). Such measures reaffirm the power of citizens to regulate consumption, even when this implies a reduction of choice for the individual consumer or costlier products. One is denied the option of choosing to pollute, just as one may on public health grounds be denied the right to spit on pavements.

The diverging outlooks of consumer and citizen over the environment is encapsulated in the notion of 'environmental space' or 'ecological footprints' (van Brakel and Buitenkamp, 1992; van Brakel and Zagema, 1994). This notion proposes that every consumer action leaves a 'footprint' on the ecological system and that every consumer takes up a certain amount of ecological space. By using a battery, by driving a car, by purchasing a computer, or by eating meat every day, contemporary Western consumers are leaving disproportionately large and deep imprints on the environment, in comparison with earlier generations and with the vast majority of the world's consumers. To achieve any goal of sustainable development, rich Northern consumers will have to reduce their consumption of the earth's resources. In the Netherlands, for instance, it has been calculated that consumers will have to reduce their freshwater usage by 30 per cent by the year 2010, and reduce their consumption of meat and milk (the production of which are notoriously heavy users of agricultural space and energy) if the drop in available Netherlands land per citizen is to be met without using other countries as 'hidden' supporters of supposed Netherlands' farming efficiency (van Brakel and Zagema, 1994: 18). With targets such as these emerging, some environmentalists have argued that Western consumption (including its consumer organizations) has become part of a new class system, in which the new ruling class, the 'consuming class' oppresses everybody else both materially and ideologically, consuming unequally while selling an impossible dream of happiness through consumption. Political economy in the twenty-first century will be dominated by this new class of dynamic and rich consumers, who unless they have a change of political heart and re-orient what they define as a good quality of life, will argue for a retention of their 'rights' to consume unequal shares of resources. Consumerism and citizenship, according to this view, are incompatible (Durning, 1992). Consumer capitalism, say these environmental thinkers, cannot continue at the current pace without meeting its nemesis – resources will run out, the eco-sphere will be irreparably damaged, and the choices of future generations severely curtailed to the point, say the more apocalyptic proponents of this view, at which life itself is threatened (see also Chapter 1: 'The Emergence of Contemporary Consumerism). Elite consumers have to do more than adopt a token 'green' product if a more just citizenship is to be available for all:

On the basis of massive borrowing and massive sales of national assets, Americans have been squandering their heritage and impoverishing their children. They have done so for the sake of present consumption, the enjoyment of shopping that accompanies it, and most of all as a way to postpone questioning the efficacy of free trade and continuous growth. (Daly and Cobb, 1990: 367)

From this perspective, the Western citizen's paramount duty is to alter and reduce consumption and to help change the rules, such as taxes and laws, to this end. Failure to do so would lead to what Meadows et al., authors of the pioneering *Limits to Growth* report in the 1970s, in a review 20 years later called 'overshoot', a style of living running beyond its limits (Meadows et al., 1992).

There can be little doubt that the efforts of environmentalists and the more radical elements of the consumer movement have played a part in the rediscovery of the citizen in recent years. However, is it possible for this idea to have any practical value in the modern world when politics itself threatens to collapse into an offshoot of consumption? 'The culture and entertainment industry has helped make politics a spectator sport. The pursuit of happiness now means amusement and diversion . . .' (Barnet and Cavanagh, 1994: 41). When politicians compete for votes through sound-bites and television commercials, and when political debate is conducted at the level of slogans, does not the idea of citizenship itself collapse too? When so many political decisions are taken outside the public's view, could it even be that the idea of citizenship has become a smoke-screen behind which green fundamentalists are pushing their own political agendas, as the ideologues of the free market sometimes claim? And could the idea of the European Union as a forum for the new citizenry not be laughed out of court by those who have sought to portray all European institutions as parapets on Bluebeard's bureaucratic castle? Finally, can it not be argued that behind the ideal of the European citizen, unelected civil servants and unaccountable politicians keep themselves in jobs by dreaming up unwarranted regulations and standards which tie up the hands of business and restrict the choice of European consumers? Second wave consumer groups in Europe, for example, persistently bemoan the quota system on imported cars which, they say, denies consumers the chance to purchase cheaper vehicles, a fine illustration of the clash of citizen and consumer outlooks (Locke, 1994b: 159–160).

The question of whether the battle over the citizen is worth fighting against the narrow self-interest of the consumer is not one that environmental groups and other progressive forces have resolved yet. Some are arguing that instead of setting up the citizen to fight the beast of consumerism, as a latter-day St George against the Dragon, a preferable strategy might be to tame the beast and redirect its powers. Why not combine an effective consumer education campaign about the environmental impact of consumption, for example, and tap its market potential at the same time? One application of this strategy was the initiative of Greenpeace Germany which saved an East German refrigerator plant from closure by the Treuhand by using it to produce a radically new environmentally-friendly product, called the Greenfreeze, which it successfully marketed to its membership. With one stroke, this assured first, the factory's future; second, it proved that refrigerators need not use ozone depleting CFCs; third, forced other mainstream manufacturers to produce similar models which they had previously denied was commercially possible; and fourth, offered a more benign technology for use in developing countries (Lang and Hines, 1993: 90–1). In this way, an environmental group turned green entrepreneur. Is this the spearhead of a new form of environmental consumerism or is it, too, doomed to be marginalized as yet another green niche in saturated markets? Hawken argues that this kind of action prefigures what he calls the 'restorative economy', arguing that if business thinks more about its waste and takes longer-term responsibility for products, not only will this be good for it, but it will allow buyers to become customers rather than consumers of the earth's resources (1993: 155–7). But the leap from present economics to future economics envisaged by Hawken or Daly and Cobb (1990: 355–75) and Lang and Hines (1993: 117–49) is daunting. The question of strategy for progressive social movements as to whether to champion the green consumer or the citizen remains open.

Conclusion

In this chapter, we have examined the battle which is being fought over the concept of the citizen. We have considered the efforts to present the consumer-as-citizen as a force which may potentially oppose contemporary Western consumerism, as well as those forces which seek to reduce the citizen to but another face of the consumer, like those investigated in other chapters of this book.

At the moment, the prospects for the citizen do not look good. Throughout the 1980s and 1990s, voters in Western countries have listened to appeals to act in more socially responsible ways. However, in the privacy of the ballot booth they have generally voted for governments which promise lower taxes and increased opportunities for individuals to spend their pay packets as they wish.

The flow of history in the West seems to be undermining the capacity of citizens to control their economies through the ballot box. Government in the global age and global marketplace is increasingly driven by large corporations and groupings of the powerful such as the G7 and OECD groups of rich countries. Power is exercised in transnational fora, such as GATT's new World Trade Organization, and through global institutions such as the World Bank and International Monetary Fund, founded in the mid-twentieth century, but hugely more powerful at its end.

Even if people wish to be citizens, the flow of economic history appears to offer them little choice but to be more or less socially aware consumers. This pessimistic assessment suggests that a majority of people may give strong backing to broader notions of civic responsibility in opinion polls, while voting against those who point out the consequences. As one commentator noted:

> Our collective hypocrisy about the state needs no encouragement. We already treat government spending as if it were gold from a magic sack hidden under the Bank of England, while treating attempts to tax us as confiscation, to be avoided by all means possible. (Marr, 1994)

At the moment the consumer-citizen appears as a timid figure at the borders of contemporary consumption. Embarrassed by the Right's attempts to embrace them or set them up as a bulwark against unwanted aliens, citizens feel uneasy amidst the din of modern advertising and the clamour of the mass media. Yet, citizens are figures who from time to time raise their voices, to the surprise of many. It is too early to assess their ultimate impact, but at the end of the twentieth century, all over the world citizen-like protests and demands for new rights, as well as the assertion of old ones, were heard in response to the economic restructuring and globalization of decision-making (see for examples, Council of Canadians, 1994; Korten, 1995). Some targeted governments and others business, seeking, for instance, to inject more 'transparency' into the process of granting companies charters of incorporation (Grossman and Adams, 1993). Whether to protect a piece of countryside from a proposed commercial development, or to stop the export of live animal stock (from becoming foreign consumers' cheap beefsteak or veal escalope) or to protest against the introduction of identity cards, citizens can make their presence felt, refusing to surrender to the rhetoricians of the New Right or to be consigned to history books.

It can be argued that today people make their presence felt as citizens only in marginal activities, which are themselves instantly trivialized and commodified by the mass media. The sacrifices of hunt saboteurs, environmental and nuclear protesters or animal activists are decoded as media stunts and attempts at sensation, devoid of suffering, commitment and moral force. No sooner do individuals discover in citizenship one of the last remaining defences against the rule of markets, than they also discover what a precarious defence it turns out to be. All the same, it is telling that whenever a vocabulary of organized and conscious opposition to consumer capitalism and its powerful accoutrements is required, citizenship, especially global citizenship, citizenship without frontiers, even if it is an assertion and celebration of the local, of the community, invariably appears on the agenda. It remains to be seen whether, under the force of things to come, the idea of citizen, redefined and reformulated, can form the basis of an alliance which mounts a serious challenge to consumer capitalism.

11

The Twilight of Consumerism

The world is too much with us; late and soon,
Getting and spending, we lay waste our prowess:
Little we see in nature that is ours;
We have given our hearts away, a sordid boon!

William Wordsworth

Few concepts have been claimed by so many interest groups, ideologies and academic traditions as that of the consumer. It is rare for an idea to have such diverse meanings as 'to consume'. As we have seen, economists, sociologists, social psychologists, cultural critics, postmodernists, Marxists, conservatives, advertisers, journalists, pop-semioticians, marketers and marketeers, historians of ideas, environmentalists and activists all come up with their 'own' visions and images. The consumer has become a cultural fetish.

This book has, from the beginning, brought together traditions which do not normally address each other enough. Each chapter of this book has critically assessed a core idea of who consumers are, how they behave, what drives them, what concerns them and how they see the world. Each one can be thought of as a landscape of consumption, highlighting different features and disguising others. We have disagreed with some, supported others, offered our own. We are not suggesting that contemporary consumption is the totality of these, nor do we recommend that readers should pick and choose which image they most or least identify with and discard the others. What we are suggesting is that each image represents a position within a contested terrain. It is what the French refer to as a *prise de position*, in other words an initial gambit on which one is prepared to place a stake.

Why has the consumer become such a hotly contested terrain, the point where so many contradictions of contemporary society converge? Why do so many claim it as their own and, if it is not, struggle to appropriate it? Why do so many political parties now claim to speak on his or her behalf? Why do so many different academic traditions seek to define the consumer, criticize the consumer or praise the consumer? At the outset of the book, we stated that numerous historical factors have contributed to raising the consumer to the first line of recent academic and political debates. These include the decline of the Protestant Work Ethic in the West, the ideological role of Western consumerism throughout the Cold War, the adoption of the consumer by the political Right which sought to redefine itself as the party of the consumer rather than just the party of business, as well as the emergence of new forms of mass communication and information.

Through the pages of this book we have established that much hinges on the consumer, whether for example, he or she is seen as sovereign (requiring no self-appointed spokespeople to defend his or her interests) or victim (easily manipulated and outwitted by the apparatuses of capital), explorer (thirsting after new experiences and meanings) or activist (campaigning on behalf of collective rights), communicator (using objects as bridges to relate to fellow humans) or rebel (using objects to express rejection and rage), identity-seeker (trying to find a real self in the objects which he or she consumes) or hedonist (concerned above all with personal pleasure). These are all attempts to frame the consumer, and, more often than not, to sell particular self-views to the consumers themselves, either by flattery, by cajoling, by moralizing, by seduction or by straight manipulation.

But while all these battles are raging above and around the heads and wallets of the consumer, people get on with their everyday lives, trying to make the best of them, whatever their lot, and also to make sense of them. It would be plausible and attractive to envisage consumers in this way, that is, as oblivious to the consternation they are causing to the chattering classes and discourse makers. At a stroke, this analysis would halt any systematic attempt to understand people's behaviour as reflexive, self-conscious consumers, leaving the terrain to those who have an interest in defining them in particular ways. Market researchers and opinion pollsters, for instance, would claim the consumer as theirs, but so too would consumer activists and political parties. We are profoundly opposed to ending our pursuit of the consumer in this fashion, by abandoning him or her to those who claim to speak on his or her behalf.

For better or for worse, many of us think of ourselves, at least part of the time, as consumers. Whether reading the consumer pages of newspapers, listening to exhortations from politicians or consumer organizations, visiting theme parks and supermarkets, or trying to stretch the family budget at the end of a week, we unavoidably have to confront ourselves as consumers, and make decisions as consumers. Why else do individuals become so preoccupied with what they buy, give and eat? Why do they seek advice, turning to the consumer agony aunts who fill the media? One cannot opt out of being a consumer, living in a non-consumer fashion, in a non-consumer landscape. Consumerism, in the diverse forms examined in this book, has become part of our daily reality.

Yet, this reality is currently threatened from a number of quarters – technological factors, globalization of production, environmental and psychological limitations, widening social inequalities and cultural fatigue. We began this book by suggesting that the modern consumer has to be understood in his or her relation to production, as the outcome of what we called the Fordist Deal. By this we meant the unwritten understanding that ever-increasing living standards and continuing employment would be the reward for accepting alienating work without excessive dissent. From birth, the modern consumer has been connected to the methods and politics of mass production, just as in a different way, earlier generations of consumers, too, had been dependent on production, harvests and warfare for their subsistence.

The Fordist bargain is currently being tested by the extraordinary capacity of modern production to shed its workforces or move at will across continents. Political economists talk of the emergence of two divisions of workers, the highly paid, knowledge-rich workers on the one hand, and the restricted, low paid, casualized, more menial workers, on the other hand. Whole nations are being consigned to core or peripheral status in the globalized economy. Regions vie with each other to court the attentions of passing transnational corporations. The world's economic map is being redrawn, with enormous implications for work, consumption and culture. This process even divides controllers of capital; some it suits, but others are threatened as the process contains the germs of the unmaking of the Fordist Deal, upon which the entire project of Western consumerism in the twentieth century was contingent. Jobless growth could accelerate concerns about the effects of inequalities on the social fabric.

The future: the vanishing consumer

Inequalities among consumers are already sharp, leaving substantial numbers of them window-shopping with only restricted opportunities to make a purchase and many, in the Third World, without even windows to window-shop. This is contributing to the fragmentation of consumers' experiences. It accounts, at least in part, for the diversity of images of the consumer pursued by intellectuals and cultural commentators. While some consumers, in the First as well as in the Third Worlds, may spend inordinate amounts of time deliberating whether to invest in a new swimming pool, a new yacht or a second home abroad, others have to choose between feeding their children or buying them a new pair of shoes. Given such social chasms, it is difficult to talk about all consumption and all consumers as coming under the same ethos or constraints, that is, as being uniform entities or acting as a unified force. We can now see why the fragmentation of images of consumption is itself a symptom of the malaise of contemporary consumerism. Under the accelerating influence of environmental factors, growing Third World anger, and increasing social fragmentation within the West's own backyard this malaise is likely to get worse.

The same fragmentation of the consumer may keep academics busy, since each tradition can claim the consumer for itself, exaggerating those features which fit its arguments, while blatantly disregarding the rest. But this stops them from recognizing the overall historical trend. Just as most Marxists were censorious about consumption, many cultural theorists have tended to celebrate it. Neither is adequate. We recognize that the fragmentation of consumption is itself a feature of contemporary society. But the matter does not rest there. The weakening of the Fordist Deal suggests to us that Western consumerism has entered a twilight phase. During the high noon of consumerism, its Golden Age, the face of the consumer was clear, as was the significance of his or her every movement. The pursuit of happiness through consumption seemed a plausible, if morally questionable, social and personal project. Today, this is far more problematic. The economic conditions have become fraught, the social inequalities have once again widened, insecurity is experienced across social classes, poverty and homelessness have resurfaced on a massive scale. Cultural fatigue threatens to overcome even the well-off. The brashness has been knocked off the consumer society. To many, experimenting with drugs may be more exciting than the wares of the fashion industry. Today, images of consumers, like those caught in surveillance cameras, are often ill-defined, their movements and motives unclear. Proponents of consumerism live in hope that tomorrow will see another bright day. We think that this vision is the product of wishful thinking, at least for the West.

A far more realistic picture is that casualization of work will be accompanied by casualization of consumption. Consumers will lead precarious and uneven existences, one day enjoying unexpected boons and the next sinking to bare subsistence. Precariousness, unevenness and fragmentation are likely to become more pronounced for ever-increasing sections of Western populations. Marginality will paradoxically become central. Our approach has suggested that a better understanding of future consumption can be gained through the notion of unmanageability. In a world where everyone claims the consumer for her- or himself, the consumer must now be deemed *unmanageable*, claimed by many, but controlled by few, least of all by consumers themselves. The notion of unmanageability seems to us to be entirely appropriate for an era where the capacity to plan must give way to opportunism. In a world where future labour is exhorted to be flexible, multiskilled, taking each day as it comes, what calculations can consumers make about the day after?

To retailers and producers of goods and services, this may not be a terminal difficulty. So long as a certain proportion of the population at any one time is in a position to consume, there will be markets. To increasing numbers of consumers, however, a future based on mortgages, careful husbanding of resources and long-term financial commitments will become problematic. Opportunism will feature on an ever-increasing scale.

This fragmentation and opportunism in consumption casts serious doubt on the aspirations of politicians who are currently hoping to appeal to consumers as a collective force or even as a new social class, pursuing common interests and applying uniform pressures. It also casts doubts on those voices currently calling for a more caring, community-based and home-orientated approach to consumption. 'Look inwards' is a nostalgic hark-back to a past era where people supposedly functioned in a stable domestic setting in settled households. We are surprised that such romantic nonsense is being considered as potentially a Big Idea for a new politics, which might even transcend the old Left–Right distinctions. We are not for one minute suggesting that people will cease to consume, that they will stop furnishing their houses, clothing their children and enjoying themselves. We do, however, think that such consumption will become increasingly spasmodic, ad hoc and reversible.

What then does the future hold? We are wary of making any more precise prognoses about the future shape of either consumption or the consumer. Market researchers and the agents of production endlessly pursue this Holy Grail, seeking to anticipate consumer trends on behalf of capital, which stands to gain massively from accurate predictions, coupled with investment in attempts to shape or tempt consumption to its benefit. The task of those who seek to anticipate trends is inevitably partisan, their goal to mould the future to their ends.

But planning a future for the consumer is one thing, delivering it is another. Even at the mundane level of anticipating what objects will be popular in the future, prognostication is fraught with danger. The history of consumption is full of dead-ends. Products that pundits were once sure would become objects of mass consumption and desire in the future now stand as quaint reminders of the pitfalls of futurology. In the 1960s, for instance, the merchants of tomorrow's world were offering us throw-away paper clothes, holidays on the moon, living in geodesic domes, eating food in tablet form, undertaking less work. In practice today, precious few houses are in dome form; there has been a meteoric rise in nutritional supplements but only in addition to more 'ordinary' food; no one has been to the moon almost since the first landings; mountains of paper are thrown away, but not having been worn on human bodies; and people who are in work often work harder and longer. The future of the 1960s failed to materialize, in more senses than one. Equally, we suspect, the future as envisaged by today's brave prognosticators has more to do with their own fantasies and wishes than future facts.

There is a disparity, however, between the fantasies of industrialists and retailers and those of consumers themselves. The former ever dream of managing consumers, while the latter's dreams make them ever un-manageable. The former seek to put their vision into practice; the latter subvert, refuse, accept, interpret, surrender or embrace, in the manner this book has explored. Consumers have proved that in spite of the best efforts to constrain, control and manipulate them, they can act in ways which are unpredictable, inconsistent and contradictory. If during the high noon of Fordism, consumers seemed temporarily to share visions and dreams, today, there is no single entity, the consumer. Consumers are divided by income, aspiration, culture. The more politicians, industry and consumer organizations try to manage consumers, the more unmanageable they seem to be. No wonder, wiser heads these days are wary of extrapolating future trends from current ones. One thing is certain, the consumer of tomorrow will not be the same as the consumer of today. The endlessly mutating meanings of 'the consumer' – now destroyer, now generator of waste, now creator – suggest that for all we know the consumer, in the senses we have explored in this book, may vanish altogether.

References

Aaker, David A. and Day, George S. (eds) (1982). *Consumerism: Search for the Consumer Interest*. New York: The Free Press.

Aaker, David A. and Biel, Alexander L. (eds) (1993). *Brand Equity and Advertising: Advertising's role in Building Strong Brands*. Hillsdale, NJ: Lawrence Erlbaum Associates.

Abercrombie, Nicholas (1994). Authority and consumer society. In Russell Keat, Nigel Whiteley and Nicholas Abercrombie (eds), *The Authority of the Consumer*. London: Routledge.

Abolafia, Mitchel and Biggart, Nicole (1992). Competitive systems: a sociological view. In Paul Ekins and Paul Max-Neef (eds), *Real-life Economics: Understanding Wealth Creation*. London: Routledge, 315–322.

Abrahams, P. (1994). The dye is cast by growth and costs. *The Financial Times*, 31 May.

Adams, Richard, Carruthers, Jane and Fisher, Charlie (1991). *Shopping for a Better World: a Quick and Easy Guide to Socially Responsible Shopping*. London: Kogan Page.

Allain, Annelies (1991). Breastfeeding is politics: a personal view of the international baby milk campaign. *The Ecologist*, 21, 5, September/October, 206–13.

Anderson, B. (1983). *Imagined Communities*. London: Verso.

Anderton, Alain G. (1991). *Economics*. Ormskirk: Causeway Press.

Andreasen, Alan R. (1982). The differing nature of consumerism in the ghetto. In David A Aaker and George S. Day (eds), *Consumerism*, 4th edn. New York: Free Press, 96–107.

Andrews, G. (ed.) (1990). *Citizenship*. London: Lawrence and Wishart

Anthias, F. (1992). Connecting race and ethnic phenomena. *Sociology*, 26, 3, 421–38.

Armistead, Nigel (1974). *Reconstructing Social Psychology*. Harmondsworth: Penguin Education.

Aron, Raymond (1967). *18 Lectures on Industrial Society*. London: Weidenfeld and Nicolson.

Balls, Edward and Gregg, Paul (1993). *Work and Welfare: Tackling the Jobs Deficit*. London: Institute for Public Policy Research.

Barker, I. (1991). Purchasing for people. *Health Services Management*, 87, 5, October, 212–15.

Barker, Paul (1994). Is Which? still best buy? *The Times*, 8 June, 15.

Barnet, Richard and Cavanagh, John (1994). *Global Dreams*. New York: Simon and Schuster.

Barratt Brown, Michael, (1993). *Fair Trade: Reform and Realities in the International Trading System*. Zed Press. London.

Barthes, Roland (1973). *Mythologies*. London: Paladin Books.

Barwise, Patrick (1994). *Children, Advertising, and Nutrition, A commentary on the 1993 National Food Alliance report Children: Advertisers Dream, Nutrition Nightmare?* The Advertising Association. London, January.

Bateson, Gregory (1972). *Steps towards an Ecology of Mind*. London: Intertext Books.

Baudrillard, Jean (1968/1988). The system of objects. In Mark Poster (ed.), *Jean Baudrillard: Selected Writings*. Cambridge: Polity Press.

Baudrillard, Jean (1970/1988). Consumer society. In Mark Poster (ed.), *Jean Baudrillard: Selected Writings*. Cambridge: Polity Press.

Baudrillard, Jean (1972/1988). For a critique of the political economy of the sign. In Mark Poster (ed.), *Jean Baudrillard: Selected Writings*. Cambridge: Polity Press.

Baudrillard, Jean (1983a). *In the Shadow of the Silent Majorities*. New York: Semiotext(e).

Baudrillard, Jean (1983b). *Simulations*. New York: Semiotext(e).

Bauman, Zygmunt (1988). *Freedom*. Milton Keynes: Open University Press.

Bauman, Zygmunt (1992). *Intimations of Postmodernity*. London: Routledge.

Baumeister, Roy F. (1986). *Identity: Cultural Change and the Struggle for Self.* Oxford: Oxford University Press

Becker, E. (1962). *The Birth and Death of Meaning.* Harmondsworth: Penguin.

Beishon, John (1994). Consumers and power. In Robin John (ed.), *The Consumer Revolution: Redressing the Balance.* London: Hodder and Stoughton. 1–11.

Belk, Russell W. (1979). Gift giving behaviour. *Research in Marketing*, 2, 95–126.

Belk, Russell W. (1982). Gift giving behaviour. *Research in Marketing*, 2, 95–126.

Belk, Russell W. (1988). Possessions and the extended self. *Journal of Consumer Research*, 15/2, 139–168.

Bell, Daniel (1976). *The Cultural Contradications of Capitalism.* London: Heinemann.

Bello, Walden and Rosenfeld, Stephanie (1992). *Dragons in Distress: Asia's Miracle Economies in Crisis.* San Francisco: Food First/Institute for Food and Development Policy.

Benson, John (1994). *The Rise of Consumer Society in Britain 1880–1980.* London: Longman.

Berger, Peter L. and Luckmann Thomas (1967). *The Social Construction of Reality: A Treatise in the Sociology of Knowledge.* Harmondsworth: Penguin.

Best, Arthur (1981). *When Consumers Complain.* New York: Columbia University Press.

Bettman, James R. (1979). *An Information Processing Theory of Consumer Choice.* Reading, MA: Addison-Wesley.

Beveridge, Sir William (1942). *Social Insurance and Allied Services,* Cmd 6404. London: HMSO.

BEUC (1994). *Consumer Guarantees and After-Sales Services*, report and press release, 18 July 1994, Brussels: Bureau Européen des Unions de Consommateurs.

Bingham, Lord (1992). *The Inquiry into the Supervision of The Bank of Credit and Commerce International* (the Bingham Report), HC 198. London: HMSO.

Birchall, Johnston (1994). *Co-op: the People's Business.* Manchester: Manchester University Press.

Blackwell, Trevor and Seabrook, Jeremy (1985). *A World Still to Win: the Reconstruction of the Post-War Working Class.* London: Faber and Faber.

Bloom, Paul N. and Greyser, Stephen A. (1981). *Exploring the Future of Consumerism.* Cambridge, MA: Marketing Science Institute (USA). Research Program, July 1981.

Bloom, Paul N. and Stern, Louis W. (1978). Consumerism in the year 2000: the emergence of anti-industrialism. In Norman Kangun and Lee Richardson (eds), *Consumerism: New Challenges for Marketing.* Chicago: American Marketing Association.

Board of Trade (1962). Final Report of the Committee on Consumer Protection (the Molony Committee). Cmnd 1781. London: HMSO.

Bocock, Robert (1993). *Consumption.* London: Routledge.

Booth, Eric (1994). Linking farmers and consumers. *Living Earth and Food Magazine* 3(24), 8–10.

Bourdieu, Pierre (1979). *Outline of a Theory of Practice.* Cambridge: Cambridge University Press.

Bourdieu, Pierre (1984). *Distinction: A Social Critique of the Judgement of Taste.* London: Routledge.

Brandt, W. (Chair) (1980). *North–South: A Programme for Survival.* London: Pan Books.

Brewer J. and Porter, R. (1993). *Consumption and the World of Goods.* London: Routledge.

Brimelow, Peter and Spencer, Leslie (1990). Ralph Nader, Inc. *Forbes*, 146, no. 6, 17 September, 117–29.

Britt, Steuart Henderson (ed.) (1966). *Consumer Behavior and the Behavioral Sciences: Theories and Applications.* New York: J. Wiley.

Britt, Steuart Henderson (ed.) (1970). *Psychological Experiments in Consumer Behavior.* New York: J. Wiley.

Brown, Donna M., Cameron, Bruce A. and Meyer, Sonya S. (1993). A survey of commercial laundry detergents – how effective are they? Part 1: powders. *Journal of Consumer Studies and Home Economics* 17, 145–52.

Brown, D.H. (1991). Citizens or consumers: US reactions to the European Community's Directive on Television. *Critical Studies in Mass Communication* 8, 1–12.

Brown, R.L. (1958). Wrapper influence on the perception of freshness in bread. *Journal of Applied Psychology*, 42, 257–60.

Brunner, Eric (1988). Bovine Somototropin: A Product In Search of a Market. London Food Commission.

Bryant, Arthur (1929). *The Spirit of Conservatism*. London: Methuen.

Buckley, N. (1994). UK Retailers hit by £2bn cost of crime last year. *The Financial Times*, 19 January 1.

Bull, David (1982). *A Growing Problem: Pesticides and the Third World Poor*. Oxford: Oxfam.

Burnett, John (1966/1979). *Plenty and Want: A Social History of Diet in England from 1815 to the Present Day*. London: Scolar Press.

Burnett, John (1969). *A History of the Cost of Living*. Harmondsworth: Penguin.

Burton, S. and Babin, L.A. (1989). Decision-making helps make the sale. *The Journal of Consumer Marketing* 6, Spring, 2, 15–25.

Cairncross, Frances (1991). *Costing the Earth*. London: Business Books and The Economist Books.

Cameron, Bruce A., Brown, Donna M. and Meyer, Sonya S. (1993). A Survey of commercial laundry detergents – how effective are they? Part ll: liquids. *Journal of Consumer Studies and Home Economics* 17, 267–73.

Campbell, Colin, (1987). *The Romantic Ethic and the Spirit of Modern Consumerism*. Oxford: Macmillan.

Camus, Albert (1971). *The Rebel*. Harmondsworth: Penguin.

Carruthers, Ian and Holland, Patsy (1991). Quality assurance for the individual. *International Journal of Health Care Quality Assurance* 4, 2, 9–17.

Carter, M. (1994). Advertising's lost generation. *The Guardian*, 2 May.

Cavanagh, John and Broad, Robin (1994). Understanding North–South Political Economy in the 1990s. Paper to International Forum on Globalization. Washington DC: Institute for Policy Studies.

Chase, Stuart (1927). *Your Money's Worth: A Study in the Waste of the Consumer's Dollar*. New York: The Macmillan Company.

Chaudhuri, S. and Ravallion, M. (1994). How well do static indicators identify the chronically poor? *Journal of Public Economics*, 53, 3, 367–94.

Chesterfield Evans, A. (1987). Confessions of a Simple Surgeon, Video tape. Sydney: Technical and Further Education Association (TAFE).

Clammer, John (1992). Aesthetics of the self: shopping and social being in contemporary Japan. In Rob Shields (ed.), *Lifestyle Shopping: The Subject of Consumption*. London: Routledge.

Cole, Nicola (1994). Protect your homestead from cowboy builders. *The Guardian*, 27 August, 31.

Commission of the European Communities, (1993). *Growth, Competitiveness, Employment: the Challenges and Ways Forward into the 21st Century*. White Paper. Brussels/Luxembourg: Bulletin of the European Community, Supplement 6/93.

Consumers Union (nd). *The Early Years Remembered*. Yonkers: Consumers Union.

Cook, W. (1994). In on the joke of a funny game. *The Guardian*, 2 May.

Co-op Union (1994). *Information Pack: Co-operation 150*. Manchester: Co-operative Union.

Coote, Anna (1992). *The Welfare of Citizens*. London: Rivers Oram.

Cornia, G.A. (1994). Poverty, food consumption, and nutrition during the transition to the market-economy in Eastern Europe. *American Economic Review*. 84, 2, 297–302.

Council of Canadians (1994). *The Citizens' Agenda for Canada*. Working Document, Annual General Meeting, 14-16 October. Ottowa: Council of Canadians.

Coupey, E. and Jung, K. (1993). *Influences of Category Structure on Brand Positioning and Choice*. University of Illinois, College of Commerce and Business Administration, Faculty Working Paper, April 1993.

Cranston, Ross (1979). *Regulating Business*. London: Macmillan.

Cranston, Ross, (1984). *Consumers and the Law*, 2nd edn. London: Weidenfeld and Nicolson.

Crawford, Robert (1977). You are dangerous to your health: the ideology and politics of victim blaming. *International Journal of Health Services* 7, 4, 663–80.

Csikszentmihalyi, M. and Roschberg-Halton, E. (1981). *The Meaning of Things*. Cambridge: Cambridge University Press.

Culler, Jonathan (1981). *The Pursuit of Signs: Semiotics, Literature, Deconstruction*. London: Routledge.

Cunliffe, Vanessa, Gee, Richard and Ainsworth, Paul (1988). An investigation into some aspects of the efficiency of low-temperature laundering. *Journal of Consumer Studies and Home Economics* 12, 95–106.

Daly, Herman E. and Cobb, John B. (1990). *For the Common Good: Redirecting the Economy towards the Community, the Environment and a Sustainable Future*. London: Green Print.

DaSilva, F.B. and Faught, J. (1982). Nostalgia: a sphere and process of contemporary ideology. *Qualitative Sociology*, 5, 1, 47–61.

Davidson, Ann (1992). *International Trade and the Consumer: Growing out of Poverty – The International Consumer Interest in World Trade*. London: National Consumer Council.

Davidson, Martin P. (1992). *The Consumerist Manifesto: Advertising in Postmodern Times*. London: Routledge.

de Certeau, Michel (1984). *The Practice of Everyday Life*. Berkeley, CA: University of California Press.

de Tocqueville, Alexis (1956 (1835, 1840)). *Democracy in America*. New York: Mentor.

Deaton, Angus (1992). *Understanding Consumption*. Oxford: Clarendon Press.

Deaton, Angus and Muellbauer, John (1980). *Economics and Consumer Behavior*. Cambridge: Cambridge University Press.

Deighton, J., Henderson, C.M. and Neslin, S.A. (1994). The effects of advertising on brand switching and repeat purchasing. *Journal of Marketing Research*, 31, 1, February, 28–44.

Delbridge, Rosemary and Smith, Martin (eds) (1982). *Consuming Secrets: How Official Secrecy Affects Everyday Life in Britain*. London: Burnett Books.

Delhausse, B., Luttgens, A. and Perelman, S. (1993). Comparing measures of poverty and relative deprivation – an example for Belgium. *Journal of Population Economics*, 6, 1, 83–102.

Dibb, Susan E. (1993). *Children: Advertisers Dream, Nutrition Nightmare?* London: National Food Alliance.

Dickenson, Nicole (1993). Management (Marketing and Advertising). Catering for the ethical shopper: a look into a growing consumer trend. *The Financial Times*, 15 April.

Dickinson, Roger and Hollander, Stanley C. (1991). Consumer votes. *Journal of Business Research*, 23, 1, 9–20.

Dinham, Barbara (1993). *The Pesticide Hazard*. London: Zed Books.

Dittmar, Helga (1992). *The Social Psychology of Material Possessions*. Hemel Hempstead: Harvester Wheatsheaf.

Douglas, Mary (1972). Deciphering a meal. First published in *Daedalus*, 101: 61–82. Reprinted in M. Douglas (1975), *Implicit Meanings: Essays in Anthropology*. London: Routledge.

Douglas, Mary (1982). *In the Active Voice*. London: Routledge.

Douglas, Mary and Isherwood, Baron (1978). *The World of Goods: Towards an Anthropology of Consumption*. London: Allen Lane.

Doyal, Len and Gough, Ian (1991). *A Theory of Human Need*. London: Macmillan.

Durning, Alan Thein (1992). *How Much is Enough?* London: Earthscan.

ECRA (1993). Consumerism and happiness. *Ethical Consumer*, 27, 11–12.

ECRA (1994). Culture jamming. *Ethical Consumer*, 29, 20–1.

Ehrenreich, Barbara (1994). Smoke signals of defiance. *The Guardian*, 19 March.

Ekins, Paul (1992). Towards a progressive market. In Paul Ekins and Manfred Max-Neef (eds), *Real-life Economics: Understanding Wealth Creation*. Routledge. London and New York.

Ekins, Paul, Hillman, Meyer and Hutchison, Robert (1992). *Wealth Beyond Measure: An atlas of new economics*. London: Gaia.

Elkington, John and Hailes, Julia (1988). *The Green Consumer Guide*. London: Victor Gollancz.

Engel, James F., Blackwell, Roger D. and Miniard, Paul W. (1990). *Consumer Behavior*, 6th edn. Orlando, Florida: Dryden Press (Holt, Rinehart and Winston).

Erikson, Erik H. (1968). *Identity: Youth and Crisis*. London: Faber and Faber.

Ethical Consumer, (1993). *The Ethical Consumer Guide to Everyday Shopping.* Manchester: Ethical Consumer Research Association.

Ethical Consumer (1994). Special Anti-Consumerism Issue, No. 27.

Evans, Phillip (1994). *Unpacking the GATT: A Step by Step Guide to the Uruguay Round.* London: International Organization of Consumers Unions.

Evans-Pritchard, E.E., (1940). *The Nuer: A Description of the Modes of Livelihood and Political Institutions of a Nilotic People.* London: Oxford University Press.

Ewen, Stuart (1990). Marketing dreams: the political elements of style. In Alan Tomlinson (ed.), *Consumption, Identity and Style: Marketing, Meanings and the Packaging of Pleasure.* London: Routledge.

Ewen, Stuart (1992). From citizen to consumer? *Intermedia,* 20, 3, 22–3.

Fairlie, Simon (1992). Long distance, short life: why big business favours recycling. *The Ecologist,* 22, 6, November/December, 276–83.

Featherstone, Mike (ed.) (1990). *Nationalism, Globalization and Modernity.* London: Sage.

Featherstone, Mike (1991). *Consumer culture and Postmodernism.* London: Sage.

Fernandez Kelly, Maria Patricia (1994). Making sense of gender in the world economy: focus on Latin America. *Organization,* 1, 2, 249–275.

Fernstrom, Meredith M. (1984). *Consumerism: Implications and Opportunities for Financial Services.* US: American Express Company.

Festing, Harriet (1993). Is there life after supermarkets? *New Economics,* 28, Winter, 8–9.

Financial Times (1994). Full-time worker numbers reduced, 7 July.

Firat, A. Fuat (1992). Fragmentations in the postmodern. *Advances in Consumer Research,* 19, 203–6.

Fiske, John (1987). *Television Culture.* London: Methuen.

Fiske, John (1989). *Understanding Popular Culture.* London: Unwin Hyman.

Fleishman, Edwin A. (1951). An experimental consumer panel technique. *Journal of Applied Psychology,* 35, 133–5.

Fleishman, Edwin A. (ed.) (1967). *Studies in Personnel and Industrial Psychology.* Homewood, Il: The Dorsey Press.

Forbes, J.D. (1987). *The Consumer Interest.* Beckenham. Croom Helm.

Forman, A.M. and Sriram, V. (1991). The depersonalization of retailing. *Journal of Retailing,* 67, 2, Summer, 226–44.

Foxall, Gordon R. (1977). *Consumer Behaviour: A Practical Guide.* Corbridge, Northumberland: Retail and Planning Associates.

Frean, A. (1994). Boasting thief draws record TV audience. *The Times,* 18 February, 9.

Freud, Sigmund (1920). *Beyond the Pleasure Principle.* Standard edition. Vol. 18. London: Hogarth.

Freud, Sigmund (1914). *On Narcissism,* Standard Edition, Vol. 14. London: Hogarth.

Freud, Sigmund, (1921). *Group Psychology and the Analysis of the Ego,* Standard Edition. London: Hogarth.

Freud, Sigmund, (1930). *Civilizations and its Discontents,* Standard Edition. London: Hogarth.

Friedman, Milton (1985). Consumer boycotts in the United States, 1970–80: contemporary events in historical perspective. *Journal of Consumer Affairs,* 19, 1, 96–117.

Friedman, Milton and Friedman, Rose D. (1980). *Free to Choose.* London: Secker and Warburg.

Fritsch, Albert J., (1974). *The Contrasumers: A Citizen's Guide to Resource Conservation.* New York: Praeger.

Fromm, E. (1942). *Fear of Freedom.* London: Routledge and Kegan Paul

Fukuyama, Francis (1992). *The End of History and the Last Man.* Harmondsworth: Penguin.

Fulop, Christina (1977). *The Consumer Movement and The Consumer.* London: Advertising Association, Research Studies in Advertising, no.10.

Gabriel, Yiannis (1982). Freud, Rieff and the critique of American culture. *Psychoanalytic Review,* 69/3, 341–66.

Gabriel, Yiannis (1983). *Freud and Society.* London: Routledge.

Gabriel, Yiannis (1984a). *The Law as an Instrument of State Intervention in Industrial Relations*. London: Thames Polytechnic Business Paper no 3.

Gabriel, Yiannis (1984b). A psychoanalytic contribution to the sociology of suffering. *International Review of Psychoanalysis*. 11, 467–80.

Gabriel, Yiannis (1991). Organizations and their discontents: a psychoanalytic contribution to the study of corporate culture. *Journal of Applied Behavioural Science*, 27, 318–36.

Gabriel, Yiannis (1993). Organizational nostalgia: reflections on The Golden Age. In Stephen Fineman (ed.), *Emotion in Organizations*. London: Sage.

Gabriel, Yiannis, (1995). The unmanaged organization. *Organization Studies*, 16, 3, 481-506.

Galbraith, John Kenneth (1967). *The New Industrial State*. New York: Signet.

Galbraith, John Kenneth (1974). *Economics and the Public Purpose*. London: Andre Deutsch.

Galbraith, John Kenneth (1979). *The Affluent Society*. Harmondsworth: Penguin.

Gane, M. (1993). *Baudrillard Live: Selected Interviews*. London: Routledge.

Gardner, Carl and Sheppard, Julie (1989). *Consuming Passions*. London: Unwin.

Garnett, Dennis E. (1987). The Effectiveness of marketing policy boycotts: environment opposition to marketing. *Journal of Marketing*, 51, 46–57.

Gelb, B.D. (1992). Why rich brands get richer. *Business Horizons*, 35, 2, September/October, 43–47.

George, Susan (1988). *A Fate Worse than Debt*. Harmondsworth: Penguin.

George, Susan (1992). *The Debt Boomerang: How Third World Debt Harms Us All*. London: Pluto.

Gershuny, Jonathan (1978). *After Industrial Society? The Emerging Self-service Economy*. London: Macmillan.

Gershuny, Jonathan (1988). Lifestyle, innovation and the future of work. *International Journal of Development Banking*, 6, 1, January, 65–72.

Gershuny, Jonathan (1989). Technical change and the work/leisure balance: a new system of socio-economic accounts. In A. Silberston (ed.), *Technology and Economic Progress*. London: Macmillan, 181–215.

Gershuny, Jonathan, (1992). Are we running out of time? *Futures*, January/February, 3–22.

Giddens, A. (1991). *Modernity and Self-Identity*. Cambridge: Polity Press.

Ginzburg, C. (1980). Morelli, Freud and Sherlock Holmes: clues and scientific method. *History Workshop*, 9, 5–36.

Goffman, E. (1959). *The Presentation of Self in Everyday Life*. Garden City, NJ. : Anchor.

Goldsmith, Edward, Allen, Robert Allaby, Michael, Davoll, John and Lawrence, Sam (1972). A blueprint for survival. *The Ecologist*, 2, 1, January, 1–43.

Goldsmith, James (1994). *The Trap*. London: Macmillan.

Gorey, Hays (1975). *Nader and The Power of Everyman*. New York: Grosset and Dunlap.

Gott, Richard (1993). *Land Without Evil*. London: Verso.

Goulart, Ron (1970). *Assault on Childhood*. London: Victor Gollancz.

Gray, John (1994a). *Beyond the New Right: Markets, Government and the Common Environment*. London and New York: Routledge.

Gray, John (1994b). *The Undoing of Conservatism*. London: Social Market Foundation.

Greider, William (1992). *Who will Tell the People?: The Betrayal of American Democracy*. New York: Simon and Schuster.

Greyser, S.A. and Diamond, S.L. (1983). U.S. Consumers' view the marketplace, *Journal of Consumer Policy* 6, 3-18.

Grossman, Richard L. and Adams, Frank T. (1993). *Taking Care of Business: Citizenship and the Charter of Incorporation*. Cambridge, MA: Charter Ink.

Gussow, Joan Dye (1991). *Chicken Little, Tomato Sauce and Agriculture: Who will Produce Tomorrow's Food?* New York: The Bootstrap Press.

Guzzardi, Jr, Walter (1982). The mindless pursuit of safety, In David A. Aaker and George S. Day (eds), *Consumerism*, 4th Ed. New York: Free Press, 363–75.

H.M. Government (1991). *The Citizen's Charter*. White Paper, July 1991, Cmnd 1599. London: HMSO.

H.M. Treasury (1993). *Financial Statements and Budget Report 1994–95*. London: HMSO.

Hair, Jay D. (1989). Changing from 'Consumers' to citizens. *EPA Journal*, 15, 4, July/ August, 37–39.

Hall, Stuart (1988). New times. *Marxism Today*, October, 24.

Hall, Stuart (1989). New ethnicities. Black film, Black cinema. London: *ICA Documents*, 27–31.

Hall, Stuart (1991). Brave new world. *Socialist Review*, 21, 57–64.

Hall, Stuart and Jacques, Martin (eds) (1989). *New Times*. London: Lawrence and Wishart.

Hambleton, R. (1988). Consumerism, decentralization, and local democracy. *Public Administration*, 66, 2, Summer, 125–48.

Hambleton, Robin and Hoggett, Paul (1993). Rethinking consumerism in public services. *Consumer Policy Review*, 3, 2, 103–11.

Hampden-Turner, Charles and Trompenaars, Fons (1994). *The Seven Cultures of Capitalism*. London: Piatkus.

Handy, Charles (1994). *The Empty Raincoat: Making Sense of the Future*. London: Hutchinson.

Harrison, Paul (1992). *The Third Revolution: Environment, Population and a Sustainable World*. London: Taurus.

Harvey, David (1990). *The Condition of Postmodernity: An Enquiry into the Origins of Cultural Change*. Cambridge, MA and Oxford: Blackwell.

Harvey, David (1991). Flexibility: threat or opportunity? *Socialist Review*, 21, 65–78.

Hawken, Paul (1993). *The Ecology of Commerce: A Declaration of Sustainability*. New York: HarperBusiness.

Hennessey, Peter (1993). *Never Again: Britain 1945–1951*. London: Vintage.

Herrmann, Robert O. (1982). The consumer movement in historical perspective. In David A. Aaker and George S. Day (eds), *Consumerism: Search for the Consumer Interest*. New York: Free Press, 23–32.

Herrmann, Robert O. (1993). The tactics of consumer resistance: group action and marketplace exit. *Advances in Consumer Research*, 20, 130–4.

Hetherington, Kevin (1992). Stonehenge and its festival: spaces of consumption. In Rob Shields (ed.), *Lifestyle Shopping: The Subject of Consumption*. London: Routledge.

Hewitt, J. (1984). *Self and Society: A Symbolic Interactionist Social Psychology*, 3rd edn. Boston, MA: Allyn and Bacon.

Hewitt, Patricia (1993). *About Time: The Revolution in Work and Family Life*. London: Rivers Oram Press.

Himmelstein, D. and Woolhandler, S. (1986). Costs without benefits: administrative waste in US health care. *New England Journal of Medicine*, 314, (7, 13 February). 41–5.

Hines, Colin (1976). *Food Co-ops: How to Save Money by Getting Together and Buying in Bulk*. London: Friends of the Earth

Hirsch, Joachim (1991) Fordism and post-Fordism: the present social crisis and its consequences. In W. Bonefeld and J. Holloway (eds), *Post-Fordism and Social Form*. London: Macmillan.

Hobsbawm, E. (1983). Inventing traditions. In E. Hobsbawm (ed.), *The Invention of Tradition*. Cambridge: Cambridge University Press.

Hobsbawm, E. (1994). *Age of Extremes: The Short Twentieth Century*. London: Michael Joseph.

Holyoake, G. (1872). *The History of Co-operation in Rochdale*. London: Trubner and Co.

Homer (1974). *The Iliad*. Oxford: Oxford University Press.

Homer (1988). *The Odyssey*. Harmondsworth: Penguin.

Horkheimer, M. and Adorno, T. (1972). *The Dialectics of Enlightenment*. New York: Herder

Hull, Clark L. (1964). *A Behaviour System*. New York: Science Editions (John Wiley & Sons).

Hutton, Will (1995). *The State We're In*. London: Jonathan Cape.

Iacocca, Lee (1984). *Iacocca: An Autobiography*. London: Bantam Books.

IOCU (1987a). *Moving Forward*. Report to the 12th IOCU World Congress 1985–7. The Hague: International Organisation of Consumers Unions.

IOCU, (1987b). *Statement of Rights and Responsibilities.* International Organisation for Consumer Unions Papers for 1987 12th World Congress, Madrid, Spain, September 15–20, 1987. The Hague: International Organisation of Consumers Unions.

IOCU, (1993). *Time to Put Consumers First: Statement on the Uruguay Round.* 20 October. The Hague: International Organisation of Consumers Unions.

Irvine, Sandy (1989). *Beyond Green Consumerism.* Friends of the Earth, Discussion Paper no. 1, September. London: Friends of the Earth.

Isaac, Katherine (1992). *Civics for Democracy: A Journey for Teachers and Students.* The Center for Study of Responsive Law and Essential Information, Washington, DC: Essential Books.

James, Jeffrey (1983). *Consumer Choice in the Third World.* New York: St. Martin's Press.

James, William (1891). *Principles of Psychology,* Vols 1 and 2. London: Macmillan & Co.

James, William (1892/1961). *Psychology: The Briefer Course.* New York: Harper and Row.

Jameson, Fredric, (1983). Postmodernism and consumer society. In H. Foster (ed.), *The Anti-Aesthetic: Essays on Postmodern Culture.* Port Townsend, WA: Bay Press.

Jencks, Charles (ed.) (1992). *The Post-modern Reader.* London: Academy Editions, and New York: St Martin's Press.

Jenkins, Richard (1992). *Pierre Bourdieu.* London: Routledge.

Jenkins, Robin (1992). *Bringing Rio Home: Biodiversity in our Food and Farming.* London: Sustainable Agriculture, Food and Environment Alliance (SAFE).

Jessop, B. (1988) Neo-conservative regimes and the transition to post-Fordism: the cases of Great Britain and West Germany. In M. Gottdiener (ed.), *Modern Capitalism and Spatial Development: Accumulation, Regulation and Crisis Theory.* New York: St. Martin's Press.

Jessop, B. (1991) Regulation theory, post-Fordism and the state: more than a reply to Werner Bonefeld. In W. Bonefeld, and J. Holloway (eds), *Post-Fordism and Social Form.* London: Macmillan.

Jeyararatnam, J. (1990). Acute pesticide poisoning: a major problem. *World Health Statistics Quarterly,* 43, 139–44.

Johansson, J.K. (1982). The theory and practice of Swedish consumer policy. In David A, Aaker and George S. Day (eds), *Consumerism,* 4th edn. New York: Free Press, 62-75.

John, Robin (ed.) (1994). *The Consumer Revolution: Redressing the Balance.* Hodder and Stoughton. London.

Johnson, Victoria (1992). *Lifestyle Overload? Population and Environment in the Balance.* A report of the ActionAid seminar held at Commonwealth House. London, on 20 November 1991.

Julius, DeAnne and Brown, Richard (1994). From Third World to world class. *The Observer,* 21 November.

Jung, Allen F. (1988). Car prices and the degree of buyer satisfaction. *Journal of Consumer Studies and Home Economics,* 12, (3 September), 237–46.

Kaplinsky, Raphael (1993). TNCs in the Third World: stability or discontinuity? In Loraine Eden and Evan H. Porter (eds), *Multinationals in the Global Political Economy.* London: Macmillan.

Kapuscinski, R. (1983). *The Emperor.* London: Picador.

Kardon, Brian E. (1992). Consumer schizophrenia extremism in the marketplace. *Planning Review,* 20, 4, August/September, 18–22.

Keat, Russell, Whiteley Nigel and Abercrombie Nicholas, (1994). Introduction. In Russell Keat, Nigel Whiteley and Nicholas Abercrombie (eds), *The Authority of the Consumer.* London: Routledge.

Kellaway, Lucy (1993). Twelve acorns for a haircut. *The Financial Times,* 30 November, 13.

Kellner, Douglas (1989). *Jean Baudrillard: From Marxism to Postmodernism and Beyond.* Cambridge: Polity Press.

Kennedy, Paul (1994). The ethical and environmental revolution and its implications for business with special reference to radical enterprises in Northern Britain. Paper to Conference: The Politics of New Cultural Movements, University of Lancaster Centre for the Study of Environmental Change, July 1994. Manchester: Department of Social Science, Manchester Metropolitan University.

Keyfitz, Nathan (1992). Consumerism and the new poor. *Society*, 29, 2, 2–7.

Korten, David (1995). *The Tyranny of the Global Economy*. West Hartford, CT: Kumarian Press.

Krebs, A.V. (1992). *The Corporate Reapers: The Book of Agribusiness*. Washington, DC: Essential Books.

Lacan, J. (1953). Some reflections on the ego. *International Journal of Psychoanalysis*, 34.

Lang, Tim (1991). Consumers or Citizens? *The Ecologist*, 21, 4, July/August, 154–5.

Lang, Tim and Baker Lara (1993). The rise and fall of domestic cooking: turning European children into passive consumers? *Proceedings of the Xlllth International Home Economics and Consumer Studies Research Conference – The European Consumer*, September 8–10, Leeds.

Lang, Tim and Clutterbuck, Charlie (1991). *P is for Pesticides*. London: Ebury.

Lang, Tim and Hines, Colin (1993). *The New Protectionism: Protecting the Future Against Free Trade*. London: Earthscan.

Lang, Tim and Raven, Hugh (1994). From market to hypermarket: food retailing in Britain. *The Ecologist*, 24, 4, July/August, 124–9.

Langman, Lauren (1992). Neon cages: shopping for subjectivity. In Rob Shields, (ed.), *Lifestyle Shopping: The Subject of Consumption*. London: Routledge.

Lansley, Stewart (1994). *After the Gold Rush: The Trouble with Affluence: Consumer Capitalism and the Way Forward*. London: Century (Business Books).

Lasch, Christopher (1980). *The Culture of Narcissism*. London: Abacus.

Lasch, Christopher (1984). *The Minimal Self: Psychic Survival in Troubled Times*. London: Pan Books.

Lasch, Christopher (1991). *The True and Only Heaven: Progress and Its Critics*. New York: Norton.

Lash, Scott and Urry, John (1987). *The End of Organized Capitalism*. Cambridge: Polity Press.

Lawlor, Eamonn (1988). *Individual Choice and Higher Growth: The Task of European Consumer Policy*. Luxembourg: Commission of the European Communities.

Le Bon, Gustave (1960). *The Crowd: A Study of the Popular Mind*. New York: The Viking Press.

Lebergott, Stanley (1993). *Pursuing Happiness: American Consumers in the Twentieth Century*. Princeton: Princeton University Press.

Lee, Martyn (1993). *Consumer Culture Reborn: The Cultural Politics of Consumption*. London: Routledge.

LETSLINK (1994). *LETS Information Pack*. 61 Wood Park Road, Warminster, Wiltshire.

Levi-Strauss, Claude (1978). *Myth and Meaning: The 1977 Massey Lectures*. London: Routledge.

Levy, S. (1982). Symbols, selves and others. *Advances in Consumer Research*, 9, 542–3.

Levy-Bruhl, L. (1966). *The Soul of the Primitive*. London: Allen and Unwin.

Light, R., Nee, C. and Ingham, H. (1993). *Car Theft: The Offender's Perspective*. Home Office, Research and Planning Unit 130. London: HMSO.

Lipietz, Alain (1989/1992). *Towards a New Economic Order: Postfordism, Ecology and Democracy*. Cambridge: Polity Press.

Lister, Ruth (1990). *The Exclusive Society: Citizenship and the Poor*. London: Child Poverty Action Group.

Locke, Stephen, (1994a). Future directions for consumerism and their implications for business. In J. Robin, (ed.), *The Consumer Revolution: Redressing the Balance*. London: Hodder and Stoughton. 173–202.

Locke, Stephen, (1994b). A new approach to competition policy. *Consumer Policy Review*, 4, 3, 159–68.

Loudon, David L. and Della Bitta, Albert J. (1993). *Consumer Behavior: Concepts and Applications*, 4th edn. New York: McGraw-Hill.

Luesby, J. and de Jonquieres, G. (1994). Big assumptions made on costs and demand. *The Financial Times*, 31 May.

Lynch, Roberta and Makusen, Ann (1993). Can markets govern? *The American Prospect*, 16, Winter, 125–34.

McCarney, W.G. (1981). Joy-riding: a quest for identity. *Youth in Society*, 53, April, 16–17.

McCracken, Grant (1988). *Culture and Consumption: New Approaches to the Symbolic Character of Consumer Goods and Activities*. Bloomington: Indiana University Press.

McGregor, P.P.L. and Borooah, V.K. (1992). Is low spending or low-income a better indicator of whether or not a household is poor – some results from the 1985 Family Expenditure Survey. *Journal of Social Policy*, 21, 1, 53–69.

Mack, Joanna and Lansley, Stewart (1985). *Poor Britain*. London: George Allen and Unwin.

Mack, Joanna and Lansley, Stewart (1992). *Breadline Britain in the 1990s*. London: Harper Collins.

McKendrick, N., Brewer, J. and Plumb, J.H. (1982). *The Birth of Consumer Society: The Commercialization of Eighteenth-century English*. Bloomington: Indiana University Press.

McRae, Hamish (1994). Brands suffer consumer promiscuity. *The Independent*, 12 July.

Madge, John (1963). *The Origins of Scientific Sociology*. London: Tavistock.

MAFF (1994). *National Food Survey 1993*. London: HMSO.

Maffesoli, Michel (1988). Jeux de masques. *Design Issues IV*, 1 and 2, 141 ff.

Mander, Jerry (1991). *In the Absence of the Sacred*. San Francisco: Sierra Club Books.

Mannoni, O. (1971). *Freud*. New York: Vintage Books.

Marcuse, Herbert (1964). *One Dimensional Man*. Boston, MA: Beacon Press

Marcuse, Herbert (1969). *An Essay on Liberation*. London: Allen Lane.

Margolius, Sidney (1982). The consumer's real needs. In David A. Aaker and George S. Day (eds), *Consumerism*, 4th edn. New York: Free Press, 48–56.

Marr, Andrew (1994). Any tax of mine must be yours, too. *The Independent*, 18 August.

Martin, Charles L. (1992). Perspectives of service consumers: their multiple roles and challenges. *Journal of Consumer Studies and Home Economics*, 16, 139–49.

Marx, Karl (1867/1967). *Capital*, Vol. 1. New York: International Publishers.

Marx, Karl (1972). Economic and philosophic manuscripts of 1844. In Robert C. Tucker (ed.), *Marx-Engels Reader*. New York: Norton.

Maslow, Abraham (1970, (1954)). *Motivation and Personality*, 2nd edn. New York: Harper and Row.

Mather, Graham (1991). The race to improve public services. In: *Empowerment: The Theme for the 1990s*. London: Adam Smith Institute 9–15.

Matsu, K. (1994). Demarketing. *The Ethical Consumer*, 27, January, 14.

Matthews, Douglas (1973). *Sue the Bastards: A Victim's Handbook*. New York: Arbor House.

Matza, David (1964). *Delinquency and Drift*. New York: J. Wiley.

Mauss, Marcel (1925/1974). *The Gift: Forms and Functions of Exchange in Archaic Societies*. London: Routledge.

Meadows, Donella H., Meadows, Dennis L., Randers, Jorgen and Behrens, William W. (1972). *The Limits to Growth*. London: Earth Island Ltd.

Meadows, Donella H., Meadows, Dennis L., and Randers, Jorgen, (1992). *Beyond the Limits: Global Collapse or a Sustainable Future*. Earthscan. London.

MEC (1994). *Spring and Summer Catalogue*. Vancouver, Canada: Mountain Equipment Co-op.

Mendelson, R.A. (Chair, Committee on Communications) (1992). The Commercialization of children's television. *Pediatrics*, 89, 2, 343–4.

Mick, David Glen (1986). Consumer research and semiotics: exploring the morphology of signs, symbols and significance. *Journal of Consumer Research*, 13, 196–213.

Miliband, R. (1969). *The State in Capitalist Society*. London: Weidenfeld and Nicolson.

Miller, Daniel (1987). *Material Culture and Mass Consumption*. Oxford: Blackwell.

Millis, H.A. and Brown, E.C. (1950). *From the Wagner Act to Taft-Hartley*. Chicago, Il: Chicago University Press.

Mishan, E.J. (1967). *The Costs of Economic Growth*. Harmondsworth: Penguin.

Mitchell, V.-W. and Boustani, P. (1992). Consumer risk perceptions in the breakfast cereal market. *British Food Journal*, 94, 4, 17–27.

Moyle, Franny (1990). Morals of a modern major marketer, *Marketing Week*, 13, 4, 6 April. 36–40.

Mukerji, Chandra (1983). *From Graven Images: Patterns of Modern Materialism*. New York: Columbia University Press.

Mulatuli (1987 (1860)). *Max Havelaar or the Coffee Auctions of the Dutch Trading Company*. Harmondsworth: Penguin.

Murphy, D.J.I. (1986). *Customers and Thieves: An Ethnography of Shoplifting*. Aldershot: Gower.

Murray, Robin (1985). Benneton Britain: the new economic order. *Marxism Today*, November, 28–32.

Myers, Bill (1993). *Food Retail*, 17, 10 August, 3.

Nadel, Mark V. (1971). *The Politics of Consumer Protection*. Indianapolis, IN: Bobbs-Merrill.

Nader, Ralph (1968). The great American gyp. *New York Review of Books*, 11, 21 November, 28.

Nader, Ralph (1970). Foreword. In James S. Turner (ed.), *The Chemical Feast: the Ralph Nader Study Group Report on Food Protection and the Food and Drug Administration*. New York: Grossman.

Nader, Ralph (1991). Keynote speech to World Consumer Congress. International Organization of Consumers Unions, Hong Kong.

Nader, Ralph (1991/1966). *Unsafe at Any Speed: The Designed-in Dangers of the American Automobile*. New York: Knightsbridge Publishing.

Nader, Ralph and Smith, Wesley J. (1992). *The Frugal Shopper*. Washington, DC: Center for Study of Responsive Law.

National Consumer Council (1977). *The Fourth Right of Citizenship: A Review of Legal Advice Services*. London: National Consumer Council 18–21.

National Consumer Council (1978). *Real Money, Real Choice*. London: National Consumer Council. London.

National Consumer Council (1979). *The Consumer and the State: Getting Value for Public Money*. London: National Consumer Council.

National Consumer Council (1981). *Shopping*. London: National Consumer Council.

National Consumer Council (1991). *The Citizen's Charter: Getting it Right for the Consumer*. London: National Consumer Council.

National Consumer Council (1993). *International Trade: The Consumer Agenda*. London: National Consumer Council.

National Consumer Council (1994). *Annual Report*. London: National Consumer Council.

Nelson, Daniel (1991). The seikatsu club consumers' co-operative: activism for alternatives. *World Consumer*, December, 4–5.

New Consumer (1991). The great Japanese supermarket revolt. *New Consumer*, 7, Spring, 14–15.

Nicholson-Lord, David (1994). Consumerism with a shrunken vision. *The Independent*, 25 May.

Nixon, Sean (1992). Have you got the look? Masculinities and shopping spectacle. In Rob Shields (ed.), *Lifestyle Shopping: The Subject of Consumption*. London: Routledge.

Norberg-Hodge, Helena (1991). *Ancient Futures*. San Francisco, CA: Sierra Club Books.

Nove, Alec (1983). *The Economics of Feasible Socialism*. London: George Allen and Unwin.

NRDC Earth Works Group (1989). *50 Simple Things You can do to Save the Earth*. Berkeley, CA: Earth Works Press.

O'Connor, James (1973). *The Fiscal Crisis of the State*. New York: St. Martin's Press.

Office of Fair Trading (1994). *A Buyer's Guide*. London: HMSO.

Omi, M. and Winant, H. (1987). *Racial Formation in the United States*. London: Routledge.

Orbach, S. (1978). *Fat is a Feminist Issue*. London: Hamlyn.

Orbach, S. (1986). *Hunger Strike: The Anorectic's Struggle as a Metaphor for our Age*. London: Faber and Faber.

Orwell, George (1962). *The Road to Wigan Pier*. Harmondsworth: Penguin.

Osborne, David and Gaebler, Ted (1992). *Reinventing Government*. New York: Addison-Wesley.

O'Shaughnessy, John (1987) *Why People Buy*. New York: Oxford University Press.

Otker, Ton (1990). The highly-involved consumer: a marketing myth? *Marketing and Research Today*, 18, 1, February, 30–36.

Packard, Vance (1981, (1957)). *The Hidden Persuaders*, 2nd edn. Harmondsworth: Penguin.

Pandya, Anil and Venkatesh, A. (1992). Symbolic communication among consumers in self-consumption and gift-giving: a semiotic approach. *Advances in Consumer Research*, 19, 147–54.

Pantzar, Mika (1992). The growth of product variety – a myth? *Journal of Consumer Studies and Home Economics*, 16, 345–62.

Parker, H.J. (1974). The joys of joyriding. *New Society*, 3 January.

Parsons, Patrick R. and Rotfeld, Herbert J. (1990). Informercials and television station clearance practices. *Journal of Public Policy and Marketing*, 9, 62–72.

Paulus, I. (1974). *The Search for Pure Food*. Oxford: Martin Robertson.

Paxton, Angela (1994). *Food Miles*. London: Sustainable Agriculture, Food and Environment Alliance (SAFE).

Penz, G. Peter (1986). *Consumer Sovereignty and Human Interests*. Cambridge: Cambridge University Press.

Perry, Sir Michael (1994). The Brand – Vehicle for Value in a Changing Marketplace, Advertising Association, President's Lecture. London, 7 July 1994.

Peters, T.J. and Waterman, R.H. (1982). *In Search of Excellence*. New York: Harper and Row.

Pines, A. and Aronson, E. (1988). *Career Burnout*. New York: Free Press.

Pirie, Madsen (Ed.) (1991). *Empowerment: The Theme for the 1990s*. London: Adam Smith Institute.

Pook, Sally (1993). Ram-raids spark talks on security. *Bath Evening Chronicle*, 2 August.

Poster, Mark (1988). Introduction. In Mark Poster (ed.), *Jean Baudrillard: Selected Writings*. Cambridge: Polity Press.

Postman, Neil (1986). *Amusing Ourselves to Death*. London: Heinemann

Potter, J. (1988). Consumerism and the public sector. *Public Administration*, 66, 2, Summer, 149–65.

Poulantzas, N. (1975). *Political Power and Social Classes*. London: New Left Books.

Powderley, John and MacNulty, Christine (1990). A turbulent time ahead. *Marketing*, 11 October, 33–4.

Ramsay, Iain (1989). *Consumer Protection*. London: Weidenfeld and Nicolson.

Ravallion, M., Datt, G. and Vandewalle, D. (1991). Quantifying absolute poverty in the developing-world. *Review of Income and Wealth*, 4, 345–61.

Raven, Hugh and Lang, Tim (1995). *Off our Trolleys? Food Retailing and the Hypermarket Economy*. London: Institute for Public Policy Research.

Redfern, Percy (1913). *The Story of the C.W.S.* Manchester: Co-operative Wholesale Society.

Redfern, Percy (1920). *The Consumers' Place in Society*. Manchester: Co-operative Union.

Reekie, Gail (1992). Changes in the Adamless Eden: the spatial and sexual transformation of a Brisbane department store 1930–90. In Rob Shields (ed.), *Lifestyle Shopping: The Subject of Consumption*. London: Routledge.

Reich, Robert (1981). Business is asking for it again. *New York Times*, 22 November.

Reich, Wilhelm (1970). *The Mass Psychology of Fascism*. New York: Farrar, Straus and Giroux.

Resenthal, Pam (1991). Jacked in: Fordism, Cyberpunk, Marxism. *Socialist Review*, 21, 79–104.

Rieff, David (1993). Multiculturalism's silent partner: it's the newly globalized consumer economy, stupid. *Harper's Magazine*, August, 62–72.

Rieff, Philip (1959). *Freud: The Mind of a Moralist*. New York: Doubleday.

Rieff, Philip (1966). *The Triumph of the Therapeutic*. New York: Harper and Row.

Rifkin, Jeremy (1992). *Biosphere Politics: a New Consciousness for a New Century*. Harper Collins. New York.

Robertson, Roland, (1992). *Globalization: Social Theory and Global Culture*. London: Sage.

Robins, David and Cohen, Phil (1978). *Knuckle Sandwich: Growing Up in the Working-class City*. Harmondsworth: Penguin.

Rock, Stuart (1989). Are greens good for you? *Director*, January, 40–3.

Rogers, Carl (1951). *Client-centred Therapy*. Boston: Houghton Mifflin Co.

Rose, G. (1978). *The Melancholy Science: An Introduction to the Thought of Theodor W. Adorno*. London: Macmillan.

Rudé, George (1959). *The Crowd in the French Revolution*. Oxford: Oxford University Press.

Rustin, M. (1992). Citizenship and Charter 88. *New Left Review*, 191, 37–48.

Rutherford, Jonathan (1990). A place called home: identity and the cultural politics of difference. In Jonathan Rutherford (ed.), *Identity: Community, Culture, Difference*. London: Lawrence and Wishart, 1–20.

Ryle, Sarah (1992). Crowds cheer as gang hits Jolly's. *Bath Evening Chronicle*, 23 October.

Sahlins, M. (1972). *Stone Age economics*. Chicago: Aldine Atherton.

Sampson, P. (1993). A better way to measure brand image. *Admap*, 28, 7, July/August, 19–24.

Samuelson, Paul A. (1970). *Economics*, 8th edn. New York: McGraw-Hill.

Schofield, J. (1993). A brave new world to exploit. *The Guardian*, 26 August.

Schwartz, Howard S. (1990). *Narcissistic Process and Corporate Decay*. New York: New York University Press.

Scitovsky, Tibor (1976). *The Joyless Economy: An Inquiry into Human Satisfaction and Consumer Dissatisfaction*. New York: Oxford University Press.

Seabrook, Jeremy (1979). *What Went Wrong? Working People and the Ideals of the Labour Movement*. London: Victor Gollancz.

Seabrook, Jeremy (1985). *Landscapes of Poverty*. Oxford: Blackwell.

Secord, Paul F. and Backman, Carl W. (1964). *Social Psychology*. New York: McGraw-Hill.

Sheth, J.N. (1991). Why we buy what we buy. *Journal of Business Research*, 22, 2, March, 159–71.

Shields, Rob (1992). Spaces for the subject of consumption. In Rob Shields (ed.), *Lifestyle Shopping: The Subject of Consumption*. London: Routledge.

SIB (1993). *Pension Transfers*. Report to the Securities and Investments Board by KPMG Peat Marwick. London, December.

Sievers, Burkard (1986). Beyond the surrogate of motivation. *Organization Studies* 7, 4, 335–51.

Simmel, Georg (1903). The metropolis in mental life, reprinted in D. Levine (1971), *Georg Simmel: On Individuality and Social Form*. Chicago, IL: Chicago University Press.

Simmel, Georg (1904). Fashion, reprinted in D. Levine (1971), *Georg Simmel: On Individuality and Social Form*. Chicago, IL: Chicago University Press.

Simmel, Georg (1978). *The Philosophy of Money*. London: Routledge and Kegan Paul.

Simmonds, Diana (1990). What's next? Fashion, foodies and the illusion of freedom. In Alan Tomlinson (ed.), *Consumption, Identity and Style: Marketing, Meanings and the Packaging of Pleasure*. London: Routledge.

Simon, Herbert A. (1947). *Administrative Behavior*. New York: Macmillan.

Sinclair, Upton (1906/1985). *The Jungle*. Harmondsworth: Penguin.

Singh, Jagdip (1990). A typology of consumer dissatisfaction response styles. *Journal of Retailing*, 66, Spring, 57–99.

Sklair, Leslie (1991). *The Sociology of the Global System*. Hemel Hempstead: Harvester Wheatsheaf.

Slesnick, D.T. (1994). Consumption, needs and inequality. *International Economic Review*, 35, 5, 677–703.

Smith, Adam (1776). *The Wealth of Nations*. Harmondsworth: Penguin 1970.

Smith, N. Craig (1990). *Morality and the Market: Consumer Pressure for Corporate Accountability*. London: Routledge.

Society of Labour Lawyers (1968). *Justice for All*. Report for Fabian Society, Fabian Research Series 273. London: Fabian Society.

Stouffer, S.A., Guttman, L., Lazarsfeld, P.F. and Star, S.A. (1949–50). *Studies in Social Psychology in World War II*, Vols 1–4. Princeton, NJ: Princeton University Press.

Suerdem, Ahmet and Sinan, Mimar (1992). What are you doing after the orgy? Or, Does the consumer really behave, (well)? *Advances in Consumer Research*, 19, 207–12.

Taylor, Joan and Taylor, Derek (eds) (1990). *The Safe Food Handbook*. London: Ebury.

Taylor, I., Walton, P. and Young, J. (1973). *The New Criminology*. London: Routledge.

Thompson, David (1994). *Weavers of Dreams: Founders of the Modern Co-operative Movement*. Davis, CA: Center for Co-operatives/University of California.

Thompson, E.P. (1993 (1971)). The moral economy of the English crowd in the eighteenth century. In E.P. Thompson, (1993), *Customs in Common*. Harmondsworth: Penguin 185–258.

Thurow, Lester (1993). *Head to Head: The Coming Economic Battle Among Japan, Europe and America*. London: Nicholas Brealey Publishing.

Tiemstra, John P. (1992). Theories of regulation and the history of consumerism. *International Journal of Social Economics*, 19, 6, 3–27.

Tilman, R. (1992). *Thorstein Veblen and his Critics, 1891–1963: Conservative, Liberal, and Radical Perspectives*. Princeton, NJ: Princeton University Press.

Tomforde, Anna (1994). Fast food loses to 'rubbish tax'. *The Guardian*, 22 August.

Tomlinson, Alan (1990). Introduction: consumer culture and the aura of commodity. In Alan Tomlinson (ed.), *Consumption, Identity and Style: Marketing, Meanings and the Packaging of Pleasure*. London: Routledge.

Townsend, Peter (1979). *Poverty in the United Kingdom*. Harmondsworth: Penguin.

Townsend, Peter (1993). *The International Analysis of Poverty*. Hemel Hempstead: Harvester Wheatsheaf.

UNICEF (1992). *Food, Health and Care: The UNICEF Vision and Strategy for a World Free from Hunger and Malnutrition*. New York: United Nations Childrens Fund.

United Nations and UNEP (1990). *The Public Health Impact of Pesticides Used in Agriculture*. Geneva: World Health Organization.

van Brakel, Manus and Buitenkamp, Maria (1992). *Sustainable Netherlands: A Perspective for Changing Northern Lifestyles*. Amsterdam: Friends of the Earth Netherlands/Milieu Difensie.

van.Brakel, Manus and Zagema, Bertram (1994). *Sustainable Netherlands*. Amsterdam: Friends of the Earth/Vereniging Milieudifensie.

Vanhonacker, W.R. (1993). *What does the multinomial logit model really measure?* INSEAD. Research and the Development of Pedagogical Materials Working Paper, February.

van Vucht Tijssen, Lieteke (1990). Women between modernity and postmodernity. In Bryan S. Turner (ed.) *Theories of Modernity and Postmodernity*. London: Sage.

Veblen, Thorstein (1899/1925). *The Theory of the Leisure Class: An Economic Study of Institutions*. London: George Allen and Unwin.

Venkatesh, Alladi (1992). Postmodernism, consumer culture and the society of the spectacle. *Advances in Consumer Research*, 19, 199–202.

Walker, A. and Walker, C. (1987). *The Growing Divide*. London: Child Poverty Action Group.

Walsh, D.P. (1978). *Shoplifting: Controlling a Major Crime*. London: Macmillan.

Warde, Alan (1994). Consumers, identity and belonging: reflections on some theses of Zygmunt Bauman. In Russell Keat, Nigel Whiteley and Nicholas Abercrombie (eds), *The Authority of the Consumer*. London: Routledge.

Webb, Tony and Lang, Tim (1990). *Food Irradiation: The Myth and the Reality*. Wellingborough: Thorsons.

Weir, David and Schapiro, Mark (1981). *Circles of Poison: Pesticides and People in a Hungry World*. San Francisco: Institute for Food and Development Policy.

Wells, Phil and Jetter, Mandy (1991). *The Global Consumer: Best Buys to Help the Third World*. London: Victor Gollancz.

Wernick, Andrew (1991). *Promotional Culture: Advertising, Ideology and Symbolic Expression*. London: Sage.

Wexler, Philip (1990). Citizenship in the semiotic society. In Bryan S. Turner, (ed.), *Theories of Modernity and Postmodernity*. London: Sage, 164–75.

White, Richard E. and Kare, Dilip D., (1990). The impact of consumer boycotts on the stock prices of target firms. *The Journal of Applied Business Research*, 6, 2, 63–71.

Whitfield, Dexter (1983). *Making it Public: Evidence and Action Against Privatisation*. London: Pluto.

Whitworth, Diana (1994). Promoting and representing the consumer interest. In Robin John (ed.), *The Consumer Revolution: Redressing the Balance*. London: Hodder and Stoughton.

Will, Rosalyn, Marlin, Alice Tepper, Corson, Benjamin, and Schorsch, Jonathan (1989). *Shopping for a Better World*. New York: Council on Economic Priorities.

Williams, Raymond (1976). *Keywords: A Vocabulary of Culture and Society*. London: Croom Helm.

Williams, Rosalind H. (1982). *Dream Worlds: Mass Communication in Late Nineteenth Century France*. Berkeley, CA: University of California Press.

Williamson, Judith (1986). *Consuming Passions*. London: Marion Boyars.

Willis, Paul (1977). *Learning to Labour*. London: Saxon House.

Willis, Paul (1990). *Common Culture: Symbolic Work at Play in the Everyday Cultures of the Young*. Milton Keynes: Open University Press.

Winnicott, D.W. (1958). Transitional objects and transitional phenomena. In *Collected Papers*. London: Tavistock.

Winnicott, D.W. (1964). *The Child, the Family and the Outside World*. Harmondsworth: Penguin.

Winward, John (1993). The organized consumer and consumer information co-operatives. In Russell Keat, Nigel Whiteley, and Nicholas Abercrombie (eds), *The Authority of the Consumer*. London: Routledge, 75–90.

Winward, John (1994). The rationale and forms of government intervention. In Robin John (ed.), *The Consumer Revolution: Redressing the Balance*. London: Hodder and Stoughton, 79–93.

Witkowski, Terrence H. (1989). Colonial consumers in revolt: buyer values and behavior during the nonimportation movement, 1764–1776. *Journal of Consumer Research*, 16, 2, September, 216–26.

Wolf, Stephen M. (1993). Keeping the competitive edge. *Hemispheres* (United Airlines magazine), July, 13.

Womack, James P., Jones, Daniel T. and Roos, Daniel (1990). *The Machine that Changed the World*. New York: Rawson Associates.

Wood, Adrian (1991). How much does trade with the South affect workers in the North? *World Bank Research Observer*, January.

Woolhandler, S., Himmelstein, D. and Lewontin, J.P. (1993). Administrative costs in US hospitals. *New England Journal of Medicine*, 329, 6, 5 August. 400–3.

Worcester, Bob (1994). Green Consumerism. Paper to United Nations Development Association conference, Royal Society of Arts. London, 2 June 1994.

Worpole, Ken (1992). *Towns for People*. Buckingham: Open University Press.

Yalch, R. and Spangenberg, E. (1990). Effects of store music on shopping behaviour. *The Journal of Consumer Marketing*, 7, 2, Spring, 55–64.

Young, R. (1994). Stores lose £516m to thieves. *The Times*, 18 February, 9.

Index

DATE DUE

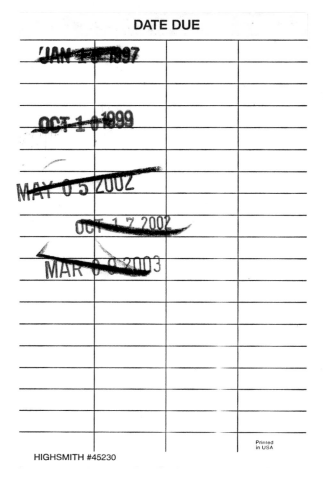